The Successful Self-Publisher

Produce and Market Your Own Best Seller

Basic Step-by-Step Techniques for Success in Designing, Typesetting, Printing, and Selling a Book

by DOROTHY KAVKA
and DAN HEISE

EVANSTON PUBLISHING, INC.
EVANSTON, ILLINOIS 60201

Portions of this book were taken from *Selling Your Book: The Writer's Guide to Publishing and Marketing* by Dorothy Kavka, Evanston Publishing, Inc., 1993

Evanston Publishing, Inc.
1571 Sherman Ave, Annex C
Evanston, Illinois 60201
1-800-594-5190

Printed in the U.S.A.
10 9 8 7 6 5 4 3 2 1

Library of Congress Card Catalog Number: 95-71949
ISBN: 1-879260-38-7

ABOUT THE AUTHORS

Dorothy Kavka is the president and senior editor of Evanston Publishing, Inc. She has a broad base of experience as a publisher, editor, writer, artist, English and creative writing teacher, and business person. A production editor for a major textbook publisher, she left to found her own publishing company ten years ago. Her small press publishes its books in the traditional way, paying its authors a royalty. It also helps writers self-publish and market their books and works with established publishers in designing, editing, and printing their publications. Ms. Kavka has produced award winning book and cover designs and is the author of the book *Selling Your Book: The Author's Guide to Publishing and Marketing*. She also founded the seminar series, "The Complete Publisher." Ms. Kavka and her company have been featured in articles in major newspapers and magazines.

Dan Heise has extensive experience working in the book trade, and has participated in almost every facet of book writing, production, marketing, and sales. As a seminar leader, marketing director, and consultant, he has made a career of teaching authors how to promote themselves and their books. Heise got his start at the age of 17, assisting a magazine editor with the premier issue of a new-age magazine. Working as a book representative for CHB Publishers, he became vice president of marketing. He also served as marketing director for Evanston Publishing, Inc. and helped to found Chicago Spectrum Press. He is currently the president of Rising Star Promotions, a Chicago-based firm specializing in assisting self-published and small press authors with sales, marketing, and promotions.

ACKNOWLEDGMENTS

We would like to thank Stan Freeman and Carol Wright, for their generous help in obtaining examples of printing materials; Rebecca Kavka, who initially edited and proofread this book; and Myra Schultz, for allowing us to reproduce her lessons on typesetting a book in WordPerfect.

Our thanks also to the following authors and publishers who let us use portions of their books for illustrations of production and marketing techniques:

P.57 .... *The Complete Book of Victims' Rights,* Debra J. Wilson, J.D., ProSe Associates, Inc., 1995 (ISBN: 0-9637285-1-2)

pp.109-116 .... *Cooking & Entertaining with Beer,* Rob Driver, ProSe Associates, Inc., 1996 (ISBN: 0-9637285-2-0)

p.42 .... *Into the Arena,* Greg A. Kinczewski, Chicago Spectrum Press, 1996 (ISBN:1-886094-26-8)

p.286 .... *The Ladder of Memory,* David Koenig, The Harp Song Press, 1994 (ISBN: 0-9637357-0-5)

pp.83-84 .... *PMS: Solving the Puzzle, Sixteen Causes of Premenstural Syndrome and What to Do About It,* Linaya Hahn, Chicago Spectrum Press, 1995 (ISBN: 1-886094-15-2)

p.74 .... *That's What Grandmothers are For,* Arlene Uslander, Chicago Spectrum Press, 1995 (ISBN: 1-886094-13-6)

p.101 .... *Voices, Insistent Voices,* Stuart McCarrell, Xenia Press, 1990 (ISBN:1-880001-07-1)

The following books used for examples are published by Evanston Publishing, Inc.

pp.72, 156, 283..*Cuckoo Forevermore,* Leonard K. Szymczak, 1996 (ISBN: 1-879260-37-9)

pp.42, 284......... *Edward Dart, Architect,* Susan Dart, 1993 (ISBN: 1-879260-09-3)

p.287 .... *Second Opinon: New Poems,* H. J. Hirshfield, 1994 (ISBN: 1-879260-33-6)

p.285 .... *To Die in Chicago: Confederate Prisoners at Camp Doublas, 1862-1865,* 1994 (ISBN: 1-879260-20-4)

pp.59, 66........... *Two Erotic Tales by Pierre Louÿs: Aphrodite and The Songs of Bilitis,* translated by Mary Hanson Harrison, 1995 (ISBN: 1-879260-24-7)

pp.70, 71........... *White-Man-Runs-Him: Crow Scout with Custer,* Dennis W. Harcey & Brian R. Croone, with Joe Medicine Crow, 1995 (ISBN: 1-879260-36-0)

CONTENTS

INTRODUCTION

So, you want to publish your own book? You are in the right place.

Do you want to learn about how books are published? You are also in the right place.

Dorothy Kavka and Dan Heise used their many years of considerable publishing talent to prepare you for the intricate, challenging, exhausting, yet exhilarating journey facing the self-publisher. This book should be your requisite companion and authoritative reference for many years to come. At times the journey may seem very lonely.

You are not alone.

You are joining an ever growing creative force of talented people determined to tell their tales and wanting to control their destinies. You want to write and publish your own book. You want to tell your story your way. You also want your book to sell. Pay attention to your trail guides, Dorothy and Dan. They give you solid directions on how to reach your destination.

You know you have a great idea for a book. You may already have a first-rate manuscript. For many writers that will suffice; they will send the tome to one or several publishers and with luck it may become one of 50,000 or so books that get published every year in the United States. They will depend on the immense publishing industry, in this ever expanding information age, to get their ideas to the reading public through sophisticated editing, marketing and distribution systems. Such writers can be very successful. After all, publishers are very good at what they do. But such writers may not always be satisfied that their book got the right attention, or got to the right niche in the market, or that the book came out at the right time, or that they were properly compensated. Writers may also feel squeezed by a publishing industry that is marked by corporate competition, mergers, and consolidations. Welcome to big business. You may be one of those writers who does not want to be part of a corporate publishing culture.

You are not alone.

Despite corporate concentrations in publishing and distribution, technology has made it possible for you to produce a book that can look, feel, and read like the best that corporate publishing has to offer. The waters may be rough in parts of the journey, but technology gives you some powerful oars to make it over the production rapids of publishing.

Just imagine the huge distance the human race has traversed since Gutenberg devised moveable type in the fifteenth century. In a short blip of history, we have made access to the printed word and printing the word almost universal. Actually, the written word is a relative newcomer as a means of transporting storytelling and culture across generations. At one time, society relied heavily on the storyteller or scribe as a venerable cultural force. Information has always been power.

Self-publishing was more the norm years ago than today. Those who controlled the presses were often those who did the writing; just consider Benjamin Franklin, who wrote, printed, and even turned out some money on his press. Other writers were often linked politically or socially to those who controlled the local press.

Self-publishing has been a noble tradition for those who want to assure that their message makes it to the public in the form it was intended. Theodore Dreiser, for example, was ignored by his first publisher of the classic *Sister Carrie;* reluctantly bound by contract, Doubleday sold only a few hundred copies because the publisher's wife thought the book immoral. Later, Dreiser invested in another book publisher and took control of the book to guarantee the next edition would successfully get out to the public. It did.

You probably already have your own heroes or heroines who defied the odds and self published to get their messages out, and changed history in the process.

You are not alone.

Technology has also given us more things to write about and more niches of readers to write for. The information revolution has given readers far greater choices than ever dreamed possible even a few years ago. With communications channels like the Internet, for example, whole communities of common interests have emerged that might never have come together otherwise; they want to read about their subjects and you can reach them with your book.

Finally, technology is giving us a more educated public that is buying more and more books. Some would say that the computer and video age means fewer books. On the contrary, the public wants more information, period. That translates into more books. Information is the great consumable of the future. With modern miracles of distribution systems and intense bookstore competition, the public has ever more titles and subjects to choose from. That translates into greater opportunities for the self-publisher — you.

You have to seize those opportunities.

You should be prepared for a lot of work and uncertainty on your journey, but you are ready for that, right?

I have known several successful self-publishers. They all shared a common drive to see their work to conclusion and they kept focused on their goal of getting as many of their books into as many hands as possible. While some went into unfamiliar or uncharted territory, particularly distribution, they all were doggedly determined to learn the routes and cross them.

You will not be alone.

The chapters you are about to traverse are very readable and understandable, despite the complexity of the self-publishing process. The great genius of this book is to make you feel comfortable with unfamiliar terrain before you actually have to travel there. You will find that the graphics and the explanations are quite effective. The sequence of the chapters follows the logical publishing process you will be facing. You will learn a lot, perhaps more than you might like to know, but what you need to know if you are serious about self-publishing. You are guaranteed to learn much from this book.

Dorothy and Dan have created an important reference for self-publishing that will set the standard for a long time.

–ROBERT REMER
Publisher, *Chicago Books in Review*

1

GETTING STARTED

Chapter 1

Publishing a book is probably one of the most exciting things that you will do in your life: not only is it a creative process, but it is a legacy for the future. As Henry Thoreau, a self-published author, wrote: "Books are the treasured wealth of the world and the fit inheritance of generations and nations...Their authors are a natural and irresistible aristocracy in every society, and more than kings or emperors, exert an influence on mankind."

A book imparts pleasure and excitement as well as ideas. It can influence the mind and heart, whether it reaches only a few readers or becomes a best seller.

Over the years, the book production process has greatly changed, beginning with scholars who spent a lifetime reproducing one book by hand. Now, publishing companies with powerful presses and large staffs turn out dozens of titles in a year.

There is still another option for publishing a book — self publishing. Until very recently, self-publishing was a field limited to vanity and subsidy presses, corporate reports, and a few instances of outstanding creative writing. An author could not easily progress from the desire to publish his or her own work to a finished book.

But quietly and very surely, the availability of reasonably priced computers with word processing and design programs has made self-publishing a respected means of book production, and a viable alternative to the fact that most major publishers will not read, much less publish, the work of unknown writers.

In the quest for professionalism, the author needs to find easily accessible information about the basics of publishing, including all aspects of production and marketing. *The Successful Self-Publisher* is more than a how-to book: it is a step-by-step guide to publishing and marketing your own book and examines the risks and rewards that are part of such a venture.

The Self-Publishing Alternative

A myth about artists is that because they are creative, they cannot possibly be practical. But people who believe this forget that the self-discipline that is necessary in any process involving skill and talent — writing, composing, painting — is the same that is needed in manufacturing and marketing the finished product. And because production is not usually an end in itself, the artist wants his or her work validated by being seen, heard, or read.

Once upon a time, publishing a book was a time-consuming process that involved many people with specialized talents and layer upon layer of specific tasks. Even now, people talk about galleys, keylining, and even casebinding as if these were all essential to the making of a book. Since the advent of the personal computer, making a book has changed so dramatically that when you have finished reading this book, you will have enough information to begin publishing your own book; a long apprenticeship is no longer necessary.

Self-publishing is an alternative that many writers turn to as traditional publishing houses close more and more doors to authors who have not yet made a name for themselves. It has an honorable tradition, as innovative authors who could not find conventional publishers printed and sold their own books until their literary worth was recognized. Mark Twain, Zane Grey, Walt Whitman, William Blake, Robert Burns, Henry Thoreau, Herman Melville, T.S. Eliot, Virginia Woolf, James Joyce, Anais Nin, Ezra Pound, Carl Sandburg, and Vladimir Nabakov were all self-publishers at one time. Some, such as Twain, Woolf, and Nin, actually went so far as to buy their own presses.

When you consider publishing your own book, you must be aware of many factors. There will be a financial investment on your part. You will have to use all of your creative abilities to get your manuscript ready to be printed. Equally important is the fact that you will be marketing your own book, which also requires a lot of time and a considerable amount of hard work.

Caveat Emptor

There are hazards to self-publishing. Choosing the self-publishing packager or printing house that will help you with your book can be your single most important decision. There are many firms that offer services to make self-publishing easier, from editing a manuscript, to designing, producing camera-ready pages, and printing the book. Thoroughly investigate any company you decide to work with and demand a contract that clearly defines every service to be performed, with a dollar amount listed for every item.

Make inquiries to many sources. You may find that a full-service self-publishing house is competitive in price with single-service companies. If you choose to buy only printing for your book, you will have to prepare your own camera-ready copy, including separations for color artwork. This book explains these techniques in detail, but if you feel unsure of your ability in any aspect of production, these services are readily available from qualified professionals.

Because self-publishing can be expensive, it is not wise to learn its liabilities from experience. It is essential that the first-time author who is going to publish a book does extensive research on the subjects of publishing and marketing.

Three Forms of Publishing

There are three major divisions in the field of publishing: traditional, vanity/subsidy, and self-publishing. The *traditional publisher* is one that contracts with a writer for a book, assumes all the costs for the book including the marketing and advertising, and pays the author a royalty on the books sold, usually eight to ten percent on the net return of the book. Major companies may also offer an advance on the royalties. The author has little to say about the look, editing, or marketing of the book, although he or she should expect to help in promoting the work.

It is easy to fall victim to unscrupulous publishing and printing companies. Advertisements abound in writers' magazines for *vanity/subsidy publishers* who promise to undertake the publishing and marketing of a book while sharing in the cost. Often, the promotional materials from these companies sound as if they are traditional presses. This is because vanity/subsidy publishers have an unsavory reputation, one that is well-deserved. The author pays for all the costs in producing and marketing the

WHEN A PUBLISHER CALLS

I had just put my daughter's lunch on the table when the telephone rang and for thirty cherished seconds, my dream came true. A small press publisher, calling long distance from Toronto, Canada, said he'd like to publish my mystery novel after minor revisions were made.

He said he could send a contract and, in the same breath, began to talk about financial pressures on small publishing houses. He estimated it would cost $12,000 for a fifteen hundred print run; and since his company didn't have the cash, he was looking for a co-publisher to invest $6,000....

An offer to publish, with a catch, wasn't the dream I'd envisioned. There'd also been something in his tone of voice and the way he kept repeating my name that made me feel I'd just been given a sales pitch....

My local writer's organization put me in touch with a small press owner who agreed that things were terrible economically, but advised me not to send the publisher any money. After contacting the editor who originally listed the publisher's address, I learned that this small press' catalog didn't name a distributor or include discount price lists for bookstores, which made us wonder if their books were sold by mail, a method I didn't think would succeed with my novel.

I wrote to the publisher, offering to help find a co-publisher and to sell five hundred copies locally. The day after I mailed this letter, my manuscript, covering letter, and CV appeared in my mailbox....

It seemed obvious that I'd never again hear from what I now suspect is a vanity press.

Should you receive a phone call from an unknown publisher, don't commit to anything verbally, and don't be afraid to contact writer's groups and organizations for information.

It could mean the difference between a profitable success and an expensive disaster.

reprinted by permission of Debra Purdy Kong
as published in Just Write, *Spring, 1995*

book, yet the publishing company owns the book. Obviously this opens up all sort of ethical questions.

As you read through the chapters on marketing in this book, you will discover how much time and effort goes into marketing. Most vanity/subsidy publishers promise they will market for you, but have no financial incentive to do so — they have been paid up front so why should they put out any extra time or money? Moreover, any publicity they might do would be thrown away by bookdealers or reviewers who would immediately recognize the publisher's name. Some of these companies are little more than scam operations and do not even print all the books that are contracted for, because they know that in all probability the books will never be sold. If the author wants to take back control of books, they would have to be purchased. These are books that were already paid for by the author.

Self-publishing is simply contracting with a self-publishing packager or a printing company to be your production department. You own all rights to the book and you only pay for what services you need to get that book into print. You have total control of every aspect of the work.

> Lately, Holocaust survivors, who want their stories to live on after them, have become very interested in self-publishing. However, usually limited by age and health considerations, they do not want to do the production and marketing of the book and thus become easy prey for vanity/subsidy presses. Our recommendation is that rather than waste their time and money with such ventures, they donate their memoirs to the Holocaust Museum or a university with a Holocaust program, so that future scholars can use their biographies as a research source.

You as the Publisher

Publishing should be a collective noun — it appears singular, but is plural in concept. A finished book is the result of teamwork: the author, designer, typesetter, and printer all become intimately involved with the production of any publication. With time and experience, you as a self-publisher can do all these tasks. However, there is no shame involved in recognizing that you are uncomfortable with some aspects of production and contracting for that part of the book to be done by someone else.

Legalities

Once your manuscript is written, and, hopefully, well edited, there are still certain steps that must be taken before you begin the production. Certain requirements are necessary for the proper protection of any publication, and you will find it almost impossible to successfully market your writing without them.

Copyright

A copyright is essential to prevent others from using any portion of a work without the copyright holder's permission. For works that were created on or after January 1, 1978, U.S. copyright law has established a "life-plus-fifty" system. This means that a work is automatically protected from the moment of its creation "in tangible form" until 50 years after the author's death. In 1989, the copyright law was amended to conform to international law, so that material published in the United States, after March 1, 1989, automatically carries international copyright protection and is protected against foreign piracy.

Even with this automatic protection, most authors choose to display the copyright notice in their work. Books print the copyright information on the reverse of the title page. This information should be "...placed on all publicly distributed copies from which the work can be visually perceived" and include the symbol © and/or the word *Copyright* or the abbreviation *Copr.*, the year of first publication, and the name of the copyright owner. It might also contain other warnings about copyright infringement. The copyright for this book reads:

> *©1996 by Dorothy Kavka and Dan Heise*
>
> *All rights reserved. Except for appropriate use in critical reviews or works of scholarship, the reproduction or use of this work in any form or by any electronic, mechanical, or other means now known or hereafter invented, including photocopying and recording, and in any information storage and retrieval system, is forbidden without written permission of the authors or publisher.*

It is to your benefit to put the copyright in your own name rather than in the name of your publisher or another person. If you are a co-author of a book or are reissuing a book that has been out of print, there are special requirements in phrasing the copyright notice. Your printer or publisher should be able to help

FORM TX
For a Literary Work
UNITED STATES COPYRIGHT OFFICE

REGISTRATION NUMBER

TX TXU

EFFECTIVE DATE OF REGISTRATION

Month Day Year

DO NOT WRITE ABOVE THIS LINE. IF YOU NEED MORE SPACE, USE A SEPARATE CONTINUATION SHEET.

1

TITLE OF THIS WORK ▼

PREVIOUS OR ALTERNATIVE TITLES ▼

PUBLICATION AS A CONTRIBUTION If this work was published as a contribution to a periodical, serial, or collection, give information about the collective work in which the contribution appeared. Title of Collective Work ▼

If published in a periodical or serial give: Volume ▼ Number ▼ Issue Date ▼ On Pages ▼

2

a NAME OF AUTHOR ▼ DATES OF BIRTH AND DEATH Year Born ▼ Year Died ▼

Was this contribution to the work a "work made for hire"? ☐ Yes ☐ No

AUTHOR'S NATIONALITY OR DOMICILE Name of Country OR { Citizen of ▶ Domiciled in ▶

WAS THIS AUTHOR'S CONTRIBUTION TO THE WORK Anonymous? ☐ Yes ☐ No Pseudonymous? ☐ Yes ☐ No If the answer to either of these questions is "Yes," see detailed instructions.

NATURE OF AUTHORSHIP Briefly describe nature of material created by this author in which copyright is claimed. ▼

NOTE

Under the law, the "author" of a "work made for hire" is generally the employer, not the employee (see instructions). For any part of this work that was "made for hire" check "Yes" in the space provided, give the employer (or other person for whom the work was prepared) as "Author" of that part, and leave the space for dates of birth and death blank.

b NAME OF AUTHOR ▼ DATES OF BIRTH AND DEATH Year Born ▼ Year Died ▼

Was this contribution to the work a "work made for hire"? ☐ Yes ☐ No

AUTHOR'S NATIONALITY OR DOMICILE Name of Country OR { Citizen of ▶ Domiciled in ▶

WAS THIS AUTHOR'S CONTRIBUTION TO THE WORK Anonymous? ☐ Yes ☐ No Pseudonymous? ☐ Yes ☐ No If the answer to either of these questions is "Yes," see detailed instructions.

NATURE OF AUTHORSHIP Briefly describe nature of material created by this author in which copyright is claimed. ▼

c NAME OF AUTHOR ▼ DATES OF BIRTH AND DEATH Year Born ▼ Year Died ▼

Was this contribution to the work a "work made for hire"? ☐ Yes ☐ No

AUTHOR'S NATIONALITY OR DOMICILE Name of Country OR { Citizen of ▶ Domiciled in ▶

WAS THIS AUTHOR'S CONTRIBUTION TO THE WORK Anonymous? ☐ Yes ☐ No Pseudonymous? ☐ Yes ☐ No If the answer to either of these questions is "Yes," see detailed instructions.

NATURE OF AUTHORSHIP Briefly describe nature of material created by this author in which copyright is claimed. ▼

3

a YEAR IN WHICH CREATION OF THIS WORK WAS COMPLETED This information must be given in all cases. ◀ Year

b DATE AND NATION OF FIRST PUBLICATION OF THIS PARTICULAR WORK Complete this information ONLY if this work has been published. Month ▶ Day ▶ Year ▶ ◀ Nation

4

See instructions before completing this space

COPYRIGHT CLAIMANT(S) Name and address must be given even if the claimant is the same as the author given in space 2. ▼

TRANSFER If the claimant(s) named here in space 4 is (are) different from the author(s) named in space 2, give a brief statement of how the claimant(s) obtained ownership of the copyright. ▼

DO NOT WRITE HERE OFFICE USE ONLY

APPLICATION RECEIVED

ONE DEPOSIT RECEIVED

TWO DEPOSITS RECEIVED

FUNDS RECEIVED

MORE ON BACK ▶ • Complete all applicable spaces (numbers 5-11) on the reverse side of this page. • See detailed instructions. • Sign the form at line 10.

DO NOT WRITE HERE

Page 1 of pages

first page of copyright form

EXAMINED BY

FORM TX

CHECKED BY

☐ CORRESPONDENCE Yes

FOR COPYRIGHT OFFICE USE ONLY

DO NOT WRITE ABOVE THIS LINE. IF YOU NEED MORE SPACE, USE A SEPARATE CONTINUATION SHEET.

5

PREVIOUS REGISTRATION Has registration for this work, or for an earlier version of this work, already been made in the Copyright Office?

☐ **Yes** ☐ **No** If your answer is "Yes," why is another registration being sought? (Check appropriate box) ▼

a. ☐ This is the first published edition of a work previously registered in unpublished form.

b. ☐ This is the first application submitted by this author as copyright claimant.

c. ☐ This is a changed version of the work, as shown by space 6 on this application.

If your answer is "Yes," give: **Previous Registration Number** ▼ **Year of Registration** ▼

6

DERIVATIVE WORK OR COMPILATION Complete both space 6a and 6b for a derivative work; complete only 6b for a compilation.

a. Preexisting Material Identify any preexisting work or works that this work is based on or incorporates. ▼

b. Material Added to This Work Give a brief, general statement of the material that has been added to this work and in which copyright is claimed. ▼

See instructions before completing this space.

7

—space deleted—

8

REPRODUCTION FOR USE OF BLIND OR PHYSICALLY HANDICAPPED INDIVIDUALS A signature on this form at space 10 and a check in one of the boxes here in space 8 constitutes a non-exclusive grant of permission to the Library of Congress to reproduce and distribute solely for the blind and physically handicapped and under the conditions and limitations prescribed by the regulations of the Copyright Office: (1) copies of the work identified in space 1 of this application in Braille (or similar tactile symbols); or (2) phonorecords embodying a fixation of a reading of that work; or (3) both.

a ☐ Copies and Phonorecords b ☐ Copies Only c ☐ Phonorecords Only

See instructions.

9

DEPOSIT ACCOUNT If the registration fee is to be charged to a Deposit Account established in the Copyright Office, give name and number of Account.

Name ▼ **Account Number** ▼

CORRESPONDENCE Give name and address to which correspondence about this application should be sent. Name/Address/Apt/City/State/ZIP ▼

Area Code and Telephone Number ▶

Be sure to give your daytime phone ◀ number

10

CERTIFICATION* I, the undersigned, hereby certify that I am the

Check only one ▶

- ☐ author
- ☐ other copyright claimant
- ☐ owner of exclusive right(s)
- ☐ authorized agent of __________

Name of author or other copyright claimant, or owner of exclusive right(s) ▲

of the work identified in this application and that the statements made by me in this application are correct to the best of my knowledge.

Typed or printed name and date ▼ If this application gives a date of publication in space 3, do not sign and submit it before that date.

date ▶

Handwritten signature (X) ▼

11

MAIL CERTIFICATE TO

Name ▼

Number/Street/Apartment Number ▼

City/State/ZIP ▼

Certificate will be mailed in window envelope

YOU MUST
- Complete all necessary spaces
- Sign your application in space 10

SEND ALL ELEMENTS IN THE SAME PACKAGE
1. Application form
2. Nonrefundable $20 filing fee in check or money order payable to *Register of Copyrights*
3. Deposit material

MAIL TO
Register of Copyrights
Library of Congress
Washington, D.C. 20559-6000

The Copyright Office has the authority to adjust fees at 5-year intervals, based on changes in the Consumer Price Index. The next adjustment is due in 1996. Please contact the Copyright Office after July 1995 to determine the actual fee schedule.

*17 U.S.C. § 506(e): Any person who knowingly makes a false representation of a material fact in the application for copyright registration provided for by section 409, or in any written statement filed in connection with the application, shall be fined not more than $2,500.

July 1993—400,000 PRINTED ON RECYCLED PAPER ☆U.S. GOVERNMENT PRINTING OFFICE: 1993-342-582/80,020

second page of copyright form

you with this wording, or write directly to the Copyright Office of the Library of Congress in Washington, D.C. and request the free information pamphlets about copyrights.

One of the only reasons to register the copyright with U.S. Copyright Office is the extra damages received if you have to sue for copyright infringement. It is rare, however, that anyone has to initiate such a lawsuit.

At the present time, fees are $20 for registration of copyright claims, and there is at least a 16-week wait for enrollment. The Copyright Office also requires that two complete copies of the best edition of all works protected by copyright be deposited in the Office within three months of publication.

ISBN

Besides putting a copyright notice within your book, it is necessary to get an ISBN number. ISBN is the acronym for *International Standard Book Number,* a numbering system of books for identification purposes. Publishers apply for and receive a set of numbers which they assign to the books they publish. Each individual title and its subsequent editions must have a new ISBN number.

The ISBN is printed under the copyright on the copyright page and on the lower right-hand corner of the outside back cover of the book or dustjacket. Once your book is assigned the ten-digit ISBN number, it is listed in *Forthcoming Books in Print,* and then in *Books in Print* and/or *Paperbound Books in Print,* source guides used by libraries and bookstores. Bookstores, distributors, and wholesalers will not handle a book without an ISBN number.

Bar Code

A bar code is now required on the back cover of every book by all distributors and wholesalers because bookstores will not buy books without one. The bar code for books is a 13-number code, called the *Bookland EAN 13,* that can be read by a cash register scanner and contains a combination of the ISBN number and the price of the work. Bar codes can be obtained from companies that specialize in producing them or you can make one yourself with a computer bar code program. However, programs that produce this EAN code are expensive, and unless you plan on publishing many books, the cost may outweigh the convenience.

0-9647418-0-6 ← *ISBN Number*

52495 ← *retail price of $24.95*

9 780964 741805

coded ISBN scan number

bar code

Library of Congress Catalog Card Number

Some authors also want a Library of Congress Catalog Card Number for their books. Issued by the Library of Congress, these are control numbers that identify the record created for each book and are sent to member libraries and book vendors to help with cataloging. Card numbers are given to those materials which are most likely to be selected and catalogued by the Library of Congress for its own collection. Being chosen for inclusion in the Library of Congress is not a judgment of the worth of the book, but only that the librarians felt it could be used by the members of Congress.

Once obtained, this number, which is not required when publishing a book, is also entered on the copyright page under the copyright notice. It can be acquired from your publisher or printer or directly from the Library of Congress. A copy of the title page of the book should be sent in with the request form. There is no charge for the number, but the Library will want a copy of the final printed book sent to them. Books with a Library of Congress number are automatically listed in *The National Union Catalogue,* a publication of the Library.

The *Preassigned Card Number* (PCN) is given to eligible books, including self-published works, *before* publication, but this category does not include cataloging. The *Cataloging in Publication* (CIP) number, with cataloging information, is issued only to large or established publishing houses for books "...most likely to be acquired by the nation's libraries."

Another way for inclusion in the Library's collection is through the Copyright Office, which is totally separate from the PCN and CIP divisions. When the required two copies of the

PLEASE FILL IN AS MUCH INFORMATION AS POSSIBLE OR APPLICABLE *RETURN ENTIRE FORM*

ADVANCE BOOK INFORMATION R.R. BOWKER DATA COLLECTION CENTER
P.O. BOX 2068, OLDSMAR, FL 34677-0103

TITLE: ______

SUBTITLE: ______

Title Volume Number: ______

PUBLISHER (Not Printer): ______

ADDRESS: ______

Is this a set? Yes☐ No☐ **Number of Volumes:** ______

PHONE: ______ **TOLL FREE:** ______

FAX: ______ **TELEX:** ______

Is Title Orig. Paperbk? ☐YES ☐NO

E-mail, Internet, etc.: ______

Pub. Date: (MM/YY) ____/____

IMPRINT (If other than company name): ______

DISTRIBUTOR (If other than publisher): ______

(If you distribute foreign books, please send us a copy of your documentation and indicate whether distribution is exclusive or non-exclusive. Currently, only exclusive distributors are included in the US portion of the BIP database.)

Copyright Date: (year) ______

Pages: ______ **Illustrated?:** ☐ YES ☐ NO

CONTRIBUTOR NAME (A=Author, E=Editor, I=Illustrator, P=Photographer, T=Translator):

Contributor ______ ☐A ☐E ☐I ☐P ☐T ☐Other ______ (check all that apply)

Contributor ______ ☐A ☐E ☐I ☐P ☐T ☐Other ______ (check all that apply)

Contributor ______ ☐A ☐E ☐I ☐P ☐T ☐Other ______ (check all that apply)

Contributor ______ ☐A ☐E ☐I ☐P ☐T ☐Other ______ (check all that apply)

Series Title: ______

Series Subtitle: ______ **Series Volume Number:** ______

Edition Info.: ☐Reprint ☐ Revised ☐ Abridged ☐Large Type ☐ Unabridged ☐ Other(specify) ______

Edition No.: ☐2nd ☐ 3rd ☐ 4th ☐ 5th ☐ 6th ☐ Other(specify) ______

Audience: (children's books require grade levels) **GRADES:** ______ **AGES:** ______

☐ Juvenile ☐ Young Adult ☐ ElHi—Reading Levels ______

☐ College ☐ Adult\General ☐Other (specify) ______

Original Title: (If previously published & changed) ______

Translated Title: ______

Current Language (If other than English): ______ **Original Language** (If translated): ______

Publisher Order No.: ______ **LCCard No(LCCN):** ______

Point Size (Large Type Bks.): ______ **Book Size:** ______ **Book Weight:** ______

For ISBN Applicants: Fill out this form for each of your titles and return with your application. When the top copy is returned to you with your ISBN log book, assign an ISBN to each title, enter it below, and return the form(s) to the R.R. Bowker Data Collection Center, Florida. This will allow us to list your title(s) with all information in our database.
ISBN Note: Write full 10-digit number in space below. The BIP system requires a separate ISBN for each edition and binding.

BINDING	ISBN	PRICE	*TYPE:	**CURRENCY	DISCOUNT
Hardcover: ☐ Trade ☐ Textbk	______	$____.____	______	______	Short____% Max____
Paperback: ☐ Trade ☐ Textbk	______	$____.____	______	______	Short____% Max____
☐Library Binding	______	$____.____	______	______	Short____% Max____
☐Mass Market	______	$____.____	______	______	Short____% Max____
☐Other: ______	______	$____.____	______	______	Short____% Max____
☐Other: ______	______	$____.____	______	______	Short____% Max____

(OTHER refers to Tchr's. ed., Wkbk., Lab Manual, Looseleaf, etc.)
*Price type refers to invoice, retail, tentative, etc.
**Currency refers to US, Canadian, etc.
(Short Discount is 20% or less)

Type of Work: ☐ Non-Fiction ☐ Fiction ☐ Poetry ☐ Drama ☐ Essay ☐ Other ______

Subject Area: ☐ Children's (CB) ☐ Law(LB) ☐ Med(MB) ☐ Relig(RB) ☐ Sci-Tech(ST) ☐ Other ______

Description of Content: ______

OVER PLEASE→

ISBN application form

REQUEST FOR PREASSIGNMENT OF LIBRARY OF CONGRESS CATALOG CARD NUMBER

NOTE: *Card numbers cannot be preassigned to books which are already published. Works that receive a preassigned Library of Congress catalog card number are not eligible to receive Cataloging in Publication data for that same edition of the work.*

FORM MUST BE TYPED DATE: ____________

PUBLISHER'S NAME ON TITLE PAGE: ____________

YOUR NAME: ____________ PHONE NUMBER: ____________

Type the complete address to which the preassigned card number should be sent. (This will be your return mailing label.)

FOR CIP OFFICE USE

Library of Congress Catalog Card Number preassigned is:

Transcribe the information in items 1-8 exactly in the form and order in which it will appear on the title or copyright pages of the printed book. Use only those abbreviations which will actually appear on these pages. (**Please attach a copy of the proposed title page, if available.**)

1. Author(s) ____________
2. Editor(s) ____________
3. Title ____________
4. Subtitle ____________
5. Edition (exactly as printed in the publication, e.g. second edition, revised edition, etc.) ____________
6. U.S. place of publication: City ____________ State ____________
7. Any copublisher(s) and place ____________
8. Series title and numbering, exactly as printed in the publication ____________
9. Approximate number of pages ____________ 10. Number of volumes ____________
11. ISBN (Hard cover) ____________ ISBN (Paperback) ____________
12. Proposed date of publication: Month ________ Year ________ 13. Language of text, if other than English ____________
14. Does (or will) the title in item 3 appear at periodic intervals, e.g. annually, quarterly, etc.? ☐ Yes ☐ No

For each title which is preassigned a Library of Congress catalog card number, the Library of Congress requires one non-returnable complimentary copy of the best edition of the published book. If selected for the Library's collections, the book will be cataloged. This copy is in addition to copyright deposit copies. Continuing participation in the PCN program is contingent on full compliance with this obligation.

Send this form to: Library of Congress
Cataloging in Publication Division
101 Independence Ave., S.E.
Washington, DC 20540-4320

FOR CIP OFFICE USE ONLY.

Searching notes:

RECD: ____________
ASGN: ____________
SENT: ____________
APIF: ____________

607-7 (rev 6/94)

Library of Congress Card Catalog application form – a copy of the title page of the book, with a publisher's name included on it, should be sent with this form best edition of work protected by copyright are deposited with the Office, they are also reviewed by staff members of the Library of Congress and may then be selected for the collection. Another way to get the finished book on the Library's shelves is to send a copy to the Exchange and Gift Division of the Library, where reviewers determine whether the book fits their requirements.

Permissions and Disclaimers

One very important requirement for book publication is the need for permissions. These are grants of approval to quote or use copyrighted material in a book. Every so often, newspapers and telecasts will report a case of plagiarism, where a writer has either failed to acknowledge sources or has claimed another person's work as his or her own. To maintain credibility and avoid potential lawsuits, always cite your research and get permission to use copyrighted material. Permissions are also needed to use photographs, music, artwork (including masterpieces owned by museums), cartoons, and even maps.

To secure authorization, send a request to the owner of the copyright, who is listed in the copyright information of every published work. There is usually a small charge to use such material. If you have strived to obtain permissions but cannot locate a specific copyright owner, you can use a disclaimer on your copyright page.

Disclaimers should also be used if your book contains specific medical or legal advice, if your story is based on true life events, or contains anything that might in anyway expose you to a lawsuit. It is always best to check with a lawyer about the exact wording for a disclaimer.

Finances

Setting yourself up as a self-publisher brings with it many decisions, not the least of which is how to present yourself. Once you begin selling your books, all the delights and aggravations that come with a business settle on your desk. As a first step, it is necessary to separate all your financial transactions from your personal accounts. Open a separate checking account just for your business income and expenses and never mix personal and business money. Some authors who sell their own books find it best to establish themselves as a company or corporation, both for tax and selling advantages. It is always more professional to send out letters to bookstores, distributors,

SAMPLE 1

PERMISSION TO QUOTE

I, [name], as Rights Editor of [company name] Publishing Co., publisher of the book[title], by [author], give[your publishing company name] permission to use the following quotation in the book [your title]:

[exact quotation to be used in your book]

This is permission for non-exclusive use. The one-time fee for usage is $[price]. Copyright and date to be given written credit. The applicant agrees to print the following in each and every copy of the book printed, either as a footnote to the first page of the selection as printed or upon the copyright page (verso of the title page), the title of the work from which the selection is taken, the title of the selection if a separate title is given, and the copyright notice as it reproduced in the original. The right to reprint the material listed in this application shall apply only to the specific edition of the book named in the application, in the English language. Permission does not extend to material from other sources included in our publication. One copy of the book is to be sent to the Permissions Department.

SAMPLE 2

PERMISSION TO QUOTE

I, [author], give [your company name] Publishing Co., publisher of [your title], permission to use excerpts from my article [title], printed in [title] magazine, on [date], without cost or obligation.

[Your company name] Publishing Co. agrees to print in each and every copy of the book the title of the work and the author's name, as well as the words "reprinted by permission of." [Your company name] Publishing Co. also agrees to send a copy of the finished book to the author upon publication.

This agreement is for this and any subsequent printings or editions of this book. This agreement shall not be assigned or transferred by [your company name] Publishing Co.

Agreed to and Accepted by

____

_________________(date)

samples of permissions forms

Every effort has been made to trace and contact copyright holders prior to publication. However, in some instances, this has proved to be impossible. If notified, the publisher will be pleased to rectify any omissions in the next edition of this book.

This book is designed to provide you with accurate information about [subject] so that you can deal more effectively with the [subject] situations that concern you. However, your own situation may be different from the ones described in this book. In addition, laws are subject to change and varying interpretations. As a result, this book is sold with the understanding that neither the author nor the publisher is engaged in rendering specific legal or other professional services to any individual.

This book is a work of fiction. Names, characters, places, and incidents either are the product of the author's imagination or are used fictitiously and any resemblance to actual persons, living or dead, events or locales is entirely coincidental.

[Your company name] Publishing Co. certifies that the recipes in this book are not intended as a medically therapeutic program, nor as a substitute for medically approved diet plans for people on fat , cholesterol-, sugar-, or sodium- restricted diets. You should consult your physician before beginning any diet plan.

Programs of this type, like diet or exercise programs, will not provide the same results for everyone. Do not start any such program without first consulting your medical advisor to be certain that you are in good health and the program will not affect you adversely.

samples of disclaimers

and libraries on company stationery, especially if you do not name the company after yourself. If you have future plans to sell more than one book, consider calling yourself a publishing company; this presents a more authoritative image and can also open some doors that are closed to mere authors.

You must also register with your state as a seller. You will be selling to people who have to pay you sales tax as well as to those who resell your books and do not have to pay taxes. Depending on your state laws, you are responsible for all the collection and bookkeeping involved with these taxes. Your accountant or lawyer can explain the laws and regulations, and the staff of your state Department of Revenue will help if you have any questions.

Setting Up an Office

If you intend to actively and aggressively sell your title and take orders by phone, you should have a *separate telephone line* just for your publishing business. Securing this second line for your phone effectively separates business and personal calls, allowing you to answer the business line in a professional manner. *Voice mail* will prevent you from missing calls if the line is in use or you have a full-time job outside your home.

A *fax machine* further expands your ability to receive documents, responses, and memos. It will also allow you to meet deadlines and get fast-breaking news to a large number of customers or media contacts in a short time.

An *800 or toll-free number* is also another way to obtain book orders in a professional way. This number is essential to any coordinated mail order or advertising campaign, and mentioning your 800 number when you are being interviewed is an excellent way to get orders directly from buyers.

Because many of your orders will be coming in by phone, you may want to invest in a *credit card processing service*. This will allow you to instantly fill most phone orders. Such a service supplies a machine that receives and verifies credit card transactions, sending the information immediately to your bank. It is easiest to get such credit card services from your own full-service bank. Credit card service fees can run as high as 4½ percent per transaction, but because credit cards are the most popular way for individuals to buy products, the transaction fees should be averaged out by the extra sales you will make.

Carefully track and double-check your credit card sales, both at the time they are processed, and when you receive your bank statement.

A *computer* expands the capabilities of an office, and gives the flexibility and power to turn out sales tools, business forms, and personalized letters, as well as setting up your book in camera-ready form. It can also help you in accounting and marketing research, automate repetitive processes, access the Internet, receive e-mail, and fax documents. To enhance the computer, you should also have a *printer* that is capable of turning out a professional-looking document.

If you want to use your computer to access the Internet, you will need a *modem* and an account with an online service such as Prodigy, America Online, Compuserve, or a local Internet service provider.

Office Tools

The basic tools of a self-publisher or small press include: a catalog or brochure describing your book or books, business cards, stationery with a distinctive letterhead, order forms, invoices, discount and returns policy statements *(see Chapter 8)*, a scheduling and appointment calendar or computer program, telephone and address file, and a ledger or computer program to record sales and returns.

You will also need a dry, secure place to store your books unless you use a fulfillment company to store and ship for you. If you will be shipping orders for yourself, set up a space that includes a table for assembling outgoing orders, padded envelopes and box mailers, packing tape, mailing labels, a postal rate scale and chart, and return address labels. You might want to set up an account with a shipping company, which is more expensive than U.S. mail, but does offer the benefit of tracking your shipments when they do not arrive when they are supposed to.

Before opening for business, it is also a good idea to subscribe to a few key industry magazines, such as *Small Press, Book Marketing Update,* and *Publishers Weekly.* These, and newsletters from small press organizations, will be an important source of information, updates, and insights into the constantly changing book trade.

The Basic Plan

Once you have established your needs, make a list of the steps you will need to take before you begin the actual production of the book. A typical list would look like this:

1. Set a budget
2. Look through writing magazines for self-publishing companies and printers and write for information about their services and pricing. Ask for sample books and names of customers for recommendations.
3. Decide on the publisher or printer you will be using. Make sure the publishing/printing contract specifies exact costs, services, and time of delivery before signing.
4. Ask publishers/printers for their specifications to produce your book. Be very specific in your inquiries and do not hesitate to call back with questions. Correcting mistakes later in the production process is always more expensive.
5. Determine the price of your book by using the formula in Chapter 8. Then check other comparable books and adjust the price of your book accordingly.
6. Obtain your ISBN number, bar code, and Library of Congress CIP number if the publisher/printer does not provide this service.
7. Have a professional editor and/or proofreader go over your manuscript, looking for errors.
8. Choose a title; check *Books in Print* and *Forthcoming Books in Print* to make sure the title has not already been used.
9. Get permissions.
10. Send copies of your manuscript to people who will give you a credible endorsement for the back of the book.

Planning the Book

Once you have accomplished the goals on your list, your manuscript is ready to go into production.

Every book consists of a title and three major sections: the front matter, the text, and the back matter. When beginning production of your book, you must keep as close as possible to this established order.

Choosing a Title for a Book

How you title your book can determine how well it will sell. *The Man Who Mistook His Wife for His Hat and Other Clinical Tales* was written by neurologist Dr. Oliver Sacks and became a best seller. It is debatable how well it would have done if it had been called *Case Studies of Brain Damage*.

When choosing a title, make sure it is easy to pronounce. It should not be the same or similar to the title of a previous book. Because a title is so important at every stage of a book's existence — getting it noticed by reviewers, distributors, and readers — keep it simple, positive, and avoid cuteness. A perfect title may connote a promise of something wanted (slim thighs, wealth, happy marriage); it is very often placed in the second person "you" (you can do something, you can win something else); it might be alliterative or use word play. Its most important aspect is to jog the mind of the passerby enough so that he or she stops to look at the book.

All books begin with a right hand page, and since the first page is always page number one, it follows that every right hand page (called a *recto*) is an odd number and every left hand page (or *verso*) is an even number. Therefore, the title page, which is almost always the first page of a book, becomes page one. The copyright page is page two. These pages are often, but not necessarily, followed by a dedication, acknowledgment, table of contents, foreword, and an introduction. All of these pages preceding the first chapter are called *front matter.*

The next group of pages, or *text*, are the chapters of the book. The final pages, which include everything after the text, are called the *back matter.* These are usually reference pages such as endnotes, the afterword, glossary, appendix, bibliography, and index.

The best way to understand the standard organization of a book is to study books in your library or bookstore. You will soon get a feel for what is necessary for inclusion in your own work.

Sources

BAR CODES

R. R. Bowker sends out a list of bar code suppliers with its ISBN application form. When you order a bar code, request a Bookland EAN 13 film master *and* duplicate master, which will give you both the bar code both on film and a positive for paste-up.

One computer program that creates bar codes is put out by Zebra Technologies VTI, Inc. and is called BAR-ONE for Windows. Whatever program you purchase, make sure it includes the EAN 13 bar code.

COPYRIGHTS

Copyright registration fees are $20. Copyrights and information about copyright law can be obtained from The Registrar of Copyrights, Copyright Office, Library of Congress, Washington, DC 20559. Phone: 202-479-0700. Hotline: 202-707-9100.

ISBN

The international standard book number (ISBN) is obtained through the Standard Book Numbering Agency, R.R. Bowker, 121 Chanlon Road, New Providence, NJ 07974. Phone: (ISBN only) 908-665-6770. They have just raised their price to $165; this charge includes a list of numbers to use for all the books you publish. Their three day rush service is now $215.

LIBRARY OF CONGRESS

The Library of Congress assigns catalog card numbers for identification of books that are in its collection. These control numbers are used by many libraries for cataloging purposes. To apply for a free Preassigned Card Number, write to the Library of Congress, Cataloging in Publication Division, 101 Independence Avenue, S. E., Washington, DC 20540. Phone: 202-707-9100. Address your request for a Library number for an already published book to the Library of Congress Exchange and Gift Division, Washington, DC 20540.

2

EQUIPMENT AND PRODUCTION BASICS

Chapter 2

Computers and Printers

Once you decide to do the production of your book yourself, you will become a production editor, typesetter, and designer. This multifaceted job can be made much easier depending on the equipment you use. First and foremost, the self-publisher must have a computer with plenty of memory. It does not matter whether the computer is a Macintosh or an IBM compatible (PC); what is important is that it has the capacity to handle book production. A typewriter or word processor will not give you a professional-looking book because neither machine has the ability to design or typeset a page adequately.

If you do plan on printing, or outputting, your own camera-ready pages, you need a printer that will give you a *minimum* of a 600 DPI (dots per inch) printout. This excludes dot matrix printers which do not have a professional graphics quality, and some ink jet printers which have a tendency to smear or form a "halo" around words. If your book is heavily designed, uses a lot of graphics or halftones (photographs), or needs unusual typefaces or font sizes, you must use a PostScript printer.

Production Choices

It will be your decision how much of your book production you will "farm out" to professional bookmakers. Some self-publishers create everything but the cover. Others contract for the typesetting or just the design of the page layout, while still others do everything themselves but the actual book printing.

If you are reasonably handy, enjoy being in control of your creative efforts, and are not afraid of making mistakes or embarrassed to correct errors, then you are a good candidate for producing your book yourself. If you do not have a computer or printer, or are working with outdated equipment, then determine the price of what it would cost to have your book professionally produced. If the cost is more than buying or upgrading a computer and/or printer, then buy the most up-to-date equipment you can afford. You will have saved the cost of a professional's bill and own equipment you can use repeatedly.

If you already have a computer but it does not have enough memory, buying a removable storage disk, such as a SyQuest, Bernoulli, or Zip or Jaz drive, will give you enough extra memory to store a complete book at a fraction of the cost of getting a new computer. These devices also give you the opportunity of handing the whole book on disk to the book printer, who in turn can output it directly to film at over 2,000 DPI. Even though commercial printers will charge you for this service, the combined costs of the removable disk and output will probably still be less than a new computer and printer.

Computer Programs

The computer program you choose to produce your book is as important as the computer itself. There are programs you can purchase that are set up to produce books — these are commonly called "desktop" or "electronic publishing" programs. Some of the most popular include Adobe PageMaker (PC and Mac), QuarkXPress (PC and Mac), Corel Ventura (PC), CorelDraw (PC), and FrameMaker (PC and Mac). Not only are these flexible programs to work with, but most come with templates that will make a book look professionally designed and typeset.

However, even a dependable word processing program can make an attractive book. It takes a little more effort, but the results can be just as good-looking as anything produced by a desktop program. WordPerfect for Windows is especially well suited for laying out and typesetting a book *(see Appendix)*.

Whichever computer and program you decide on, make sure they are flexible enough to adjust for extra space on the inside margin of each page for the binding, and that it will automatically set running heads or footers, number pages, and justify each line of type evenly without inserting extra spaces. All equipment should have enough memory to store each chapter of your book as a separate file, and run everything smoothly and cleanly when you are ready to go to camera-ready copy.

As you read through the specifications for book production in this chapter, ask yourself if your equipment can handle these requirements. Self-publishing is an important form of publishing, but you do not want your book to *look* self-published. The difference is between the professional and the amateur, and there should be nothing amateurish about your book.

Book Specifications

In order to set up the specifications, you must know the size of your book, the type of binding, and the number of copies to be run, as well as the type and weight of the paper, how many photographs are to be included, and how much color you want on the cover or dustjacket. You should also decide when you need the book. You need all this information because this is how printing costs are determined. That is why there is no real answer to the question so often asked of printers: "How much will it cost to print my book? I don't know exactly what I want, but I need to know how much money it will be." Printer quotations can only be accurate when they are based on precise specifications. *(See Chapter 6 for more about printing specifications.)*

Pages and Signatures

When you begin setting up the specifications for your book, one method of holding down costs is to keep the total number of pages divisible by 16 or 32. It is important to remember that the total number of pages includes the front and back matter; this means *everything* from the title page to the last page of the index or bibliography. A page is defined as only *one side* of each piece of paper in a book.

The pages in a finished book should not be confused with the way the pages are set up to be printed. Presses are set up to run large rolls or sheets of paper, and each side is printed with multiple pages of the book at one time — 16 and 32 pages to a sheet are the most common setups. Each of these printed sheets is called a *signature*. The printer should be the only one responsible for setting up the pages in the proper order for the signature; this specific setup is called the *imposition* of the pages.

The signature is folded so each page falls into its proper position. All the signatures are then gathered together to be cut and bound into a book. A book can be run with four- and eight-page signatures, but the cost will be close to or the same as for standard signatures because those signatures will still be printed as 16 or 32 pages, only with blank pages included. If you have ever seen a book with blank pages bound in at the end, you have seen a book where the page count did not fit the signature.

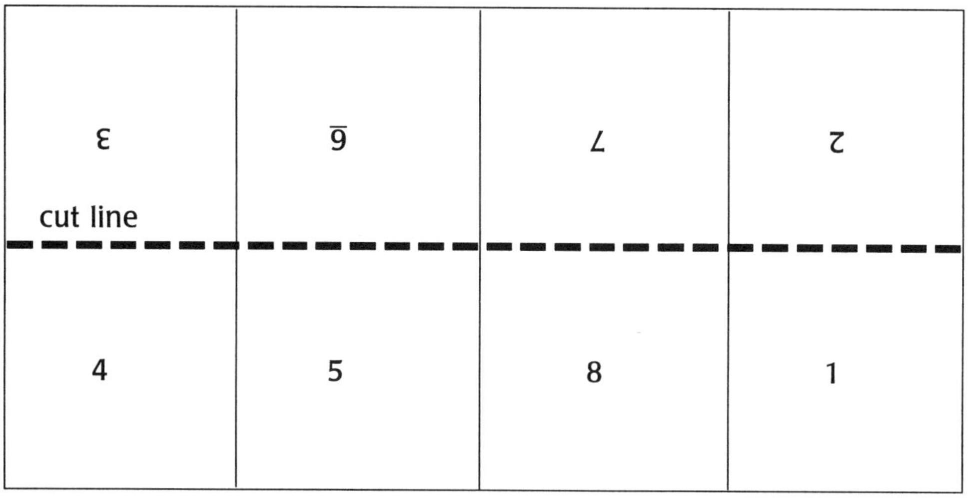

8-page imposition

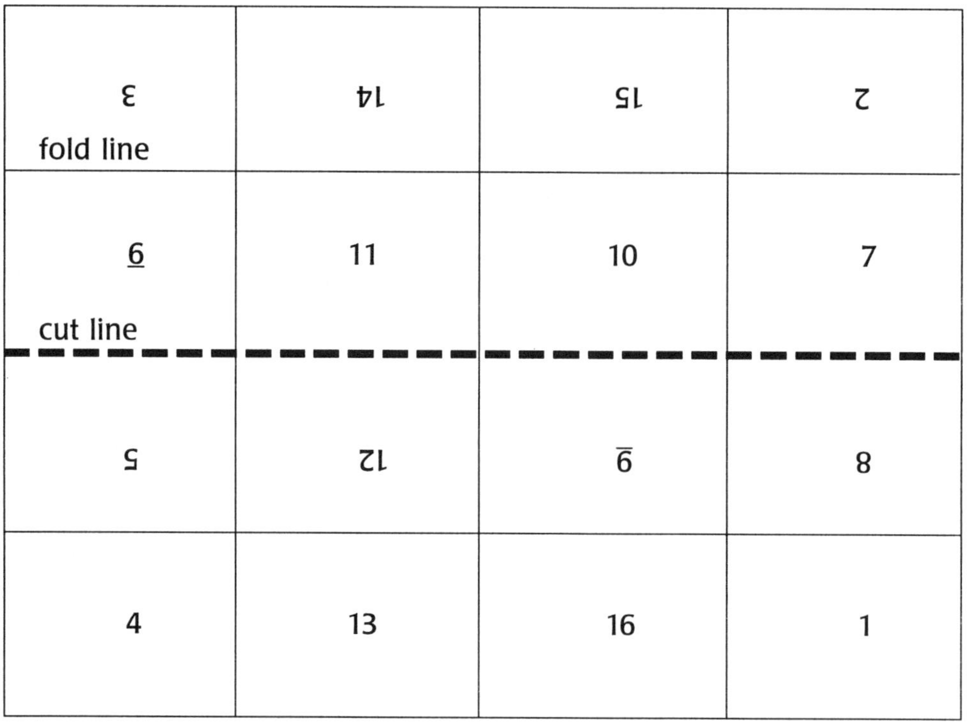

16-page imposition

signatures set up for different types of presses

Quantity

One of the major costs of printing is the setup. Your setup costs include such things as turning camera-ready pages into film, making the plates, and press preparation. These are not tasks for the self-publisher, but are done by the commercial printer, service bureau, or graphics house.

Books are printed on huge presses, which can be as large as a building. The most cost-efficient printing is done when you print at least 1,000 copies of a book. Once you reach 1,000 copies, you usually have covered the setup costs and thereafter are mainly paying for just paper and ink. The per unit cost of a book goes down the more books you print.

Binding

Often self-publishers want casebound or hardcover books because they think they will sell better at the bookstores or that libraries will not buy perfect bound, soft cover books. This was true in the past, but not any longer. In fact, libraries, with their continuing budget cuts, appreciate that a perfect bound book is less costly.

A perfect bound book has a glued spine. It is sturdy and can withstand hard use. The covers of perfect bound books are usually coated with a varnish, an ultraviolet (UV) coating, or a plastic film laminate *(see Appendix)*. The laminate offers the most protection from wear and tear. The biggest complaint about soft cover books is that their covers tend to curl over time, but there is now a non-curl laminate on the market that controls that problem.

Some soft cover books, such as workbooks, must open fully without breaking the spine, and they are specially bound with a *layflat* binding. This type of binding is cost-efficient for large runs only.

A casebound book can have either a glued or a sewn spine. The best looking, as well as the most secure spine, is one that is Smyth sewn, a method which first sews each individual signature and then sews all these signatures together. A casebound book is more expensive than a perfect bound book because of all the extra work and materials that go into making it. Other than appearance, which can be important in certain circumstances, the only other reason for opting for a casebound book is that you can charge more money for it.

There are other kinds of binding including wire stitching (also called "saddle stitching"), spiral wire, and plastic combs,

examples of different book bindings:
(top) wire-O; (middle-row left) plastic comb; (middle-row right) chapbook with wire stitching; (bottom-row left) casebound; (bottom-row right) perfect bound

but most books that are sold in bookstores or on the shelves of libraries are either perfect bound or casebound. That is because books with other types of binding are hard to shelve.

It is very difficult to perfect bind a book that has fewer than 64 pages, because the spine becomes so small, less than 1/8 of an inch. The way around this problem is to "bulk up" the book by using a much thicker paper so the spine becomes thicker. Juvenile books that are casebound can be as small as 16 pages, but use a special sewing process called *juvenile binding*.

The Run

How many books should you print? In the cost-conscious world of business, more and more small press publishers are deciding on smaller runs of anywhere from 1,000 to 3,000 books. They know that the unit cost of a book becomes lower the more books they print, but they also are painfully aware that if the book does not sell, no matter how cheap the book was to produce, they will still lose money. Therefore, print the largest, but most practical amount of books you can, knowing that you can always reprint if the orders start pouring in. The key word here is practicality — balance the cost of the book against any preorders. Know exactly how many books you must sell to make your money back for your run. If you choose a run of 1,000 copies and the book costs you $3.50 a copy to produce, you might price it at $14.95. You would have to sell at least 235 books at full cost to make your money back (original cost of $3,500 and income of $3,513.25). However, very few books are sold at full price. *(See Chapter 8 for a more precise pricing formula.)*

Size

The most common sizes for books are 5½ by 8½, 6 by 9, and 8½ by 11. The most economical and easiest to handle are the smaller sizes. Books such as "coffee-table" volumes are often printed in larger custom sizes.

There is another kind of small paperback, sometimes called a "pocketbook," which is usually sold through drugstores, supermarkets, news stands, department stores, and some chain bookstores. These books are mass-merchandised, with typical runs of 100,000 or more copies, which keeps the price per book low. The softcover books that most self-publishers contract for are larger in size, printed on heavier paper stock, and with a usual run of anywhere from 500 to 5,000 copies. These are called "trade" paperbacks.

Paper

Most publishers and printing companies offer a variety of paper stocks in different colors and weights. When choosing a paper for your book, you will have to decide on a *weight* and *PPI, or pages per inch*. The PPI will help you determine the size of the spine of the book, because the lower the number of pages per inch, the thicker the paper and the bigger the spine. The weight of the paper is its actual thickness, or how many pounds make up a ream of paper. The usual paper weight for a book is 5-pound paper. Sixty-pound paper is also used frequently, while 70# is heavier, more costly, and thus is used less often.

To keep your paper costs down, use a "house" paper, which is the paper that your printer or publisher keeps in stock and buys in quantity. Most books are printed on an *offset* paper, which has a slightly rough finish. If you are running a lot of photographs, in black and white, or especially in color, then you probably will want to go to a coated paper — this can be either matte or gloss in finish. This type of paper costs more than an uncoated paper, but it reproduces pictures much better.

Consider using acid-free paper for your books. Paper that is not acid-free turns yellow and disintegrates after a few years. Recycled paper adds a nice touch, especially to books that deal with environmental issues, but can cost more and currently is limited in the selection of finishes.

Paper color for books runs from very white to cream colored. Unless you are publishing a specialty book, do not use any other colors for your paper choice.

The paper stock for the cover of a trade paperback book is usually *10-point C1S*, or 100-pound stock, coated on one side. Some designers prefer 12-point covers (120-pound paper), but these heavier covers curl more easily than the standard weight. Coated cover paper only comes in white, which is convenient if you are trying to save money and have specified a two-color cover, because the white of the paper can be used in your cover design as an extra free color.

> Paper prices have been rising lately at a very fast rate. Because of this, some printers will not honor their quotations for more than a few days. One way around this problem is to pay for the paper you will need in advance. This way, the printing costs of the book will not go up as the production goes on. However, be sure to include rising paper prices for future reprints in your pricing.

Photographs

Photographs are one of the most misunderstood aspects of a book. *Illustrations,* such as line drawings, graphs, and maps, are treated as text and can either be generated in a computer, scanned, or glued (never taped) in place where they belong in the text. They are then considered camera-ready and incur no extra production costs. However, a photograph is *not* camera-ready and cannot be printed just as it is.

A black-and-white photograph must be converted into a *halftone* before it can be printed. This can be done with computer scanning, but the kind of equipment that gives a true photographic quality to a photograph is expensive. Most desktop publishers who scan in photographs end up with what looks like a scanned photo in their books, which does not have the clarity of a true halftone. This is better in quality than a photocopy produced on a copy machine, but often not good enough for a professional-looking book.

What is a halftone? If you look at a black-and-white photograph, you can see that it is made up of many tones of grey, black, and white. If you were to use a copy machine, you would lose those middle tones and the photo will reproduce to a muddy black. That is what your photo would look like if you tried to print it without modifications. But if you change the tones of that photograph into dots, these different sizes of black dots, when printed, fool the eye into seeing all the continuous-tones that made up the original photograph. This is then called a halftone.

Color photographs must be separated into four colors of film: cyan (blue), magenta, yellow, and black. Once these four layers of film are put together, all the colors in the original photograph are produced. Again, this can be done on a computer

scanned photo printed with PageMaker 80 line per inch screen default

photocopy of photograph

halftone

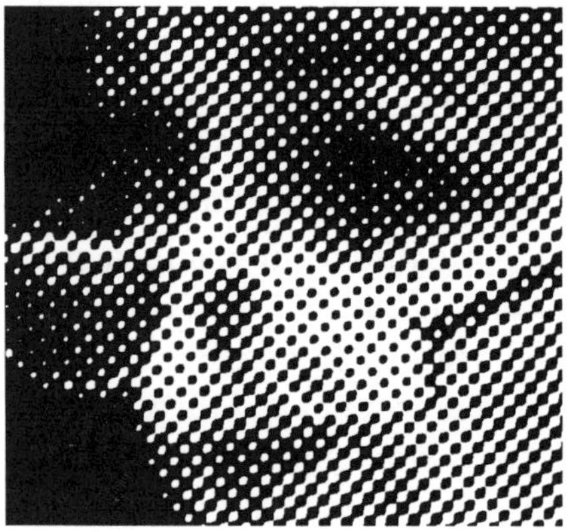

closeup of halftone showing halftone dots

computer scan, photocopy, and halftone

with a program such as Photoshop, but, unless you have high-end equipment, it is better to have a professional separator do this work. A separator's price includes a proof of what your photo will look like when printed, which is often called a *matchprint*. This proof is used to make sure the colors are accurate and as a correction source at the press when covers are printed (*see Appendix for more about color printing*).

Timing

It can take eight to ten weeks for the typesetting, design, and preparation of the book and cover to get to the camera-ready stage. Add to that about three to four weeks before the proofs (*bluelines*) are ready. Once the bluelines are approved, a perfect bound book will take another three to four weeks until its delivery, while a casebound book needs at least six to eight weeks. If your book is printed during a busy time at the presses, it can take even longer. Timing can be crucial to the success of your book on the market, so confer with your publisher or printer every step of the way about the expected delivery time of your book.

Production

Professional-looking typesetting and design are essential for a book. Often new publishers assume that an 8½ by 11 page, set in Courier type (typewriter style), with ½ inch margins looks just fine. But, typesetting your book is not the same thing as preparing a paper for a class. A book has a certain look and feel to it that readers expect, and anything less is strictly amateurish and probably unsalable.

3

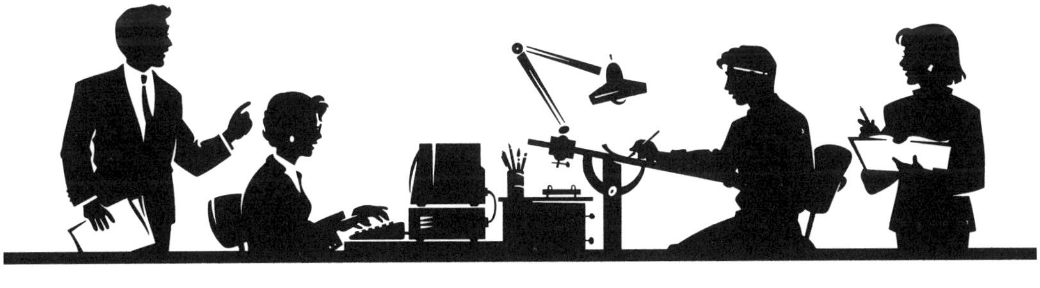

PRODUCTION, EDITING, AND DESIGN

Chapter 3

Readability

What determines the look of a book? Readability, suitability, and producibility. Readability means that the text in a book is easy to read. The type is *justified* (evenly spaced on both the right and left margins, as seen on this page), and every line does not end with a hyphen. There should be no extra spaces between words, and pages should not begin with a single word or line.

A book can be overdesigned, especially by people who own a computer program that allows them to use many different typefaces. As a rule of thumb, never use more than two typefaces on a page and keep design elements to a minimum. Nothing superfluous should come between the reader and what he or she is trying to read. If the reader notices how the words are put on the page rather than the words themselves, the book is not well designed or typeset.

Suitability

Suitability is the determination of the choice of typefaces used, and the layout and design of the pages and book in relation to the subject matter. You would not choose a small condensed typeface for a book that senior citizens are going to read, nor would you choose a fancy script for a primary school book. If you are producing a cookbook, the ingredients should be listed above the recipe instructions, not under them or three pages later. A page should be laid out so that there is room for the running heads and the page number, and these must be in the same place on every page and not placed so as to be confused with the text. There should be extra space allowed on the left or right margin for the binding, depending on whether it is a verso or recto page. The headlines, subheads, and captions should be the same style for every chapter. The most important factor in the production of a book is *consistency.*

Producibility

Producibility deals with the conflict between your wish-list and your pocketbook. The more elaborate your book, the more expensive the book will cost to produce. Set a budget for yourself and stay within it. Even if you can afford to produce a full-color text with original illustrations and a full-color cover, how much will you have to charge to just make your money back, and will prospective buyers pay that price? Once you have determined the specifications for your book and put it into production, do not change your mind about the page count, type of paper used, and colors of the cover. "Stop the presses!" is just a line from the movies. Be consistent in your work and your book will look professional and stay within budget.

Editing and Proofreading

Every book starts with a manuscript. The first step to take after writing your work is to get it edited and proofread. There is no shame in doing this. Behind every great writer looms an editor with a red pen. No professional writer does a final edit or proofread of his or her own work, because after spending hours in writing and rewriting a book, it is almost impossible for an author to see mistakes that have been made.

A professional editor or proofreader can make a difference in the quality of your work, but is not always necessary. If you have a good command of the basic rules of grammar and composition and have a friend who is well read and knows what a sentence should or should not be, you can follow that route. However, be aware that one edit and proofread is never enough. Large and small publishing houses have both copy *and* production editors. A *copy editor* reads through a manuscript, noting any alterations that should be made, such as grammatical and stylistic changes, and also double checks facts. The *production editor* reviews the copy editor's work and also inspects the way the book has been set up, looking for inconsistencies, such as headlines that are not in the same place from chapter to chapter, too much space between lines, or even a typeface change that should not have happened.

No one will ever read your book as closely or as objectively as a professional editor, who has been trained to see what is good about your manuscript as well as find ways it might be improved.

Professional editing of a manuscript often gives an author new insights into writing. *(See Appendix for proofreading symbols and how they are used.)*

Whatever your decision is about editing and proofreading, do not rely on a spell check or a grammar program. In fact, most grammar programs give Abraham Lincoln's "Gettysburg Address" a grade of D minus. Even a good spell check program doesn't know the word *homonym.*

> I have a spelling checker;
> it came with my PC.
> It plainly marks four my revue
> mistakes I cannot sea.
> I've run this poem threw it,
> I'm sure your pleased too no,
> its letter perfect in it's weigh,
> my checker tolled me sew.

Layout

There are two elements to the design of a book: the inside text design, or *layout,* and the outside cover and/or dustjacket design. Unlike the design of other works of art, the main consideration in designing a book is the reader's comfort. If he or she cannot easily read the words, then that book or cover is badly designed, no matter how pretty it appears.

Every book needs a plan before it can be made into camera-ready copy. If you are not a professional book designer, then you must do some basic homework before you begin to design the layout for your book. Go to bookstores and the library and pick up books that appeal to you and try to figure out why they "speak" to you. Look specifically at the design of the pages, the typeface that is used, and the way the page numbers, running heads, and footers are placed. Photocopy pages from the books you like and use them as a source for developing your own layout plan. (Using these pages as a source does not mean directly copying them for your own book, which is plagiarism.)

If your computer program has templates already set up for books, you may be able to use one of them for your layout; these templates can easily be adapted for different types of books. *(See Appendix for samples of layouts.)*

Certain rules are constant for all books, such as all odd-numbered pages are right-hand pages and left-hand pages are even-numbered, and the first page is always a right-hand page.

Margins

Each page in a book has certain elements that are necessary and become part of the layout. Begin with the margins surrounding the area, or block, of text. The margins surrounding the text block affect the look of the book. The larger they are, the more luxurious the book's appearance — some books of poetry have only one or two lines of text centered on a page.

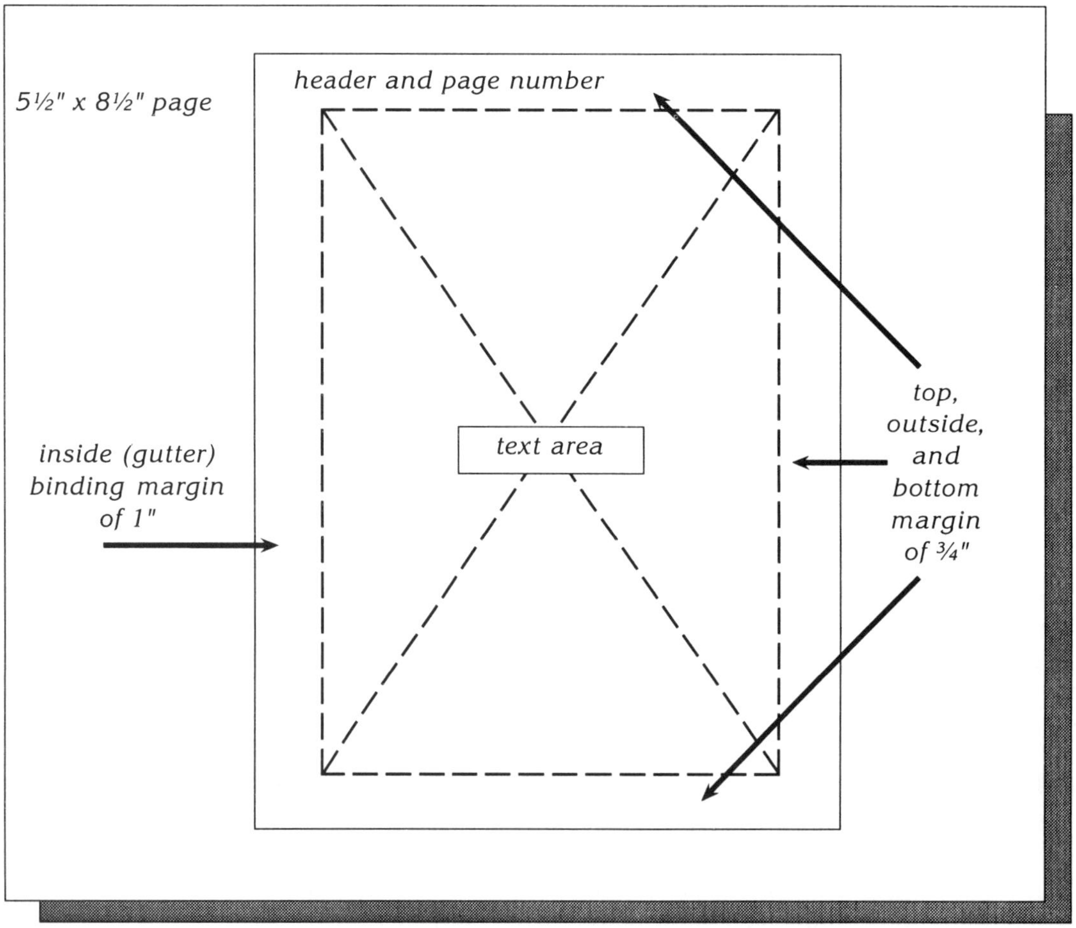

template for right hand (recto) one page spread

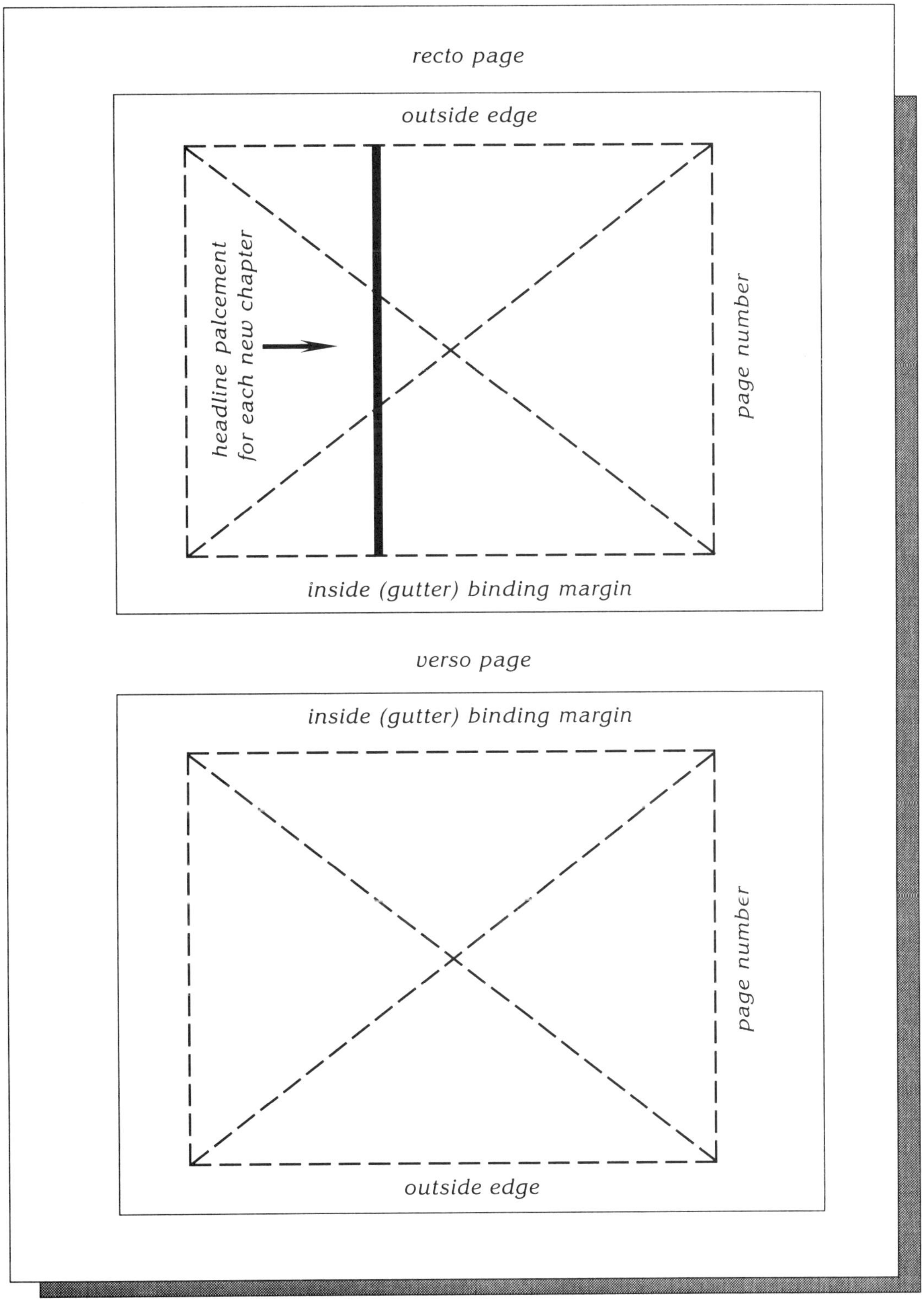

template for 2-page spread of poetry book

You must also include at least ¼ inch extra on the inside margin for a binding edge. A novel that is 5½ by 8½ inches might have a ¾ inch margin on the outside edge, bottom, and top, and a 1" margin on the inside, or *gutter,* binding margin. A 6 by 9 book should have larger margins, usually of 1inch and 1¼ inch. If you decide to vary the size of the margins, the top of the page should be the smallest, the second largest should be the gutter or inside margin, the third largest should be the outside margin, and the largest should be at the bottom of the page. Whatever margins you choose, keep them consistent throughout the book and work for a balance between the mass of the text and the white space of the margin.

The margins define the area of the text block and the size of the page. If your program can produce *crop marks* when you print, use this option. Crop marks are the indication to the printer as to where the page should be cut. The marks will help you see the actual size of the book's page so you can determine if the margins and other elements of the layout are placed correctly.

Running Heads, Feet, and Page Numbers

The running head is the line at the top of a page that indicates the chapter title or the name of the book or author. It is not a necessary element, but if you use it, make sure it is separated from the main text block. The running foot is any information repeated along the bottom of a page, and it too should be apart from the text block. The running head or foot is often separated from the main body of text by a set amount of space, a smaller font, and/or a different typeface.

Page numbers are often part of the running head or foot. They can be placed top or bottom right, left, or centered, but placing them left on a left-hand page and right on a right-hand page is best for the ease of the reader. Often, numbers are smaller than the type used in the body of the text. Make sure that whatever design you decide upon, it remains the same from page to page.

Heads and Subheads

Chapter *heads* (headlines) often use a different font or typeface than the body of the text. This is to call attention to the new chapter. As a rule of thumb, use no more than two different typefaces in a book, and the use of fonts within a typeface should also be kept at a minimum. *(See Chapter 4 for a more detailed examination of typefaces and fonts.)*

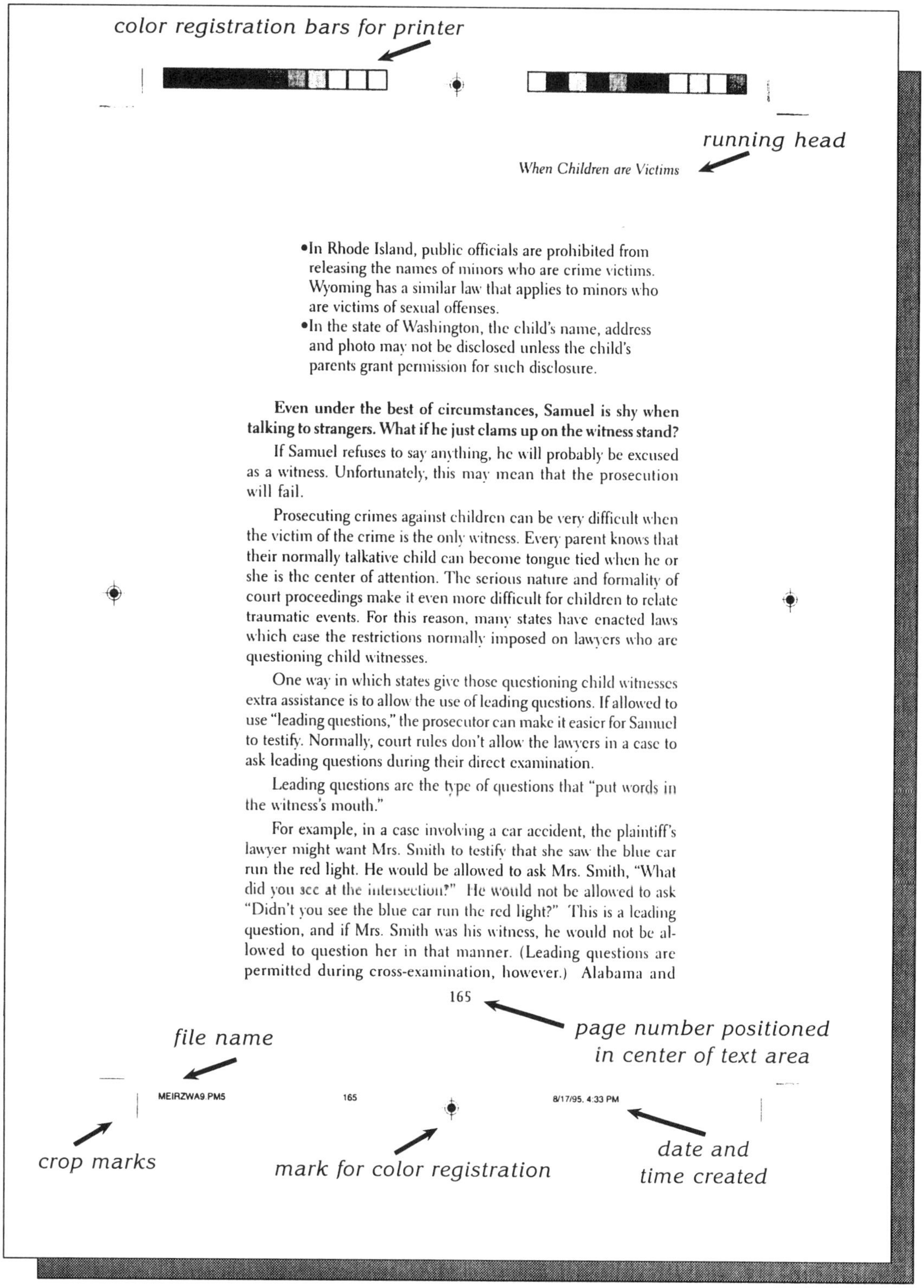

When Children are Victims

- In Rhode Island, public officials are prohibited from releasing the names of minors who are crime victims. Wyoming has a similar law that applies to minors who are victims of sexual offenses.
- In the state of Washington, the child's name, address and photo may not be disclosed unless the child's parents grant permission for such disclosure.

Even under the best of circumstances, Samuel is shy when talking to strangers. What if he just clams up on the witness stand?

If Samuel refuses to say anything, he will probably be excused as a witness. Unfortunately, this may mean that the prosecution will fail.

Prosecuting crimes against children can be very difficult when the victim of the crime is the only witness. Every parent knows that their normally talkative child can become tongue tied when he or she is the center of attention. The serious nature and formality of court proceedings make it even more difficult for children to relate traumatic events. For this reason, many states have enacted laws which ease the restrictions normally imposed on lawyers who are questioning child witnesses.

One way in which states give those questioning child witnesses extra assistance is to allow the use of leading questions. If allowed to use "leading questions," the prosecutor can make it easier for Samuel to testify. Normally, court rules don't allow the lawyers in a case to ask leading questions during their direct examination.

Leading questions are the type of questions that "put words in the witness's mouth."

For example, in a case involving a car accident, the plaintiff's lawyer might want Mrs. Smith to testify that she saw the blue car run the red light. He would be allowed to ask Mrs. Smith, "What did you see at the intersection?" He would not be allowed to ask "Didn't you see the blue car run the red light?" This is a leading question, and if Mrs. Smith was his witness, he would not be allowed to question her in that manner. (Leading questions are permitted during cross-examination, however.) Alabama and

165

MEIRZWA9.PM5 165 8/17/95, 4:33 PM

camera-ready copy with page elements in place, including crop marks, running head, and page number – some of the elements shown are optional

Heads are often dropped down on the page for visual interest. They can run flush left, right, or be centered. Often they are all in *caps* (capital letters) or *small caps* (all caps with initial letters a little larger). Again, whatever you decide to use as your design technique, be consistent — heads should fall on the same place on every page on which they appear, they should be the same size, and use the same typeface and fonts.

If your book uses subheads, they can be the same typeface as the chapter head or a font variation of the body text. They should not be as large as the chapter head. They can be placed flush left, right, or centered on the page. Usually they have extra space above them to separate out the section they are introducing. In this book they are the same typeface as the main heads, but smaller in size and are placed to the side of the main text to help the reader locate specific information more quickly.

Special Elements of Design

Sometimes a designer wants to use special elements to add interest to a book design. Underlining under a running head, unusual design elements, such as *dingbats,* between sections of the book of chapter heads, and indenting around quotations or special sections of the text are all techniques that can be used. If you choose to use these effects, be consistent in their use throughout the book.

> ▲
>
> **Reverse type is not easily read in long passages of text. Use this typesetting technique sparingly.**
>
> ▼

reverse type with dingbats above and below as extra design elements

Paragraph Spacing

Certain programs allow you to add a small amount of extra space between paragraphs. This is a technique that typesetters have always used to make a book easier to read. If your program does not allow you to do this, *do not double space between paragraphs.*

She was naked like the goddess, holding in each hand the corners of her scarlet veil which the wind unfurled in the evening sky, and the mirror, in her right hand, reflected the setting sun.

Languidly, with infinite grace and majesty, her head bowed, she climbed the outside ramp that formed a spiral band around the vermilion tower. A flame burned her half-closed eyes. The blazing sunset reddened the pearl necklace like a river of rubies. She walked in this glory; her gleaming skin took on all the magnificence of its flesh, the blood, the fire, the bluish carmine, the velvety redness, the vibrant rose, and, turning with the great, thick walls of crimson, she climbed towards the sky.

She was naked like the goddess, holding in each hand the corners of her scarlet veil which the wind unfurled in the evening sky, and the mirror, in her right hand, reflected the setting sun.
Languidly, with infinite grace and majesty, her head bowed, she climbed the outside ramp that formed a spiral band around the vermilion tower. A flame burned her half-closed eyes. The blazing sunset reddened the pearl necklace like a river of rubies. She walked in this glory; her gleaming skin took on all the magnificence of its flesh, the blood, the fire, the bluish carmine, the velvety redness, the vibrant rose, and, turning with the great, thick walls of crimson, she climbed towards the sky.

the first example is typeset with extra space (.06") before each new paragraph and the second example is typeset with no extra space between paragraphs

Inserting Illustrations and Photographs

While setting up the page layout, leave spaces where illustrations and photographs will be placed. Illustrations should be a clear black and white, with shading done with screens, crosshatching, or dots. Illustrations done in pencil or watercolor are very hard to reproduce in black and white, and should be turned into halftones to replicate the softer quality of the originals. You can reduce the size of the illustrations to fit the space allotted by having them sized to fit by turning them into photostats or photocopies. If you have access to a scanner, then illustrations can be sized, *cropped* (unnecessary elements cut out) and placed into position using your computer program. If you must place them by hand, illustrations should be pasted, never taped, into place on the page. Use a straight edge to align them on the page, always making sure they are parallel to the text lines. *(See Appendix for more complete instructions on paste-up and keylining of illustrations and photographs.)*

Photographs can be scanned into your layout for an indication of placement, sizing, and cropping. The photos themselves can then given to a commercial printer, who will turn them into halftones and insert them as you have shown in the layout. Scans and photocopies which are used in this way are called "for placement only," or FPO. *Never paste, glue, or tape the actual photograph into place on a page.*

The Template

Once you have put together a template based on the page design you like, set a few pages of text and print them out to see how they will look. Try a different size typeface and different margins: experiment until your page looks exactly as you want it to. Then start typesetting the whole book. Remember that consistency is the basis for all good book designs.

original illustration

For a cover to be considered camera-ready, every color that is used must be separated on to an overlay. Each separation contains all the parts of the text and illustrations that are one color, in their exact location in relation to the other colors on the cover. This alignment is done with registration marks which are placed on each separation in exactly the same place. When all the registration marks are placed one on another, the cover should look as if it had never been separated.

the same illustration, sized and cropped to fit the layout

this illustration is a pen and ink drawing, using crosshatching for shadows

square

vertical

horizontal

the first photograph is the original, while the other FPO photographs have been sized and cropped – notice how the dimensions of the photo change as it is cropped

4

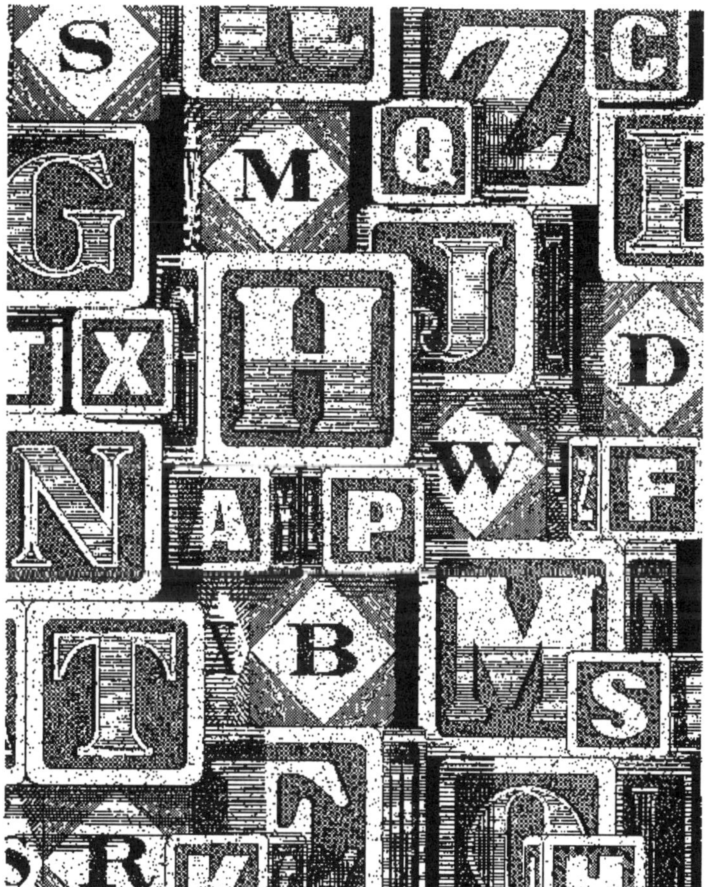

TYPESETTING

Chapter 4

Typesetting is one of the most misunderstood aspects of producing a book. There is a very real difference between typesetting and typing into a computer or word processing machine. Before the advent of personal computers, all books were typeset on a complicated typesetting machine run by a typesetter, who was thoroughly trained in design, grammar, spelling, and the intricacies of the typesetting machinery. The typesetting costs per page were high, anywhere from $35 to $50, and corrections were done by keyliners, who did a "paste up" with T-squares, glue wax, and matte knives. Manuscripts had to be marked word for word for the typesetter, indicating what size and typeface was needed for each head and subhead, what size type and typeface must be used for the text, and where italics and boldface should be placed. Even the amount of type that would fit on a page had to be calculated.

Common Mistakes

The personal computer has made this kind of typesetting obsolete, but anyone typesetting a book still needs to know grammar, design, and the basic rules of typesetting to make a book look professional. There are six giveaways to a nonprofessional typesetting job:

- dashes made with two hyphens instead of an *em dash* (a dash the length of the letter m)
- two spaces after a mark of punctuation instead of one space
- underlining words instead of using italics
- inch marks (also called *tick marks*) used instead of book or closed quotations

- the last word on a page hyphenated

- a single word or a one line end of a sentence dangling by itself at the top or bottom of a page, which is called either a *widow and/or orphan*

Another error which is very common, and which is actually a punctuation problem, is a comma placed after, instead of before, quotation marks.

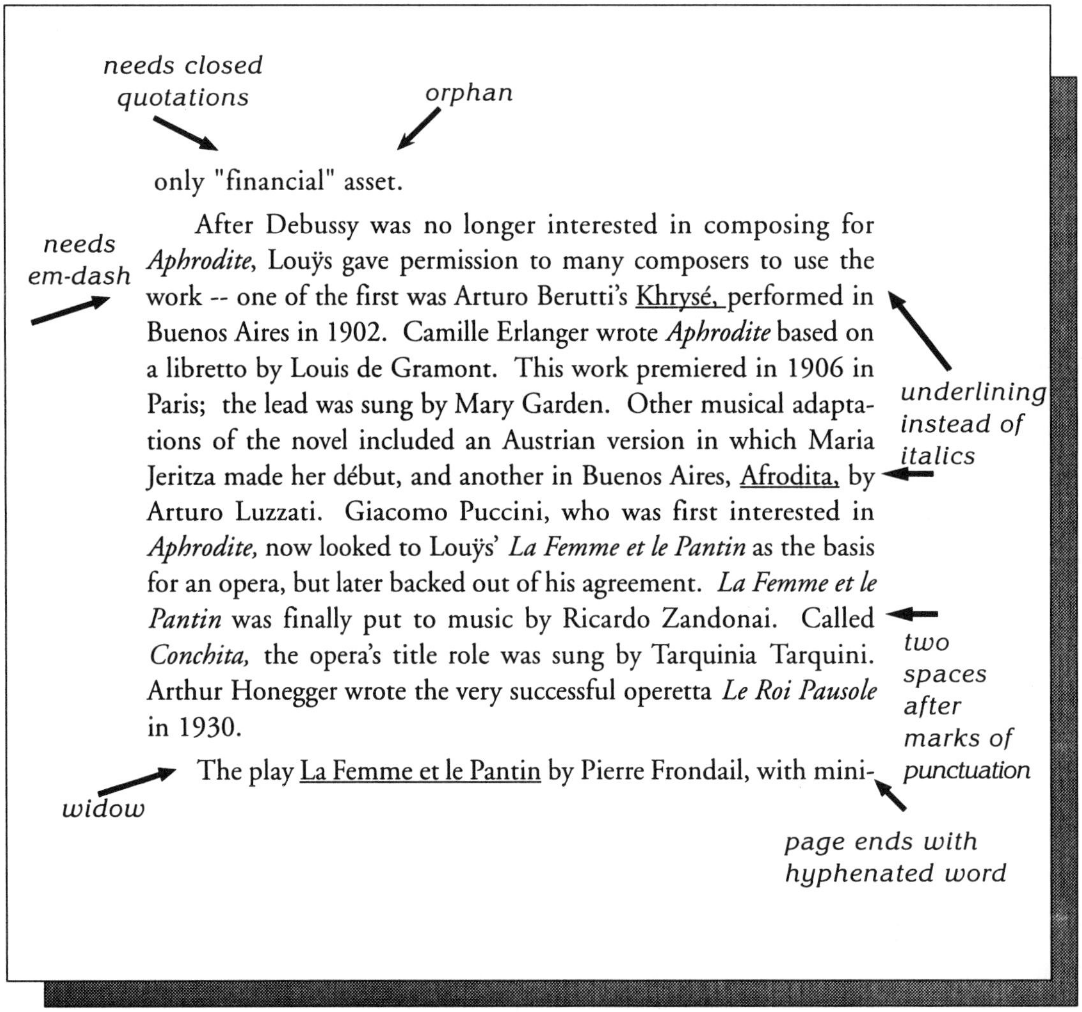

only "financial" asset.

After Debussy was no longer interested in composing for *Aphrodite,* Louÿs gave permission to many composers to use the work -- one of the first was Arturo Berutti's Khrysé, performed in Buenos Aires in 1902. Camille Erlanger wrote *Aphrodite* based on a libretto by Louis de Gramont. This work premiered in 1906 in Paris; the lead was sung by Mary Garden. Other musical adaptations of the novel included an Austrian version in which Maria Jeritza made her début, and another in Buenos Aires, Afrodita, by Arturo Luzzati. Giacomo Puccini, who was first interested in *Aphrodite,* now looked to Louÿs' *La Femme et le Pantin* as the basis for an opera, but later backed out of his agreement. *La Femme et le Pantin* was finally put to music by Ricardo Zandonai. Called *Conchita,* the opera's title role was sung by Tarquinia Tarquini. Arthur Honegger wrote the very successful operetta *Le Roi Pausole* in 1930.

The play La Femme et le Pantin by Pierre Frondail, with mini-

typical typesetting errors

Typeface Choice

There are thousands of different typefaces. Most laser printers have 35 basic typefaces, including Times (or Times Roman), Helvetica, Palatino, New Century Schoolbook, and Courier. The cost of typefaces has been dropping, and packages of typefaces can easily be purchased at a low cost.

A *typeface* is the family name of a type and a *font* is the different sizes and styles within a typeface — boldface and italics are fonts of one typeface. Typefaces are also divided into two groups: *serif* and *sans serif.* The serif is the crossbar at the ends of a letter. Sans serif is a letter without this bar.

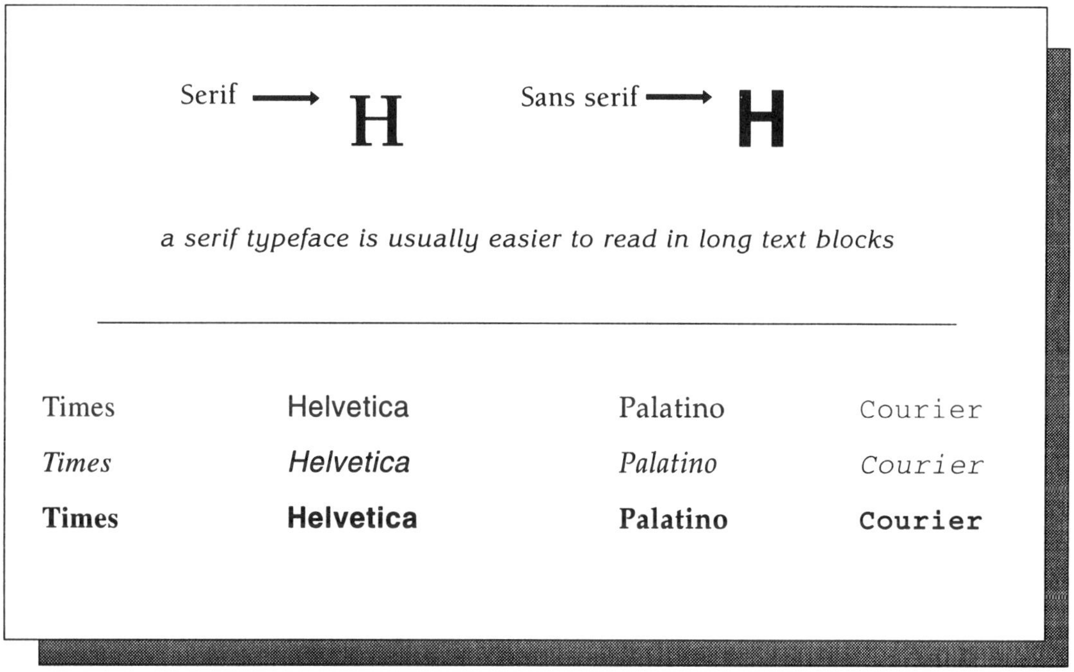

the typeface is the family name of a type and the font is each different size and style within a typeface: boldface and italics are fonts of a typeface

The choice of type for a book is important because type fills an elementary function. It is the vehicle for words; it makes those words understandable, or readable; and it enhances the message of the words. A typeface has a decided effect on the message you are conveying to your reader, very much like an actor reciting his lines — you would react differently to his bellowing "Help!" than to his whispering, laughingly, "Help?"

DANGER Danger DANGER
Danger Danger DANGER

note the different feeling about the word "Danger" that each typeface conveys

As stated before, do not mix more than two typefaces in a book. Most book designers usually vary the typefaces for the heads and text, using similar typefaces for overall consistency or contrasting faces to break up the text into smaller units. Others use different fonts of only one typeface for both heads and text, preferring the coherence and formality that comes from this look. Using many typefaces on a page may look interestingly different to the novice typesetter, but this gives a message of confusion to the reader, who wants to quickly and easily read the words on a page and does not want to be concerned about the typesetting style.

When deciding on a typeface, choose one that fits the subject of the book. You would not use a script typeface for a young child's book, or an academic-looking typeface for a book of romantic poetry.

He rounded the corner with the mouse, the cat, the girl, and the dogcatcher following close behind. There was no time to lose, not if the puppy was to be saved. Quickly he ran toward the river, pausing once only to make sure he was still being followed, never letting go of the rope.

He rounded the corner with the mouse, the cat, the girl, and the dogcatcher following close behind. There was no time to lose, not if the puppy was to be saved. Quickly he ran toward the river, pausing once only to make sure he was still being followed, never letting go of the rope.

which typeface would be the best for a young child to read

Size of Type

Once you have chosen the typeface for your text and heads, you should choose the size of the type. Type is measured in picas and points, not inches or millimeters. Roughly, there are six picas to an inch and 12 points to a pica, making 72 points to an inch.

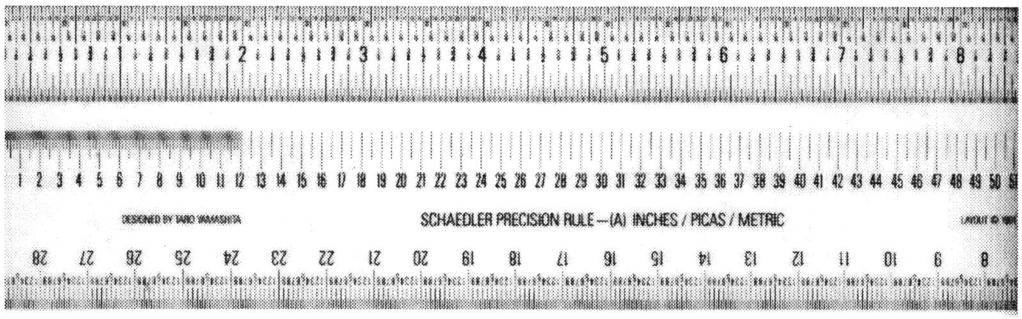

special ruler showing inches, picas, and decimal inches

Most books are printed with a 10-point to 12-point typeface. If your book is written specifically for very young people or senior citizens, use a bigger typeface size. Every typeface has certain characteristics that help determine its proper size and place. For example, Times, a very common typeface, is very condensed, so an 11 point size in this typeface looks about the same as a 10 point size in Garamond, a looser and rounder typeface.

Every typeface has certain characteristics that help determine its proper size and place. For example, Times, a very common typeface, is very small, so an 11 point size in this typeface looks about the same as a 10 point size in Garamond.

Every typeface has certain characteristics that help determine its proper size and place. For example, Times, a very common typeface, is very small, so an 11 point size in this typeface looks about the same as a 10-point size in Garamond.

the first sample is Times (11 point) and the second is Garamond (10 point) – note the differences in size, width, and overall look in a paragraph

The best rule of thumb is to try typesetting the same paragraph in different typefaces that you like. Then, once you have made your choice of typeface, set the paragraph in different sizes of that type until you get the look you want.

It is important to understand that Courier is not considered an acceptable typeface for books. It is only used to duplicate the look of typewriters.

During the regiment's advance, one of Captain Yates Company F pack mules lost a portion of the cargo. The pack mules had been behind during the entire trip. Now the pack mules had lost a box of hardtack. Sgt. William Curtis and a small detachment was sent back to find it. When they found the box, a Sioux boy, along with some friends was sitting on the box eating some of the goods. His name was Deeds, the 10-year-old nephew of Sitting Bull. When the troopers saw him, they fired their carbines. A bullet hit him in the chest killing him instantly. Two other boys ran away. The soldiers did not give pursuit, but the battle at Little Big Horn had begun.

During the regiment's advance, one of Captain Yates Company F pack mules lost a portion of the cargo. The pack mules had been behind during the entire trip. Now the pack mules had lost a box of hardtack. Sgt. William Curtis and a small detachment was sent back to find it. When they found the box, a Sioux boy, along with some friends was sitting on the box eating some of the goods. His name was Deeds, the 10-year-old nephew of Sitting Bull. When the troopers saw him, they fired their carbines. A bullet hit him in the chest killing him instantly. Two other boys ran away. The soldiers did not give pursuit, but the battle at Little Big Horn had begun.

the first sample typeface is Claredon and the second typeface is Courier — which looks like it belongs in a book and which looks like a school assignment

Leading

Leading, which is pronounced "ledding," is the space between lines of type as measured in points. The word comes from the days when type was set by hand, and the space between lines of type was separated by slugs of lead, or "leading."

The more space you allow between lines, the more "airy" your page will look. Most computer desktop publishing programs have a default that automatically places a reasonable amount of space between lines. Some desktop publishing programs, such as PageMaker and QuarkXPress, allow you to change this ratio. If you can change the leading in your program, try to allow at least two to three points more leading than the type's point size for a clean, readable line. Thus, if you are using a 10 point typeface, your leading should be at least 12 or 13 points.

The leading is indicated by a fraction (or ratio), such as 11/13, with the top number, 11, the size of the type and the bottom number, 13, the amount of leading used.

During the regiment's advance, one of Captain Yates Company F pack mules lost a portion of the cargo. The pack mules had been behind during the entire trip. Now the pack mules had lost a box of hardtack. Sgt. William Curtis and a small detachment were sent back to find it. When they found the box, a Sioux boy, along with some friends, was sitting on the box eating some of the goods. His name was Deeds, the 10-year-old nephew of Sitting Bull. When the troopers saw him, they fired their carbines.

During the regiment's advance, one of Captain Yates Company F pack mules lost a portion of the cargo. The pack mules had been behind during the entire trip. Now the pack mules had lost a box of hardtack. Sgt. William Curtis and a small detachment were sent back to find it. When they found the box, a Sioux boy, along with some friends, was sitting on the box eating some of the goods. His name was Deeds, the 10-year-old nephew of Sitting Bull. When the troopers saw him, they fired their carbines.

the first paragraph is set at 11/14 and the second paragraph is 11/18

Hyphenation and Justification

Justified type is type that is flushed evenly on both the left and right sides of a page. It is the most usual way for a book to be typeset, but it can cause some problems in hyphenation. Hyphenation is when a word breaks at the end of a line of type, as in the word *hyphenation*, two lines above. When every line is even, too many words may end up hyphenated. As a rule of thumb, there should be no more than two hyphenated words in a row. Some programs allow you to predetermine how many hyphens should follow one another. If your computer program does not have this type of flexibility, then you can adjust the tracking of individual lines so you do not end up with "rivers" of hyphens.

I slipped on the stairs as I frantically hurried to my six o'clock appointment with Melody Mill at Sydney University. For the past 18 months, ongoing therapy with the University counselor had become my salvation. Prior to seeing her, I had dissolved into a series of panic attacks. The very thought of completing my thesis had immobilized me with waves of anxiety. The text had been close to being finished, but doubts plagued my rattled mind. Who would ever care about my study "The Operant Conditioning Response with Rats Subjected to Frequent Immersions in a Water-Filled Maze"?

I slipped on the stairs as I frantically hurried to my six o'clock appoint-
ment with Melody Mill at Sydney University. For the past 18 months, on-
going therapy with the University counselor had become my sal-
vation. Prior to seeing her, I had dissolved into a series of panic attacks. The
very thought of completing my thesis had immobilized me with waves of anxi-
ety. The text had been close to being finished, but doubts plagued my rat-
tled mind. Who would ever care about my study "The Operant Condition-
ing Response with Rats Subjected to Frequent Immersions in a Water-Fill-
ed Maze"?

the first example was limited to one hypen (and used none), while the second example had no hyphen limits

Kerning and Tracking

Kerning is the spacing between two letters or characters. Words and letters are equally spaced on a typewriter. On a typeset page the letter spacing is varied depending on the width of each character while making the inter-character spacing *appear* equal. Thus, some letters would need to be spaced closer together and some further apart. *Tracking* loosens or tightens the space between letters *and* words more generally; most desktop publishing programs average out the widths of the letters and automatically determine where to break each line based on this information.

A good desktop program also kerns characters and allows the default setting for the tracking to be changed from very tight to very loose. The tracking you see on your screen may not be an accurate representation of the actual printed page, so always print out a sample to check its overall look. Tracking does not eliminate the need for kerning, and even a well-kerned type may need tracking. Generally, tracking is used to alter the general appearance of the type and kerning to correct space between individual letters.

Most word processing programs today automatically adjust difficult kerning pairs such as *Av, Tw, Wo, Wy, Tr, Ya,* and *Wr*. But each typeface has kerning pairs that still may cause problems. Sometimes the only way to adjust the kerning is by using special methods discussed in your computer program's instruction manual. This method of kerning is usually done only for heads or subheads where spacing problems are more obvious.

Tracking is also rarely adjusted, but, depending on the typeface, it may have to be loosened or tightened. The size you choose for the type is usually the determining factor. When you print your sample pages, run a few with different tracking in order to see what looks the best with the text and the heads.

Wa lk U p   **Walk Up**

the example to the left has no automatic kerning, while the one to the right was kerned by the typesetting program

Whenever your folks went out at night,
and you and I were home,
you tiptoed to my room and said,
"I don't want to sleep alone."
I put you in my great big bed;
then I gently closed the door.
We snuggled close, as warm as toast.
(That's what grandmothers are for.)

Whenever your folks went out at night,
and you and I were home,
you tiptoed to my room and said,
"I don't want to sleep alone."
I put you in my great big bed;
then I gently closed the door.
We snuggled close, as warm as toast.
(That's what grandmothers are for.)

in these two examples, just by changing the tracking from "normal" to "loose," many of the kerning problems that often happen in a script typeface are solved — those few characters in the second example that are still touching can be individually kerned

When you typeset your manuscript, be consistent, just as you should with any element in the production of your book. Typefaces, fonts, sizing, and leading must remain the same throughout the book. The typesetting, more than any other aspect of your book, gives a subliminal message to the reader. If the thoughts of the heroine are set in italics, the reader unconsciously will understand that italics will thereafter mean a silent soliloquy. If every chapter head is set in a sans serif type and the text in a serif, the reader instinctively knows when a new chapter begins, even if the chapter break is not on a separate page.

Typesetting is not difficult, but it is time-consuming and labor-intensive. Yet, when the book is laid out and typeset, it will take on a life of its own and you will be able to clearly visualize the final product — your own professional-looking book.

Final Considerations

Follow these basic typesetting rules for a clear, attractive, and easy-to-read book.

The most readable typefaces for a book are serif. The typeface should be without extreme features in its design — not too tall, thin, short, squat, or with *descenders* or *ascenders* that are overly distinctive. A descender is the part of a letter that falls below the line of text, and an ascender is the part of the letter that rises above the line: the letters *p, q,* and *y,* have descenders and *d, t,* and *b* have ascenders. A good typeface to choose for a book is one that does not call attention to itself.

1. Do not use all caps in a sentence or paragraph for emphasis. Not only is it hard to read, but emphasis should come from the quality of the writing, not typographical tricks. For the same reason, a corollary to this rule is to avoid the use (and/or overuse) of such punctuation as the exclamation mark, underlining/italics, and dashes.

2. Adjust your text lines to a readable length, neither too long (use more than one column in such a case) nor too short. Always keep in mind the comfort of the reader.

3. Keep your leading loose enough to be readable. Tight line spacing makes it almost impossible to distinguish individual words and phrases. People read in phrases, not individual words, and they need space to help them keep their place in the text.

4. Use unusual typefaces only for heads, subheads, and chapter titles. Be consistent in their use: every chapter head must be the same, as must be every head and subhead.

5. Take advantage of the special character sets within your typeface program — em-dashes, bullets, © symbol, and fractions are only a few of those available to you. Use of these special characters make a book look professionally typeset. *(See Appendix for the complete list of character sets available to Windows users.)*

HISTORICAL PERSPECTIVE

When typefaces first came into being, there were no separate fonts for each typeface. The first kind of type was *roman* (type that is vertical in shape). In the early 16th Century, *italic* (cursive) type was popularized in Italy, which gave its name to the style. These remained the only two types of typefaces until the late 1700s, when roman and italic typefaces were matched up, so that most roman typefaces then had an italic variation. As printing techniques became more sophisticated, the concepts of weights and proportions of letters influenced the design of new typefaces.

In the 20th Century, typefaces became "families," as they were carefully designed with roman and italic designs in different weights and proportions. New designs included sans serif and script typefaces, and some artists became famous for their typeface designs.

Now, with computer programs that allow anyone to design or adapt his or her own typeface and fonts, typeface designing has reached an individuality that has never been available before.

5

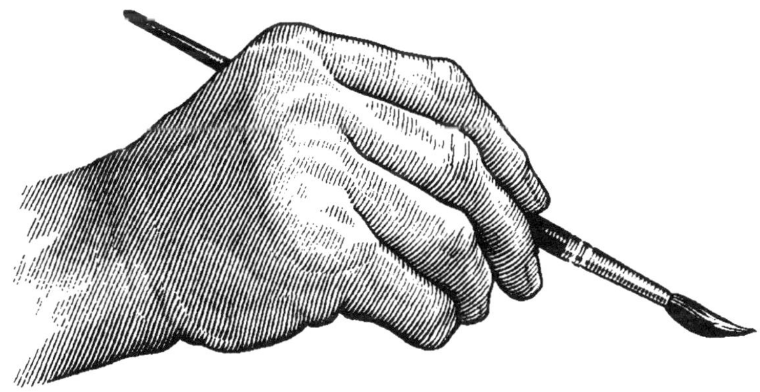

DESIGN OF COVER AND DUSTJACKET

Chapter 5

To understand the importance of the cover or dustjacket of a book, consider how you, yourself, choose a book. You see a cover that catches your eye, pick it up, look at the title, turn over the book to read what is on the back cover, and then leaf through the table of contents or read a few pages. It is the cover that catches your attention first, and that means that if you are going to put your money anywhere in your book's production, it should be in the design and color of the cover. The only time you do not have to put a lot of thought into the cover or dustjacket design is if you know you will be selling the book only through mail order or a seminar, in which case the title and contents become the most important factors.

The cover is the one part of the book which we strongly recommend you have produced professionally. Unless you are a designer or photographer by profession, it will be very difficult for you to come up with a design that will be salable. Moreover, you must be knowledgeable about color printing and color separations. If you have strong ideas about what your book's cover should look like, then tell your designer; but the suggestions from a good book cover designer are worth their weight in sales to distributors and bookstores. The success or failure of a book is often attributed to the cover design.

Color and Color Separation

The more color you can afford to put on the cover of a book, the more appealing the book will look. Two is the minimum numbers of colors any book cover should have. A two-color cover can also incorporate the white of the cover paper stock and *screens* of the main colors to produce an interesting design. Screens are tints of a color which is made lighter or darker by changing the number and size of the dots used to print the color. The larger the dot, the darker the color. Black, which is always counted as a color, does not need to be used unless there is a photograph of a person on the cover. Photographs of people, if they cannot be run in full color, should always be run in black or a color close to black.

When you think about color on the inside pages of a book, always think in terms of what a commercial printer can reproduce with ink on paper rather than what the original artwork, photograph, or your computer monitor looks like. Color must be separated out to be printed. There are two methods of color separation: *spot color* and *full color,* which is also called *process color.*

Spot Color

Spot color is the placing of individual colors in a specific location within the design. The colors can be separated by a desktop program or by hand *(see Appendix)*. The separation must be exact, so when each individual color is placed into position, the colors fit exactly. These separations are called *overlays*.

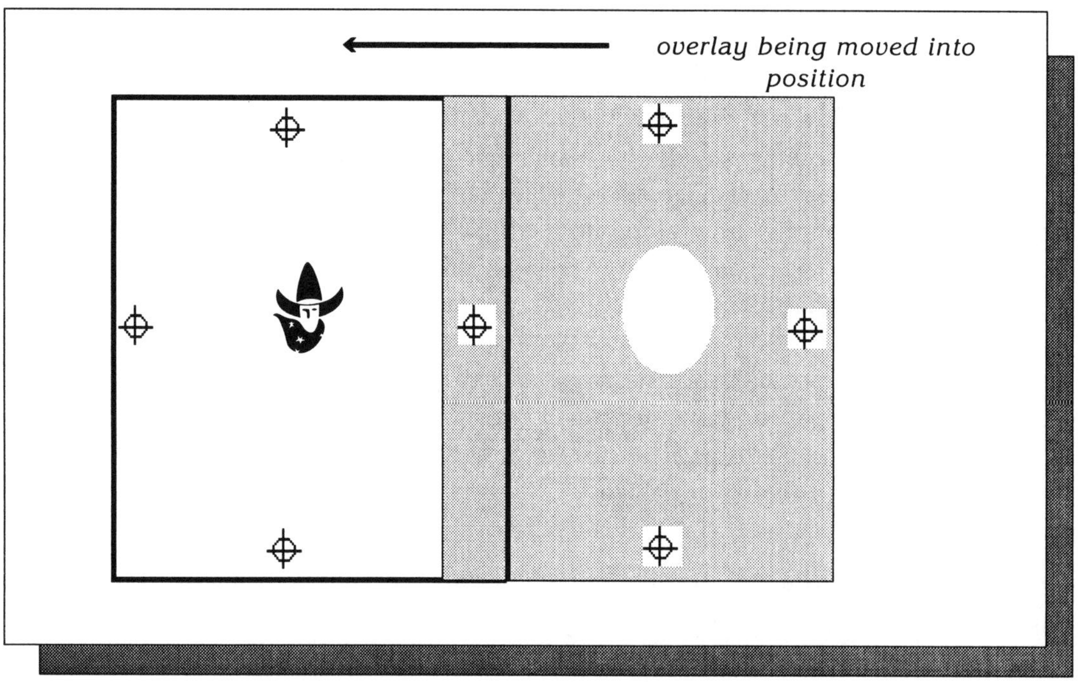

a gray overlay, with a white cutout for illustration, being placed over original artwork so all the registration marks line up, one over the other

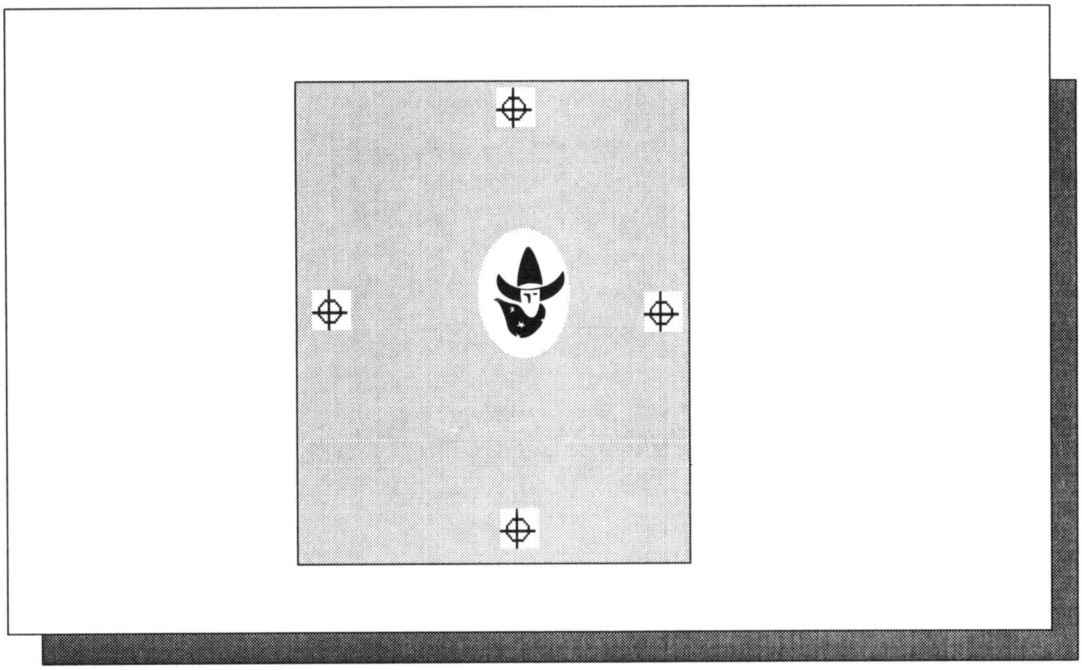

*overlay and artwork when overlay is in position –
the printer will remove registration marks*

For a *full color* or *process color* separation of a photograph or illustration, the elements to be separated are sent out to a professional separation service which uses a computer-generated laser to break down the colors into four pieces of transparent film (cyan, magenta, yellow, and black). When the pieces of film are placed together, the resulting image simulates all the colors there were in the original. *(See Appendix for an in-depth explanation of process color separation.)*

Many computer programs have the capacity to generate these full-color separations, but the final print quality will be less than professional unless you can run the separations as film. This film is used to make the proofs and the printing plates for the press.

Cover Design Elements

The title is an integral part of the design of the cover. Many powerful book covers are designed just with a title and subtitle and do not use photographs or illustrations. A designer may enlarge the first letters of a word, add graphic elements, or skew and/or shade individual letters.

When working on your cover design, just as with the text, you should not use more than two different typefaces, and the typefaces you choose should integrate well with each other.

Make sure that as you design your cover you leave enough space for all the necessary information. The *front cover* should prominently display the title, subtitle, and author's name. The subtitle's importance must not be underestimated. Use it to tell the readers exactly what they are going to get out of reading the book, or to explain an ambiguous title. *Bashful Buttons and Clouds of Lace,* a book of poetry with a cover done in primary colors, at first glance looks as if it might be a children's book. Its subtitle now proclaims it to be "Poetry for Romantic Evenings."

Often, other pertinent information may appear on the front cover, such as the publishing company's name, any literary awards the book has won, and the name of the person who wrote the introduction.

The *back cover* usually contains "ad copy" describing the book, endorsements from well-known people, a short, pertinent biography of the author and his or her photograph, the bar code, and the price. The subject of the book should appear on the upper left hand section of the back cover; this will help the bookstore or library shelve it in the proper department.

The *spine* rarely has room for more than the title of the book, the author's name, and the *colophon* (imprint) of the publishing company. Design the spine of the book to look as interesting as possible, because when a book is shelved, all the buyer usually sees is the spine.

The main objective in designing a book cover is to make it attractive and give an immediate sense of its subject to a potential buyer. If you plan on incorporating more than type into the cover design, you can commission an artist's illustration, buy clip art, use public domain art, or use non-copyrighted photographs that come with many computer programs. The clip art now available is very sophisticated, ranging from cartoon-like illustrations to full-color photographs. Clip art packages are also very reasonable in price. Often, the suppliers of this artwork offer free suggestions and layouts for using their artwork along with the clip art package, which can be a big help when you are looking for cover design ideas.

elements of front cover including clip art (full-color cover)

Women's Issues/ Health

THE SOLUTION TO THE PUZZLE IS HERE!

If you experience fatigue, irritability, depression, headaches, or bloating, you are not alone.

PMS has long been a puzzle to the medical community and millions of women. *PMS: Solving the Puzzle* explodes the myth that PMS is untreatable. It gives women the tools to live a fuller, healthier life.

NOW READ ABOUT THE CAUSES AND THE CURES.
REGAIN CONTROL OF YOUR BODY AND YOUR LIFE!

"The text combines cutting edge research with time-tested remedies. *Solving the Puzzle* builds a partnership between women and their doctors. It is the state of the art text on PMS."

–*Jordan Goetz, M.D.*
Director, Santa Barbara Holistic Medical Center

"PMS is often ignored by the medical profession because it is difficult and complex to treat. This excellent and comprehensive book reviews the many causes of PMS and offers useful and effective advice on PMS treatment. I recommend this book highly."

–*Susan Lark, M.D.*
Author of *The PMS Self-Help Book*
and *The Menopause Self-Help Book.*

"*PMS: Solving the Puzzle* is an outstanding book! Authoritative, comprehensive, yet concise. It will help countless people."

–*William Crook, M.D.*
Author of *The Yeast Connection and The Woman*

Linaya Hahn, LNC, has experienced the pain of PMS and the triumph of its control. She says, "The two most important facts to keep in mind are: PMS is real, and you don't have to have it."

The author has addressed the American College of Obstetricians and Gynecologists, has been on "The Oprah Show," and has had articles published in professional journals and popular magazines.She is the founder of the PMS Holistic Center, where she has helped thousands of women.

ISBN: 1-886094-15-2

$16.95

back cover of book including price, bar code, and ISBN

Cover Sizing

The size of the cover is determined by set factors. For a trade paperback book, the spine size is the first component you need for your calculations. Divide the number of pages in the typeset book by the *PPI* (pages per inch) of the paper being used. Your publisher or printer can tell you the PPI of the paper you have chosen. Thus, a 160 page book using a 50 pound paper with a PPI of 530 would have a spine size of .30 inches (160÷530=.30).

Then, take the size of the book's pages and double the width. Add that number to the size of the spine. Therefore, the 160 page book that is 5½ by 8½ inches would have a cover size of 11 by 8½ plus .30 inches for the spine, or 11.30 by 8½ inches.

The dustjacket for a case bound book also must take into consideration the thickness of the *case* (built-up cover) and the size of its flaps. Flaps can be anywhere from 2½ inches to 4 inches in size, with the larger sizes used for larger books. A ¼ inch allowance is added to each point where the dustjacket folds over the case. The case is usually ¼ inch larger on each side than the page size. The safest way to measure dustjacket size is to ask your commercial printer for the exact specifications.

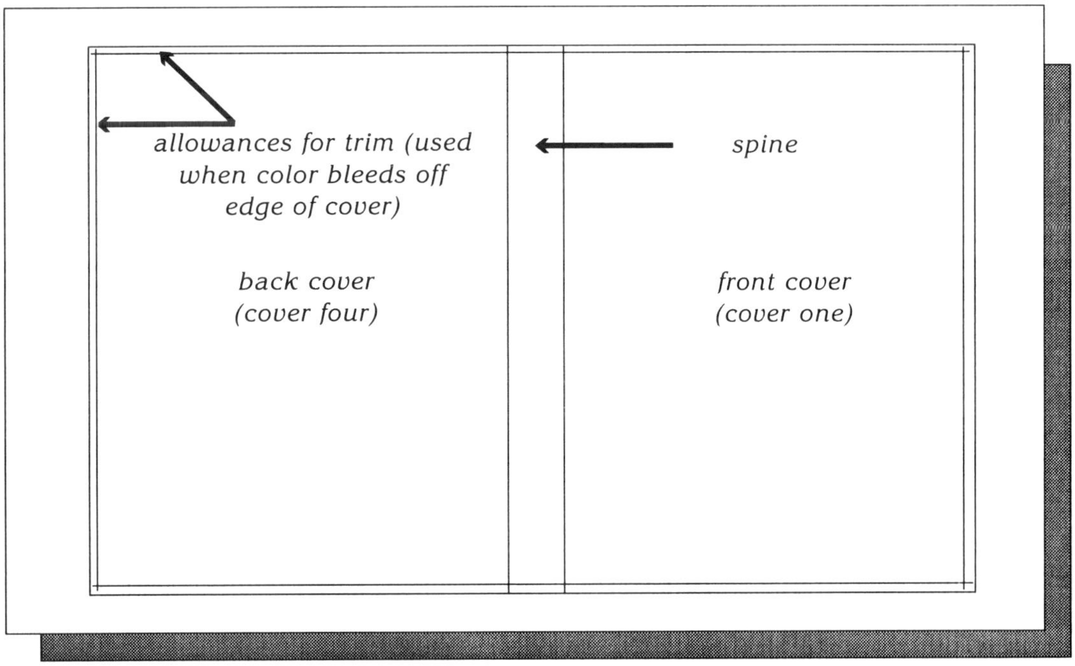

layout for perfect bound book

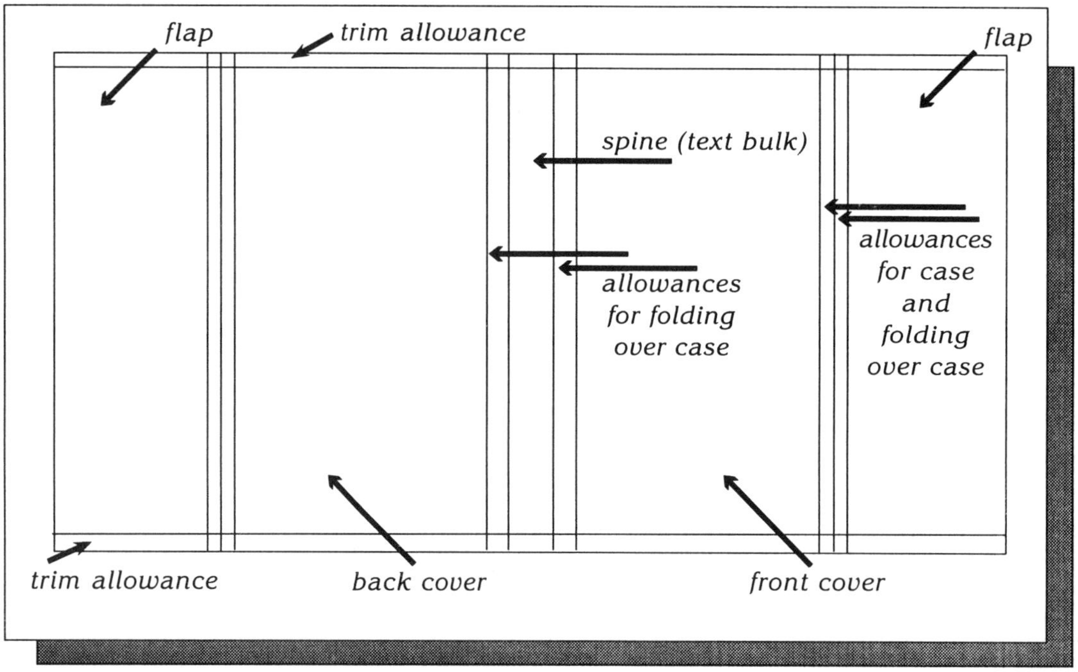

dustjacket layout

The Art of Book Covers

The main idea to focus on when designing is simplicity. In the case of a book cover, your objective is to provide a graphic element which complements and enhances the title. The design should have a single message that catches the viewer's attention. A book about running should not have a graphic of a busy park scene with a tiny runner lost in a group of picnickers. A far more powerful design element would be a close-up shot of the muscular lower torso and legs of a runner, with the title of the book in large letters.

The best cover design elements create a subtle visual relationship between the graphic element and the title. Consider what impression you want to make and use your design element to suggest that promise, benefit, or quality. Sex can be suggested by a slip strap sliding off of a woman's shoulder, wealth by the color green and an oversized dollar sign, and elegance with a string of pearls or a tuxedo. If there is a distinct object, event, or location that is central to your book, use a graphic element that suggests that theme without being too literal. The more playful, simple, and understated you can be in presenting an idea, the stronger that idea will come across.

the first example shows a book cover designed with only type, while the second example uses just one strong graphic element

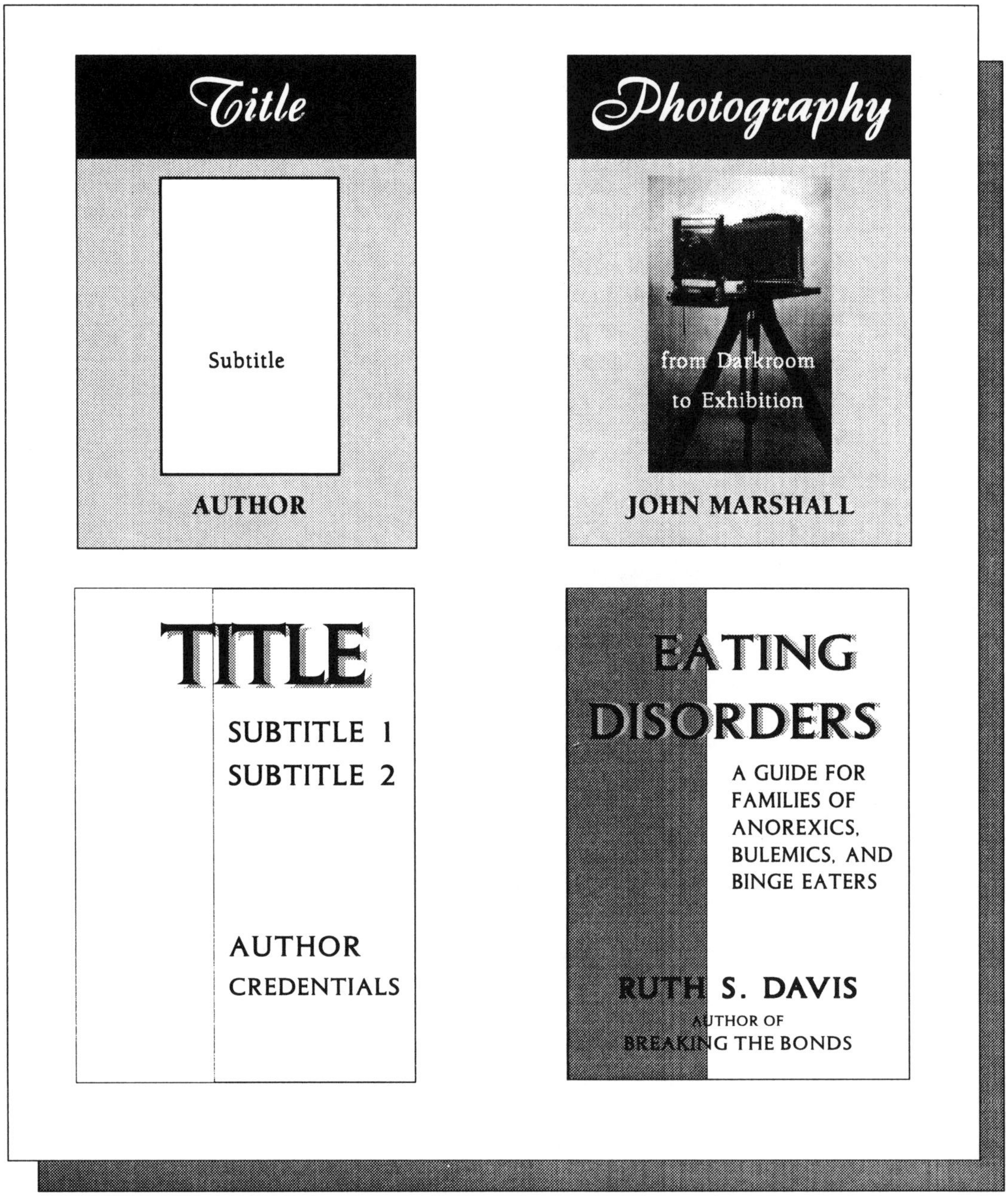

samples of book cover designs that fit many subjects

Because book cover design takes artistic ability, if you decide to create your own cover for your book, take the time to look at many books in your library and bookstore. Pick out those whose covers appeal to you and carefully consider why they are successful in their design. Do not copy these covers, but use them as a source for ideas for your own book. Make a list of these design aspects:

- What typefaces are used and how are they placed?
- If there is artwork or a photograph used, which parts are emphasized by cropping or sizing? What do you think the reasons were for the art being chosen for the cover?
- What sort of background design and colors are used?
- How are the type and artwork placed in relation to each other?
- How much "white space" is used to emphasize certain elements of the cover? *White space* is unused space between and around design elements.
- What were your exact reasons for choosing this cover as outstanding? Be specific in your answers.

Once you can answer these questions and understand fully what makes a successful cover, you should be able to design the cover of your own book.

6

WORKING WITH A COMMERCIAL PRINTER

Chapter 6

The key to getting what you want from a commercial printer is knowing what you want, understanding your options, and effectively communicating your needs in clear and concise terms. Do not be embarrassed to ask questions and do expect understandable answers. When printing a book, correcting mistakes is costly, while asking for information is free.

Printing Schedules

Trade book printers have streamlined their business operations to process camera-ready manuscripts and artwork into finished books in an organized, coordinated, and predetermined manner. Any deviation from this routine can stall the process, disrupt the press-run schedule, and cause the printer to charge you extra money.

Printing a book, from pre-press to finished product, usually takes a minimum of four months, assuming you are working from a finished manuscript that does not need heavy editing or rewriting. This time frame also assumes you are leaving some or most of the editing, designing, and other services, such as indexing, to experienced professionals.

Publishers spend a significant amount of time checking and rechecking their work for errors to ensure their finished books are professional, quality products. If your production team does not catch errors before the book goes to press, the people who are evaluating, reviewing, and reading your book will notice them later. The closer your book comes to its press date, the more time and money it takes to correct errors. Traditional publishers take a year or more to bring a book from manuscript to finished product. Because most self-published authors feel a sense of urgency about getting into print, they often do not want to take the time to proofread their work carefully more than once, if at all. If you are going to take a significant portion of the manuscript preparation into your own hands, give yourself the time to do it right, and double check yourself every step of the way.

Price Quotations

For the commercial printer, your book production begins when you call to request a quotation. The quote is a guaranteed price which is good for a set amount of time, usually for no more than a few weeks. The printer determines the price based on certain important specifications, which include:

1. Size or dimensions of the book (height and width).
2. Number of pages in the book, including front matter, back matter, and blank pages (calculated by signatures).
3. Quantity of finished books (the press run).
4. Weight, finish, and brand of paper stock.
5. Cover stock and cover coating.
6. Type and quality of the binding.
7. Number of ink colors required.
8. Pre-press work (including creating halftones of photographs and separations of artwork).
9. Any extras (such as dustcovers, shrink-wrapping, foil stamping, and perforated tear-out pages).
10. Shipping instructions.

Once these variables have been determined and the quote is issued and accepted, the printer waits for the camera-ready copy and artwork to arrive. Printers use standard quotation sheets to record the specifications of each job. The following are terms they use that you should understand.

> *New book:* A book for which no work has been done before by the printer.
>
> *Exact reprint:* All pre-press work has been done before for a previous run of this book. The existing plates simply need to be pulled and rerun.

☐ ______ (SALESMAN) Account

Request for Quotation

Date ______

☐ House Account

☐ Deliver ☐ Call In ☐ Mail ☐ Fax

Quote Due ______

BILLING: **DATE COPY/ART IN** ______ **DELIVERY DATE** ______

Customer ______

Address ______

City ______ State ______ Zip ______

ITEM DESCRIPTION: ______

☐ New ☐ Exact Repeat ☐ Repeat w/Changes ☐ Exact Sample ☐ Same as Sample w/Changes ☐ Similar to Sample, All New

PAPER — PRINTING: No. of Copies ______, ______, ______, ______

Text: No. of Pages ___ / ___ / ___, No. of Sheets ___ / ___ / ___, No. of Panels (1 Side of Sht) ___ / ___ / ___

Finish Size ______ Flat Sheet Size ______

Type Paper ______ (WEIGHT) (COLOR) (TYPE) (FINISH)

☐ Printed 1st Side — ☐ Black ______ (INK COLOR(S)) ☐ Printed 2nd Side — ☐ Black ______ (INK COLOR(S))

☐ Close Registration ______ ☐ Solids ______ ☐ Reverses ______ ☐ Screens ______ ☐ Bleeds ______

Cover: Pages Printed ______

Finish Size ______ Flat Sheet Size ______

Type Paper ______ (WEIGHT) (COLOR) (TYPE) (FINISH)

☐ Printed Cover 1 & 4 — ☐ Black ______ (INK COLOR(S)) ☐ Printed Cover 2 & 3 — ☐ Black ______ (INK COLOR(S))

☐ Close Registration ______ ☐ Solids ______ ☐ Reverses ______ ☐ Screens ______ ☐ Bleeds ______

ARTWORK PREPARATION:

☐ Negatives Furnished ______

☐ Camera Ready Artwork Furnished ______

☐ Typesetting and Paste-up ______

PHOTOGRAPHS:

B & W ______; Duotones ______; Outline ______;

Knockouts ______; Other ______

COLOR SEPARATIONS:

______ Number Furnished By Customer

______ Number To Make From ______

Sizes ______

PROOFS: ☐ None ☐ Galley ☐ Page ☐ Blueline ☐ Color Key ☐ Composite Matchprint ☐ Matchprint of Color Seps

BINDERY/FINISHING:

☐ Fold — Type ______

☐ Perforate/Score ______

☐ Collate/Staple ______

☐ Saddle Bind ______

☐ Perfect Bind ______

☐ Spiral Wire Bind ______

☐ Wire-O Bind ______

☐ Plastic Comb Bind ______

☐ Shrink Wrap ______ Per Pkg. ☐ Trim ______ Sides

☐ Laminate ______

☐ Number — Starting Number ______ End Number ______

☐ Drill — No. Holes ______ Spacing ______ Size ______

☐ Die Cut ______

☐ Glue Tabs ______

☐ Punch/Round Corner ______

☐ Other ______

☐ Pad — (☐ Top, ☐ Side) ☐ Regular ☐ Carbonless No. Sheets/Pad ______ No. Pads ______

☐ Box/Wrap — Special Instructions ______

☐ **SALESMAN DELIVER** **DELIVER** ☐ **U.P.S.** ☐ **FREIGHT** ☐ **CUSTOMER PICKUP**

Deliver To: (Address, Person, Phone No.) ______

COMMENTS: ______

QUOTE RECEIVED BY: ______

Item	Price
______	______
______	______
______	______

standard printers' quote sheet

Repeat with changes: A repeat run with one or more of the pages to be corrected, shot to film, stripped into place, new plates made, and the book reprinted.

Sample: A sample of the previous run of the book is being sent to provide a model for the printer to work from. Film and plates still need to be prepared.

Number of copies: The size of the press run, or the number of copies you want. Because the more copies you run the cheaper the unit cost becomes, request prices for at least two or three size runs.

Overrun/underrun: There is always an underrun/overrun clause in a standard printer's contract. When books are run on a large press, there is wastage, whether through tearing, spotting, or any of a dozen other common printing problems. Extra copies are run to make sure that there are enough usable books to fill an order. If the number of salable books actually produced is over the number you requested, you will still have to pay for those books. If the number is less, you should only have to pay for those books you receive. This number is, by tradition, limited to 10 percent over or under the original run number.

Number of pages: The total pages in your book, including the front and back matter. This includes the title page, copyright page, introduction, table of contents, index, bibliography, and appendices. A page is one side of a single sheet of paper.

Finish size: The size of the finished book. A perfect bound book will be the exact size specified; a casebound book is a little larger because the cover is larger than the pages.

Type of paper: This term takes several variables into account, such as the paper weight, color, brand, and finish. Using the printer's "house," or standard paper, will always save money.

Ink color: The text of a book is usually printed in black ink. Other colors may be used in conjunction with black to enhance design elements, or specifically for illustrations and photographs. Each additional color in the body of the book increases the printing costs.

Close registration: Colored text, screens, or graphic elements that are very close to other elements on the page must be carefully printed so everything will be straight and fall exactly where it should on the page. A loose registration, which is color that does not have to be closely aligned to other page elements, does not require as much pre-press and press work.

Solids: Large areas of solid color, which use more ink and entail more pre-press and press work.

Reverses: Images that need to be converted, such as black reversed to white, or white objects turned into black.

Bleeds: These are used when you want an image or an area of color to extend to the edge of the text page or cover. Bleeds require printing beyond the margin of the paper so that when the page is trimmed, there are no thin lines of the original paper color showing.

Cover: A trade paperback book has a standard cover of 10 point (100 pound) white stock coated on one side. It is usually made up of one sheet of scored paper which is folded to form the spine. A case bound book has a cover made from cardboard stock which is scored to form a cover and a spine. The entire piece is covered, usually in cloth, and frequently stamped with gold or silver foil. A *dustjacket* is usually prepared with the same methods as a trade paperback cover, although with 80 pound paper, and flaps to fold over the cover.

Pre-press work: Everything necessary to make your work camera-ready. This usually includes converting photos to halftones, separating color elements, and making reductions and enlargements.

Extra covers/F&G's: Extra covers are a necessary element of marketing and should be ordered before the book goes to press. F&G's is an abbreviation for *folded and gathered pages*, which are the pages of the book cut and gathered into the signatures and ready for binding. These can be bound with index paper stock and a plastic comb and used for review copies.

Other bindings: There are bindings other than perfect bound and Smyth sewn. These include saddle stitching (wire stitching), plastic combs, and wire spirals.

Other services: For specialty books, there are foldouts for maps and oversize pages; perforations or scoring for tear-out pages; drilled holes; and specialty bindings, such a juvenile binding for a book too small for a regular spine.

Shrink wrapping: After the books are printed and bound, they can be shrink wrapped, either individually or in packages of two or more. This provides extra protection against damage during shipping and storage.

Camera-Ready Pages

Your book is ready to be made into camera-ready pages after it has been designed, typeset, and proofread. At this point, every mistake possible to correct should have been corrected. The book should then be printed on a high-resolution printer on paper that uses the heat from the printer to fuse the toner onto the paper — any major brand of coated laser paper will work. Most commercial printers prefer each page of the book to be run on a separate piece of paper.

You will want to present the printer with camera-ready pages that look exactly like the finished book will look, with each page placed in order from the first to last, and with blank pages inserted where there will be blank pages in the book. Setting up the pages in an *imposition layout,* so that the pages fall correctly for each signature, is something best left to the printing house.

As the pages are printed on your own printer, check to make sure there are no spots or wrinkles on them. Every letter should look clean, without fading, streaking, or spotting. Any instructions to the commercial printer that must be written on the pages should be carefully and lightly marked with a non-reproducing pencil or pen, preferably in the margins rather than in the text block.

Camera-ready means that each page is ready to be photographed and turned into film. The way each page looks is the way it will appear in the book. If you have done any pasteup on a page, it must be absolutely straight and parallel to the text. Any stray marks or smears must be removed.

If you have the equipment and experience, you can output your book directly to film, or send your computer files to a pre-press house that will prepare the book on "repro" paper or film.

Preparing the Film

The printer photographs the camera-ready copy and uses the negatives to make printing plates. That is why camera-ready pages should need no extra pre-press work in order to be converted into film. Photographs should already be converted into sized and cropped halftones, or the printer must be given the exact instructions for the photo specifications, so they can be converted into halftones. These are then placed on the camera-ready page. Color pages, including the cover, should be properly separated, or instructions given for their separation and placement.

Page and Cover Proofs

About three to four weeks after you have sent your camera-ready pages and cover to the printer, you will receive the page and cover proofs in the form of folded and gathered signatures on photosensitive paper. The page proofs are developed by a photographic process from the film of the camera-ready pages; these proofs are usually called *bluelines* (because they are colored blue) or *dyluxes*. Proofs can also be called *brownlines, Vandykes,* and *silvers*. All of these are names for page proofs which are meant to show you how the pages of

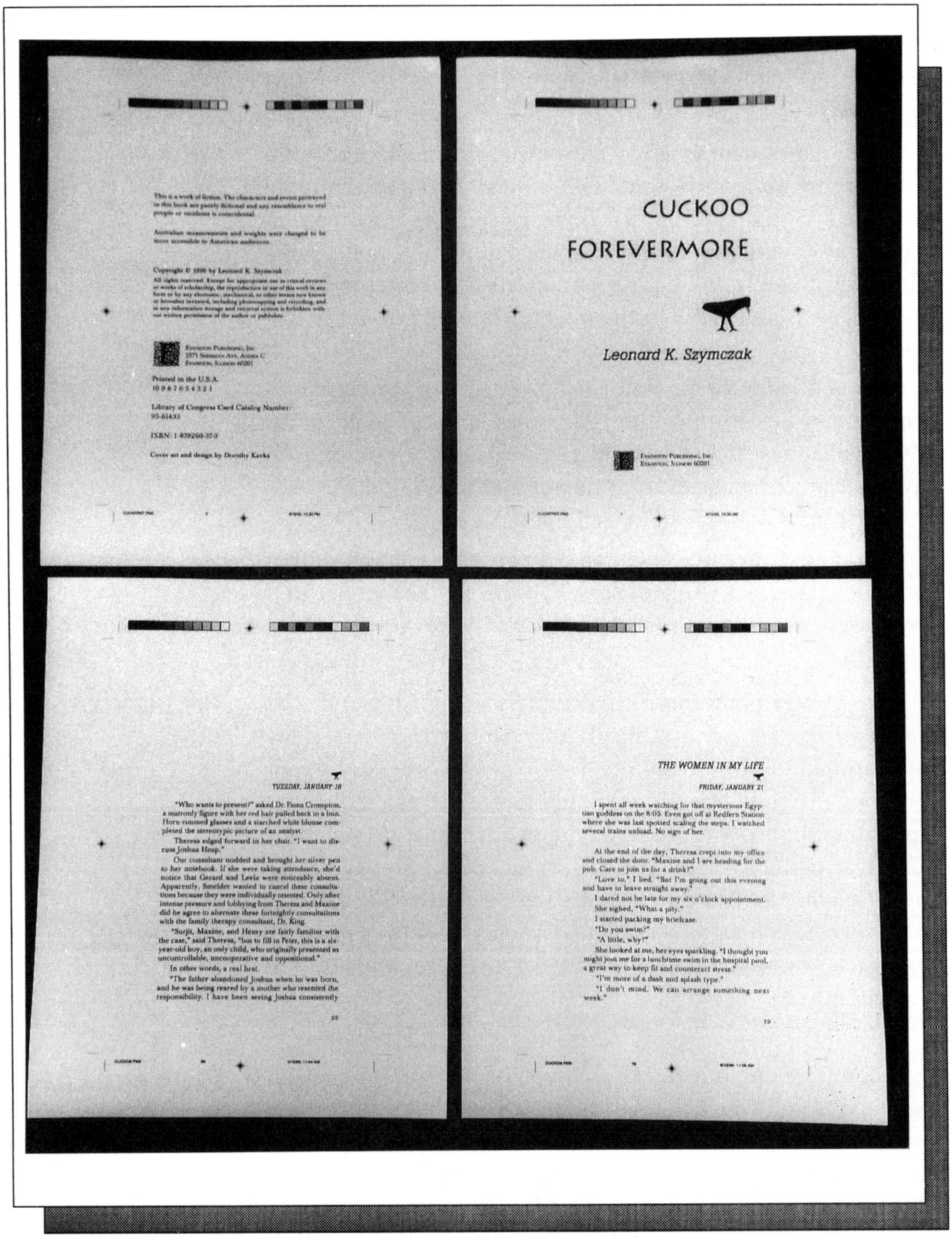

camera-ready pages

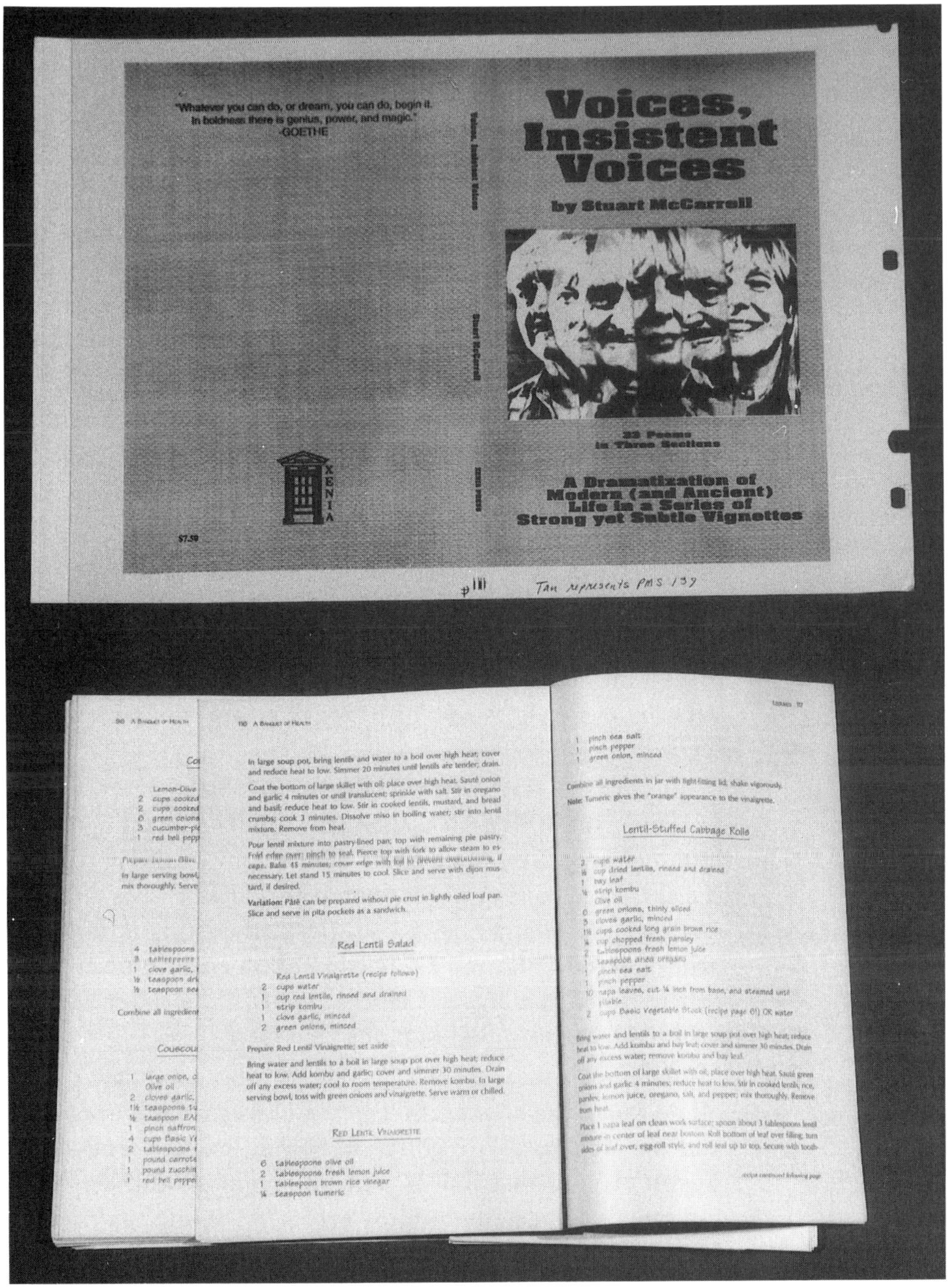

printer proofs: (top) two-color color keys and (bottom) bluelines your book will look when they are printed, cut to size, and folded into signatures.

The *color keys* are the acetate or plastic overlays that are placed together to indicate how the cover and multicolored text will look. They are also produced from the film used to create the printing plates, and are used to verify that the cover colors are in alignment and that all colors have been separated correctly. Often, the proofs are not the exact color specified by the designer, because they are used for placement correction rather than color matching.

Full or process color covers and art are usually proofed with a *Matchprint,* or *Chromalin;* this proof is used to precisely check colors, and to make sure the color match is correct as the covers come off the press.

Printer's Errors/ Author's Errors

Any mistakes you find on the bluelines and color key are mistakes that will be printed in the book. However, this is not the time to be correcting your text, which should have been done in the proofreading stage. Now you are looking for printer mistakes, such as spots on the page, missing page numbers, or even pages out of order. You are not rereading the book.

If your eye does catch a mistake you have overlooked before and cannot live with, then you can have that page reshot, but it will cost you to do so. You must supply the printer with the corrected page or pages, which are called *author alterations* (AA). If the mistake is the printer's, then this is noted as a *printer's error* (PE) and there is no extra cost involved to correct it. *Once you sign off on the proofs, the printer cannot be held liable for mistakes that you find later.*

After you return your corrected proofs and have signed off on them, the books, covers, and/or dustjackets are printed, and the signatures are collated, bound, packed, and shipped to you or your distributor. The shipment should be checked for defects, especially binding errors, with one copy reserved for noting any changes you will want in the next printing.

You are finally through creating, writing, rewriting, and have corrected your last proof. Your manuscript has become a book. You are an author, you are in print, and the time has come to get your work into the hands of the reading public. You should begin your marketing.

WHEN CHECKING BLUELINES, WHAT DO YOU LOOK FOR?

1. Holes in color, screens, etc.
2. Stray blotches, spots
3. Uniform density of color
4. Correct folding and trim
5. Proper pagination (page numbers in order)
6. Missing art or type
7. Artwork/type filling in with ink
8. Flopped photos (facing wrong direction)
9. Incorrect or transposed photos
10. Broken type
11. Crooked type
12. Sloppy corners
13. Misspellings and content mistakes
14. Proper alignment of borders and rules (especially when crossing gutters)

A blueline is a paper proof your printer makes by exposing paper (usually dylux) through the negatives which were shot from your original boards. These negatives will then be used to make your printing plates.

Since bluelines are made from your negatives, what you see is what you will get. Make sure that what you are checking is exactly the way you want it. This is your last chance to see your book before it is printed.

If an error does get by, bluelines provide tangible notice as to who is responsible, you or the printer. If it is something you neglected to correct, the printer assumes no responsibility and is under no obligation to make amends. However, if it is a printer error (PE), you marked it as such on the blueline, and it was not corrected, the error becomes the printer's responsibility to correct.

For jobs printed in more than one color, it is difficult to see separate ink colors on a blue line. However, the black plate will appear as a dark blue, while other colors will be a lighter shade of blue. Areas printed in a screen will appear slightly darker than the white areas.

When checking bluelines, do not assume anything. For example, do not assume your printer has noticed that missing page number. If something is missing, mark it. If something is there that should not be, mark it. (Use your pagination layout to help find and keep track of all problems and corrections.)

PRINTING TRADE CUSTOMS

1. QUOTATION A quotation not accepted within thirty (30) days is subject to review. C&F or CIF prices are based on current rates of sea freight, so they are subject to variations of such rates or any surcharges imposed by shipping lines at the time of shipment. The cost of advance copies, extra covers and jackets and the cost of sending them and dummies by post courier or air freight shall be added to customer's account, unless otherwise agreed in writing.

2. ORDERS Orders regularly entered, verbal or written, cannot be canceled except upon terms that will compensate printer against loss.

3. EXPERIMENTAL WORK Experimental work performed at customer's request, such as sketches, drawings, composition, plates, presswork and materials will be charged for at current rates and may not be used without consent of the printer.

4. PREPARATORY WORK Sketches, copy, dummies, and all preparatory work created or furnished by the printer, shall remain his exclusive property and no use of same shall be made, nor any ideas obtained therefrom be used, except upon compensation to be determined by the printer.

5. CONDITION OF COPY Estimates for typesetting are based on the receipt of original copy or manuscript clearly typed, double-spaced on 8½ by11 inch uncoated stock, one side only. Condition of copy which deviates from this standard is subject to re-estimating and pricing review by printer at time of submission of copy, unless otherwise specified in estimate.

6. PREPARATORY MATERIALS Art work, type, plates, color separations, negatives, positives and other items, when supplied by the printer, shall remain his exclusive property unless otherwise agreed in writing.

7. ALTERATIONS Alterations represent work performed in addition to the original specifications. Such additional work shall be charged at current rates and be supported with documentation upon request.

8. PROOFS Proofs shall be submitted with original copy. Corrections are to be made on "master set," returned marked "OK," or "OK with corrections," and signed by customer. If revised proofs are desired, request must be made when proofs are returned. Printer regrets any errors that may occur through production undetected, but cannot be held responsible for errors if the work is printed per customer's OK or if changes are communicated verbally. Printer shall not be responsible for errors if the customer has not ordered or has refused to accept proofs or has failed to return proofs with indication of changes or has instructed printer to proceed without submission of proofs.

9. PRESS PROOFS Unless specifically provided in printer's quotation, press proofs will be charged for at current rates. An inspection sheet of any form can be submitted for customer approval at no charge, provided customer is available at the press during the time of make ready. Any changes, corrections or lost press time due to customer's change of mind or delay will be charged for at current rates.

partial list of printing trade customs concerning printer's responsibilities
(continued on next page)

10. COLOR PROOFING Because of differences in equipment, paper, inks and other conditions between color proofing and production pressroom operations, a reasonable variation in color between color proofs and the completed job shall constitute acceptable delivery. Special inks and proofing stocks will be forwarded to customer's suppliers upon request at current rates.

11. OVERRUNS OR UNDERRRUNS Overruns or underruns not to exceed 10 percent on quantities ordered up to 10,000 copies shall constitute acceptable delivery. Printer will bill for actual quantity delivered within this tolerance. If customer requires guaranteed "no less than" delivery, percentage tolerance of overage must be doubled.

12. CUSTOMER'S PROPERTY Customer's property and all property supplied to the printer by or on behalf of the customer will be held, worked on, and carried at customer's risk.

13. DELIVERY Delivery of work shall be accepted when tendered and thereupon the ownership for finished work shall pass to the customer upon delivery to his place of business or to carrier at shipping point and payment shall become due. Unless otherwise specified, the price quoted is for a single shipment, without storage, FOB local customer's place of business or FOB printer's platform for out-of-town customers. C&F or CIF price includes delivery to dockside warehouse or container terminal in a seaport in customer's country, unless otherwise specified in writing. All domestic charges related to receiving the shipment, including but not limited to customs duties, broker's clearance fees, dock charges, and inland freight are charged to the customer's account. Proposals are based on continuous and uninterrupted delivery of complete order, unless specifications distinctly state otherwise. Charges related to delivery from customer to printer, or from customer's supplier to printer, are not included in any quotations unless specified. Special priority pickup or delivery service will be provided at current rates upon customer's request. Materials delivered from customer or his suppliers are verified with delivery notification as to cartons, packages or items shown only. The accuracy of quantities indicated on such tickets cannot be verified and printer cannot accept liability for shortage based on supplier's shipping information.

14. WARPING OF CASED BOOKS While every care is taken by the printer in the manufacture of casebound books, the printer cannot be held entirely responsible for warping of cases due to sudden and great differences in the temperature or humidity between the place of manufacture and the place of distribution. If warping of cases is due to faulty manufacture, claims for compensation or replacement will be considered.

15. CUSTOMER FURNISHED MATERIALS Paper stock, camera copy, film, color separations, and other customer furnished materials shall be manufactured, packed and delivered to printer's specifications. Additional cost due to delays or impaired production caused by specification deficiencies shall be charged to the customer.

7

FROM MANUSCRIPT TO BOOK: A VISUAL GUIDE

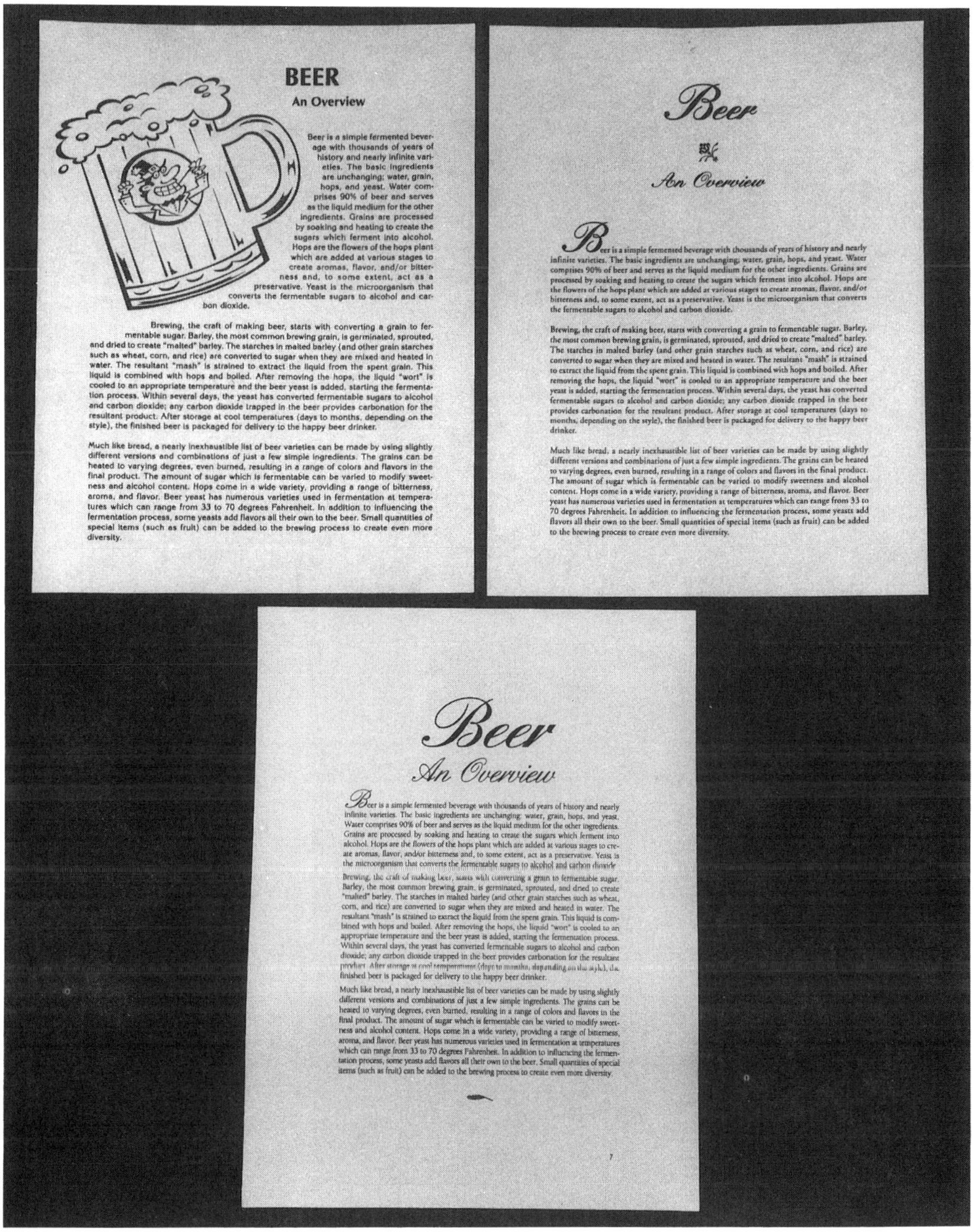

*different typesetting templates of same book prepared for style choice—
the publisher chose the bottom one*

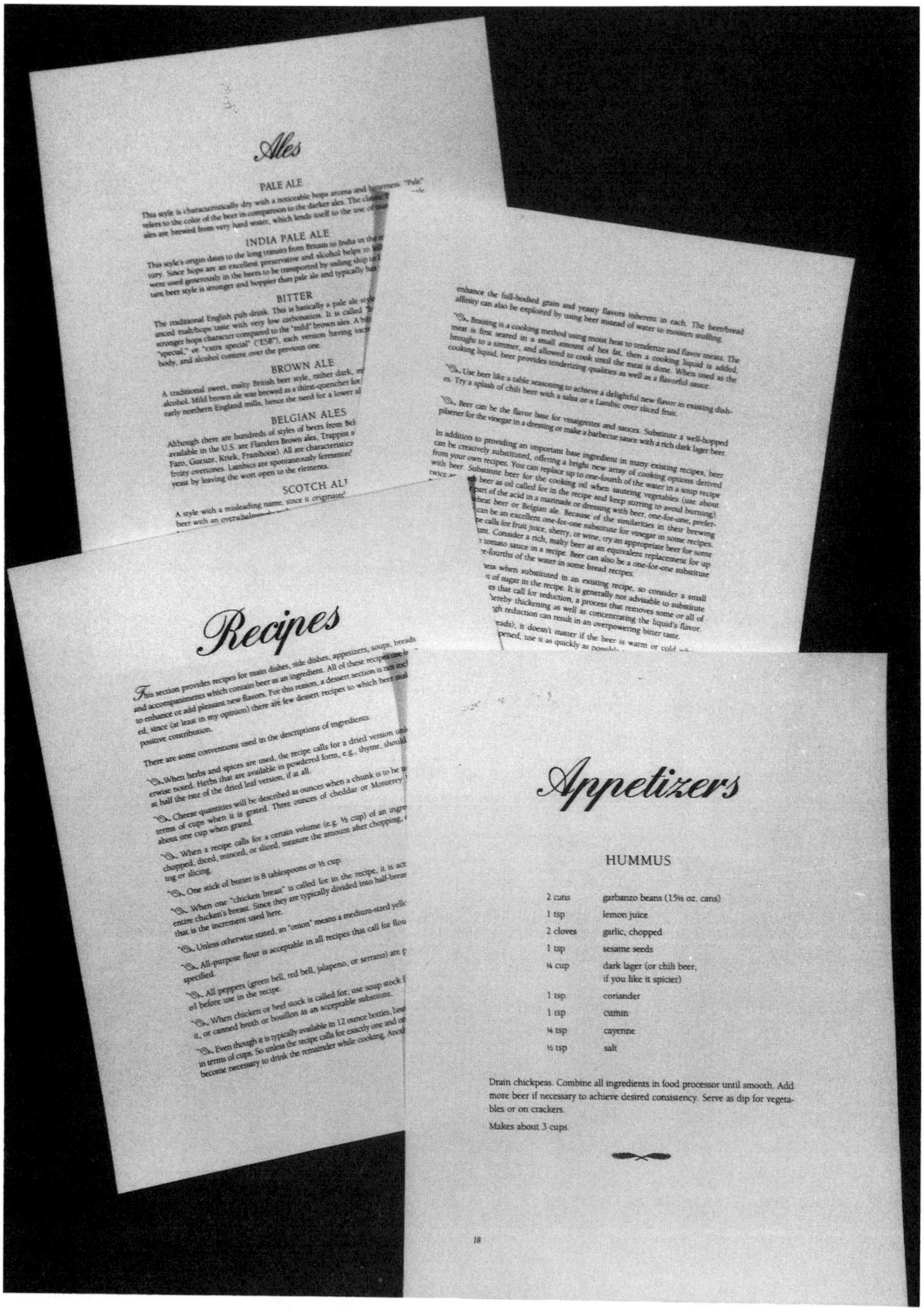

camera-ready pages

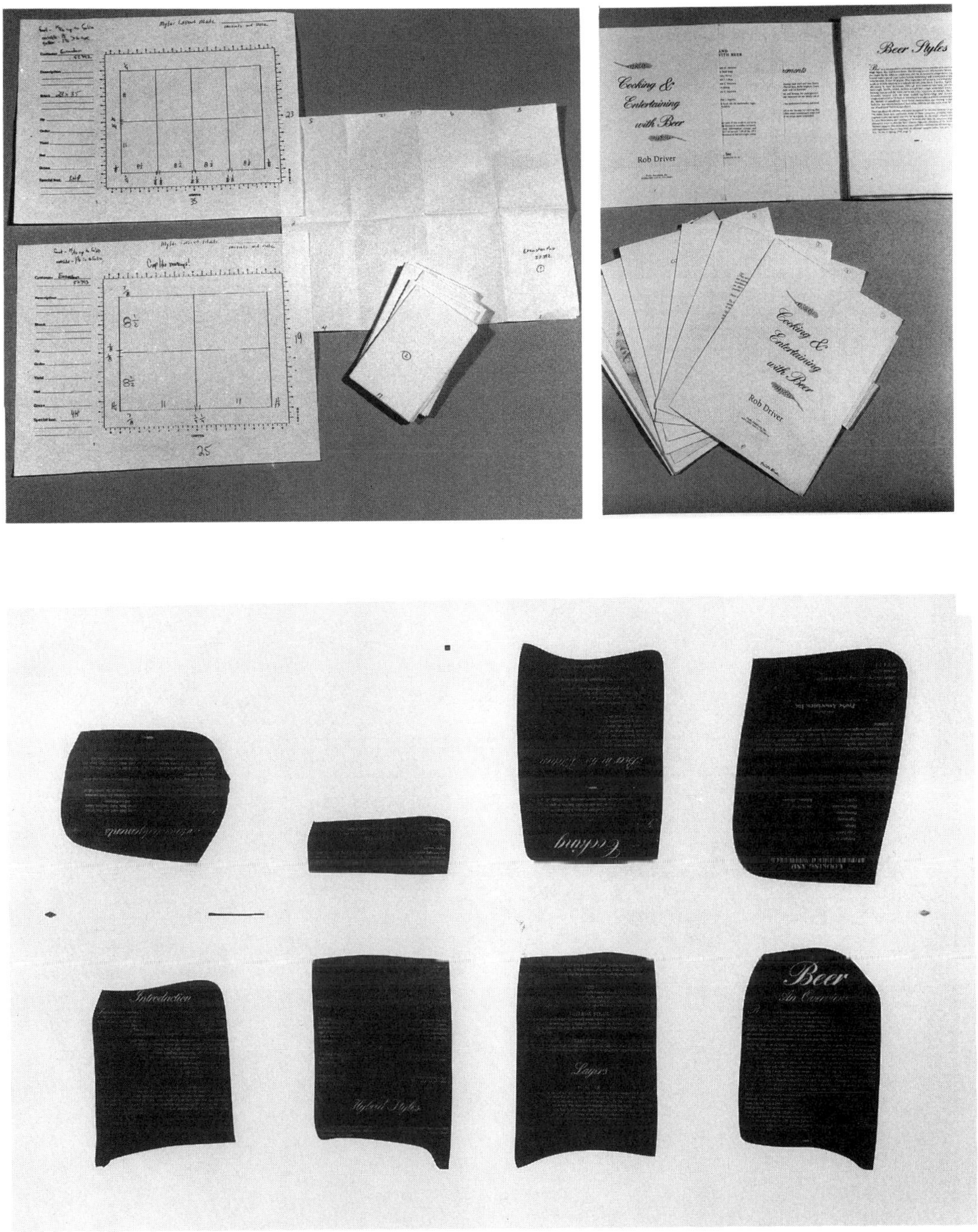

(top left) printer layout sheet and folding dummies; (top right)bluelines; (bottom) film from which printing plates are made

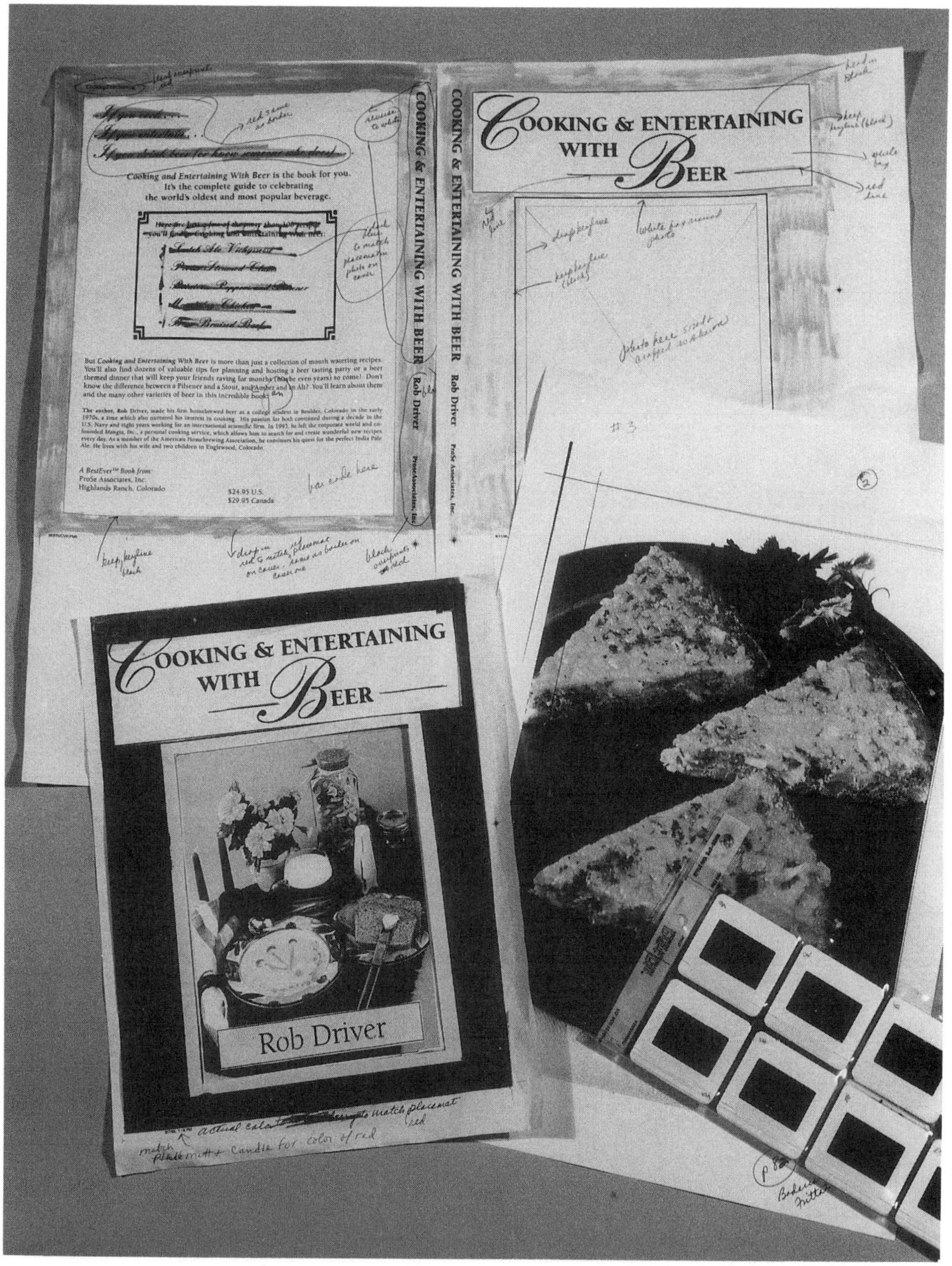

sample cover and photo specifications to show printer color layout, sizing, and cropping of photographs

(top) "random" proofs and bluelines of photos and (bottom) Matchprint proof of cover

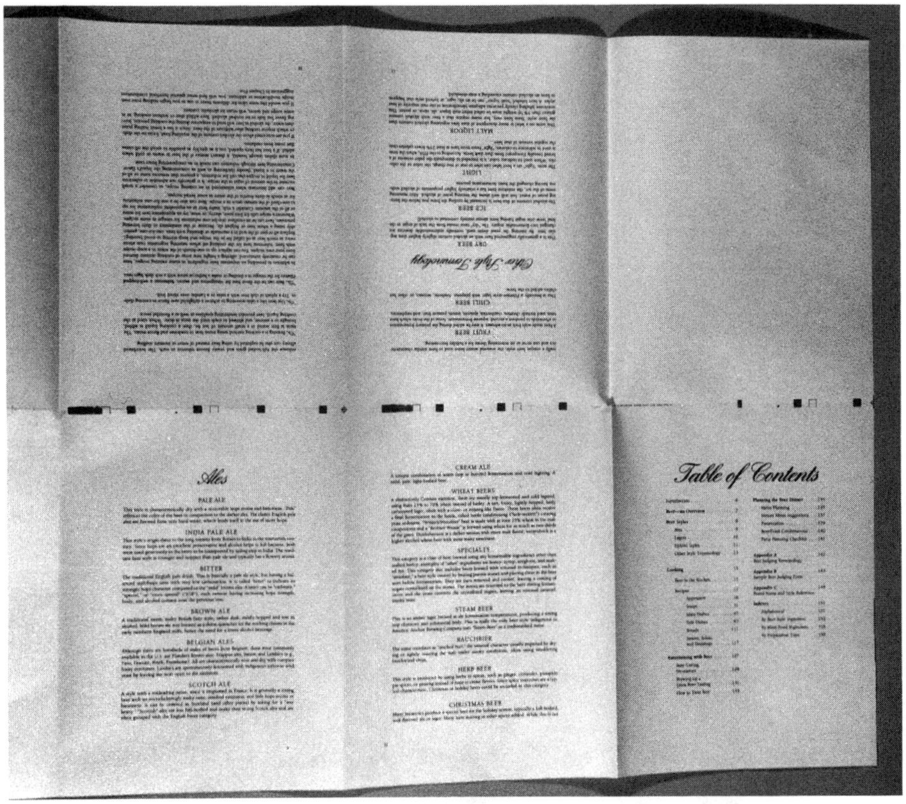

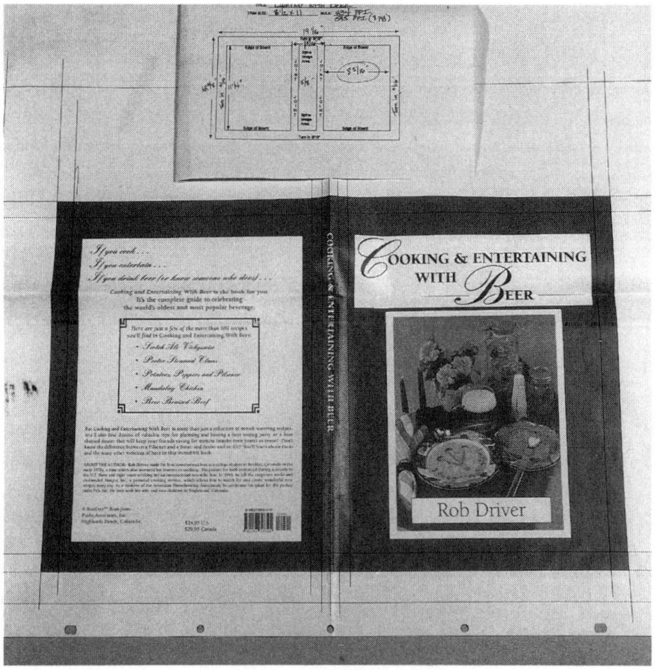

(top) signatures after printing(bottom)printer folding and cutting specs

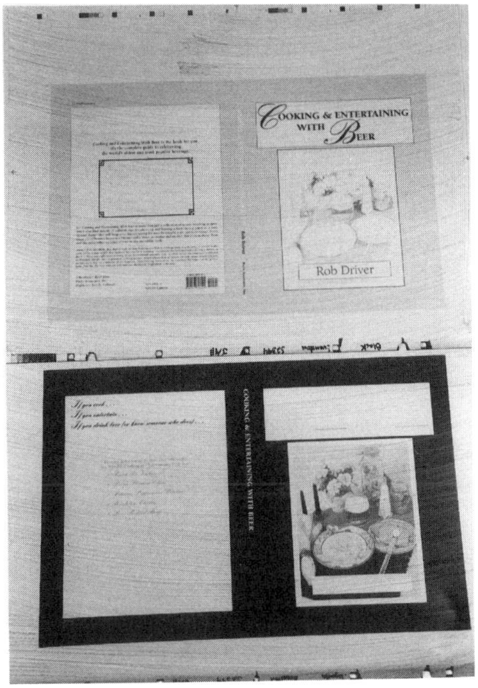

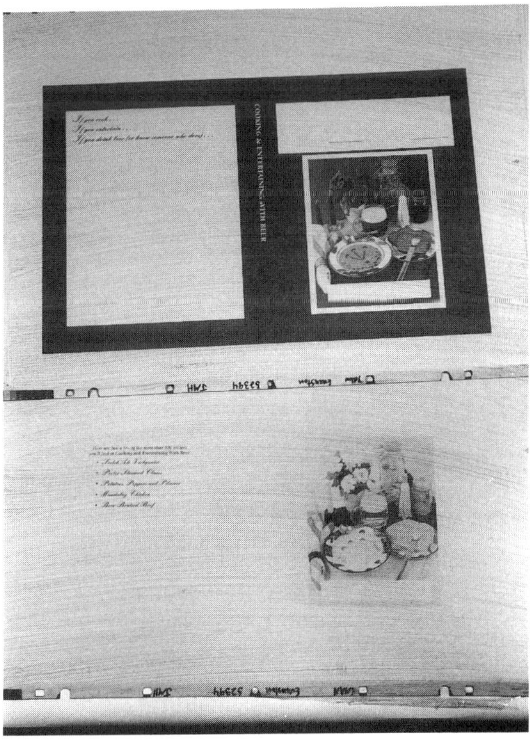

metal plates used to produce full-color cover
one plate is for black ink, one for cyan, one for yellow, and one for magenta

finished book

8

PRICING, PROFITS, AND DISCOUNTS

Chapter 8

Factors That Influence Price

Choosing a cover price for your book is not a decision to take lightly, or to leave up to guesswork. Pricing can have a very serious impact on the future of your book. Setting a low price on your book does not necessarily give it an advantage. For example, when pricing a book that is intended for sale through mail order catalogs, it is important to set a price high enough for the catalogs to make a comfortable profit. Also, since value paid is value perceived, an inappropriately low price can make a book seem worthless to a potential buyer. On the other hand, a book priced too high will give the sales advantage to a lower-priced competitor.

There are many factors that can influence the pricing of your book, including its intended markets, the cost and quality of the competition's books, the income and spending habits of the book's intended audience, and the value of the information provided. Your primary concern in pricing your book, however, is to be certain you will make a profit.

Small Press Runs

Small press runs, especially first runs, run the risk of being unprofitable. A first printing is more expensive in cost per book because of printing set-up costs. Perhaps you print 1,000 books at a per unit cost of $2.15, and price the books at $5.95 — more than twice what each book costs to produce. After you send out 50 review copies and spend $500 on promotional efforts, a national distributor picks up the book. The distributor's sales reps sell every book in the run. You break out the champagne and dream of your imminent retirement.

But then reality sets in. The distributor takes a minimum of 60percent of each sale, or $3.57 per book. Your return — 40 percent of each book sold — is $2.38 per book. Once you subtract your production costs, you will receive $111 profit on the 950 books sold, which is not even enough to cover the money you spent on advertising. So, even though you have sold out the press run and spent less than $1,000 on promotions, you will lose money on your book.

Forecasting the Profit

In the past, publishers often used simplified equations, such as "price equals five times the per unit cost of production." For the self-publisher, although helpful, this equation does not take into account enough information to prevent you from seriously mispricing your book. Consider two publishers, one who sells through a distributor, and one who sells through direct mail solicitation. The economics of selling out an entire press run varies greatly between the two, as one is receiving 100 percent of the price of each book through direct-mail sales, while the other only receives 40 percent of each sale after the distributor takes its percentage. Though their production costs and press run were the same, and the books carried the same price, one title netted less than half the total of the other. The obvious conclusion is that, however similar they might be in production costs, these books should not carry the same price.

To arrive at the right price for your book, you must first determine which combinations of book price and distribution mix will yield the largest profits on a sold-out run. Also figure in distribution price demands, competitive pricing, marketing budgets, and perceived value of the book. These variables are important in determining price; however, it is up to you to determine their importance in relation to your book and marketing strategy.

You can keep the process relatively straightforward and comprehensible by using a mathematical equation that will adjust for the variables and provide an accurate pricing forecast. All it takes to accurately price a book is some rudimentary math, patience, and thoroughness.

First, determine the per-unit cost of producing the book. To arrive at this figure, divide the total cost of producing the book — including pre-press costs, printing, and shipping the book to a storage facility — by the number of books in the press run. This is the production cost of each book. Multiply that number by five, and you will arrive at a number close to your optimal price.

> Jonathon Hacker is spending $21,500 to produce a run of 10,000 books about the Internet. By dividing $21,500 by 10,000, Hacker figures his per-unit cost to be $2.15. He then multiplies the per-unit cost by five to determine a book price that should be close to the optimal price. The result is $10.75, which Hacker then adjusts to $10.95, a price that is close to but still less than competitive books.

Distribution Mix

The next step is to decide on a distribution mix that is supported by your marketing plan. The *distribution mix* is the proportion of the press run you expect to sell through specific outlets, such as wholesalers, distributors, book clubs, or direct mail. Rank these outlets in the order of your book's highest potential sales to its lowest.

Each kind of outlet will yield a different percentage of the cover price for each book sold. Distributors generally remit 30 percent of the cover price of a book, wholesalers pay back 45 percent, bookstores send 60 percent, and direct mail yields 100 percent of the book's price. These percentages play an important role in helping you find an optimal price, just as they play an important role in the economics of selling your book.

> Jonathan Hacker intends to sell his book through a major distributor who will remit 30 percent of the cover price on each book sold. His sales through direct mail will yield him 100 percent of the cover price, and non-traditional sales will yield 70 percent of the price of each book. Hacker does not think that sales through individual bookstores, libraries, wholesalers, and catalogs will amount to much, and so leaves these outlets out of his distribution mix forecast. He then notes his mix as 0.3, 1.0, and 0.7, with each number representing sales through the distributor, direct mail, and non-traditional sales, respectively.

Forecasting Sales

The next step is to make an educated guess as to what portion of your press run you can expect to sell through each kind of outlet. This part of the forecasting process is part prophecy and part strategy. To a certain extent you are guessing at how many books you will sell through a specific channel.

If you are publishing a book specifically geared toward non-traditional markets such as gift stores, you might decide to limit the number of books you intend to sell through distributors, and put a heavy emphasis on store sales. If your book is written for a specific niche market and you have access to a large mailing list that targets your market, you would put a heavy emphasis on direct mail sales.

> Hacker has struck a deal with an Internet service provider to buy 4,000 copies of his book. This represents 40 percent of his press run being sold to non-traditional markets in the form of promotional giveaways to new Internet accounts. He intends to launch a 10,000 piece direct mail campaign, which he expects to sell 2,000 books, or 20 percent of his stock. He does not want to sell more than 3,000 books through his distributor, so he will only provide that number for warehousing. The remaining 1,000 books he has set aside for promotions, giveaways, and review copies.

The Forecast Equation

Now you are ready to begin plugging these numbers in a *forecast equation.* Begin by identifying the variables:

P = total production costs

C (proposed cover price) = 5 x pc [production cost ÷ total number of books]

X = percentage of book's cover price remitted on each sale through a specific outlet

N = number of books forecast to sell through a specific outlet

M = proposed marketing budget

The equation then looks like this:

$$\text{Profit} = (CX^1N^1 + CX^2N^2 + CX^3N^3) - (P + M)$$

Now we add the initial set of numbers to replace the variables and the equation looks like this:

Profit = (10.95 x .4 x 3,000) + (10.95 x 1.0 x 2,000) +(10.95 x .7 x 4,000) – (27,100 + 10,000)

In this equation, 10.95 is the price of the book, .4 represents the percentage (40 percent) of the cover price remitted when the book is sold through the distributor, and 3,000 represents the number of books that the distributor will sell. Next, the price is multiplied by 1.0, representing a 100 percent return on direct mail sales for 2,000 books. The third figure is the price of the book, .7 (70 percent) is the amount of the cover price remitted from non-traditional sales.

Profit = [19,710 + 21,900 + 30,640] – 37,100

In this equation, 19,710 represents the return on 3,000 books sold to the distributor at 40 percent of the cover price of $10.95. The next number of 21,900 is the return on 2,000 books sold through direct mail at 100 percent of the cover price. The last number of 30,640 represents 4,000 copies of the book sold to non-traditional markets at 70 percent. The final figure of 37,100 represents total projected production costs and the marketing budget.

Profit = $35,150

Thus, the profit projection for this set of variables can be calculated at $35,150. This is an optimistic yield, enhanced by the assumption that most of the books in the run will be sold through high-profit channels such as non-traditional outlets and direct mail sales.

Using Pricing Information

The next step is to begin changing the variables, allowing for a lower or higher price, changing the distribution mix figures, and introducing other outlets. Once you have worked through all likely distribution mixes and price combinations, *you will have a series of projected profit maximums.* This will indicate how low or high you can comfortably set the price of the book and give you an idea of what kinds of sales you need to focus on.

BOOK PRICING SUMMARY	
P	*(production expense).* This is the total amount of money invested in editing, designing, and printing your book.
pc	*(per-book production costs).* This is the total production expense P, divided by number of books in the run.
C	*(the initial proposed cover price).* Multiply the per-book production cost by five. You may want to multiply by a number as high as eight, or as low as four, depending on other valuations.
X	*(the net return on sales through each kind of outlet).* This is the return after discounts. Example: individual bookstores take an average of 40 percent of the cover price of each book sold, making your net return 60 percent of the cover price.
N	*(the number of books you expect to sell through each outlet).* Use your marketing plan when deciding on this number. Remember that this figure is based on the number of books in the initial press run only.
M	*(your proposed marketing budget).* This is the amount of money you expect to spend during the year to advertise and market your title. This figure should include postage, printing, and design costs of advertising material, and any fees associated with developing marketing tools and displaying at trade shows.
Use the equation [Profit = $(CX^1N^1 + CX^2N^2 + CX^3N^3) - (P + M)$], replacing the variables with the values you determined in the previous steps.	
Repeat the equation, altering the values to yield different profit margins.	
Keep running new numbers through the equation and comparing the results until you find a price, distribution mix, and budget that is realistic and profitable.	
Make final adjustments to the price based on the pricing of the book's specific competition.	
Stick to your final marketing budget and distribution mix as closely as possible. Just as your marketing plan is your blueprint to success in selling your entire press run, your pricing plan will ensure that you price your book correctly.	

PRICING WORKSHEET

(P) production expense ______
number of books printed ______
(P ÷ number of books equals
(pc) cost per book ______

(M) proposed marketing budget ______

(C) cover price is 5 x (pc) ______
cover price is 3 x (pc) ______
cover price is __ x (pc) ______

(X) net returns from outlet sales
X^1sale outlet______________percentage__________
X^2sale outlet______________percentage__________
X^3sale outlet______________percentage__________

(N) forecasted sales from outlet X^1 ______
forecasted sales from outlet X^2 ______
forecasted sales from outlet X^3 ______

To determine profit margins:

$(CX^1N^1 + CX^2N^2 + CX^3N^3) - (P + M) = \text{Profit}$

(___ x ___ x ____) + (___ x ___ x ____) + (___ x ___ x _____) -(_____ + _____) = Profit

(_______) + (______) - (_____) = Profit

__________ = Profit

Use this information to set goals for your sales to key outlets and monitor sales to low-return outlets; these numbers will ensure that you do not critically lower your profit margin by selling too great a portion of your press run to such customers.

Of course, the more books you run, and the higher you price them, the more profit you will make. This does not mean that you should invest in a large press run. If you cannot sell a significant portion of your press run, you will lose money. Also, do not let this formula persuade you to raise the price of the book to an unreasonable figure. The idea is to find a comfortable, realistic, and well-balanced pricing and selling strategy that will ensure a profit under a wide range of circumstances.

The most difficult part of this process is forecasting the percentages of books to be sold at various discounts. There is no way to accurately predict how many books from your initial run you will sell through each outlet. By running the numbers through the equation, you will begin to find outlet mixes that will raise your profit margin. This information should be used to influence and guide your marketing strategy. You may find that in order to price a title reasonably, you will have to limit sales of the books at high discounts to distributors and wholesalers and focus on direct-to-consumer sales, such as mail order.

Discounts

You will be expected to give a discount to most of your customers, excluding individual, direct-to-consumer sales. Discounts for direct sales to bookstores are individually set by each publisher and can be as simple as:

2–4 books .... 20 percent discount

5–99 books .... 40 percent discount

100+ books .... 50 percent discount.

Distributors will generally dictate to the publisher the terms and discount they receive, but because they are actively selling the books, giving their own discounts to buyers, and taking care of all the billing, their higher percentage is earned. There can be negotiation on discounts with distributors and wholesalers if there is a large demand for your book.

If you decide to sell your books by yourself, selling on *consignment,* where books are not paid for until they are sold, rarely works for the author or the bookseller. In such a case, because the books are not paid for, the seller feels little obligation to take care of or keep track of the books. Unless you are really desperate for the sale and prepared for the consequences, do not get talked into such an arrangement. Wholesalers and distributors technically work on consignment, but they can usually be trusted to accurately track and pay for books as they are sold.

If you are selling directly to libraries, do not discount unless they buy more than two books. Schools usually receive what is called a "short" discount of 10 to 20 percent off the retail price.

Returns

Return policies are a reality of selling books. First time publishers are often shocked to find out that returns are common practice in the book trade. Jubilance over a large sale can turn to anguish when the books are returned six to eight months later and payment must be refunded. If you are working with a distributor, a return policy will be stated in your contract. If you are selling through wholesalers or directly to the bookstores, work out a statement of return that is fair to you as well as your customers.

RETURN POLICY

Only books in resalable condition and not torn, mutilated, or defaced in any way may be returned for refund (or credit) and only if received within six months of original invoice date. The invoice must be included in return shipments and all shipments must be returned prepaid.

Terms and Policies

In order to prepare for the many kinds of accounts you will be working with, prepare a statement outlining the various discounts and sales terms you extend. These *terms and policies of sale* should be reproduced and sent along with the statement of returns to all customers. You will be asked by some buyers to make special deals in return for promises of large purchases. Do not do so, because if you give one customer special financial considerations, then by law you must do the same for all your customers, a sure way to lose your credibility and your profits.

Thirty days net is usual in this type of billing, and if payment takes more than 90 days, all discounts should be automatically canceled. You can charge interest on accounts that are overdue, but define clearly what constitutes "overdue" and state the interest percentage in your terms.

Ask for at least two references for orders over a certain amount, such as $50 or $75, and at least one banking reference. Keep careful records on customers so that you can identify those who do not or will not pay in a reasonable amount of time. Extend credit only up to a certain predetermined limit.

You will probably have to pay shipping charges on prepaid orders, but if a buyer orders on credit, he or she should expect to be responsible for those charges, and freight and postage should be added to all invoices that involve trade discounts. Requests for special handling must be received in writing, with the order and prices noted as "subject to change without notice."

TERMS AND POLICIES

Prices subject to change without notice.

Terms: Thirty days net. Publisher reserves the right to require cash with order in establishing new accounts. U.S. currency only.

Interest: Accounts more than 30 days overdue are charged interest at 1½ percent per month which is an annual rate of 18 percent.

Delivery: F.O.B. our point of origin. We pay shipping and handling on prepaid orders only.

Shipping: Our standard policy is to send by the cheapest rate available. Please specify if you prefer a special method of delivery.

Special Requests: These must be received in writing and are handled on an individual basis only.

Because of exchange rates and shipping fees, all costs should be higher outside the United States, and you may want to indicate payment only in U.S. currency. Since everyone likes a bargain, you can offer an extra 5 percent discount for anyone who pays up front and 10 percent with no returns allowed, both of which are cost efficient for you due to savings on billing and returns. Another excellent promotion that can be part of your terms is to offer a free book with a minimum order of ten or twelve books.

STOP Orders

STOP orders (for Single Title Order Plan) were developed for bookstores that order only one book from a publisher, but still need a discount. These are prepaid orders, very often accompanied by a blank check that can be filled in up to a certain amount. The publisher can set the terms for STOP orders; for example, you can offer a 20 percent discount for such an order, with the buyer paying the postage for the book, or 10 percent and you pay postage. Whatever terms you set, be consistent in applying them to all STOP orders.

If you set your policies before you begin to sell your books, you will then be able to concentrate on the more important aspects of marketing, such as preparing your marketing tools.

9

DEVELOPING A MARKETING PLAN

Chapter 9

The self-published author, poised to jump head first into the rough and tumble world of book sales and promotion, is best advised to look before leaping. The less experience you have working with the book trade, selling a title to trade buyers, or promoting yourself to the media, the more important it is that you do your sales and marketing homework before you even put your manuscript into production.

Facts about the Book Trade

A study of the U.S. book trade in its present state is a sobering experience for authors about to throw their hat, and personal savings, into this arena. The facts can be shocking:

- Every day in the United States, more than 125 books are published. That is more than 45,625 new titles a year.
- Because of fierce competition and a tendency on the part of buyers to lump books into categories, there is no such thing as a title without direct competition. You may think that your book is an "absolute first," but no one else in the trade will see it that way.
- On the average, trade buyers take discounts of over 50 percent of the cover price of your book on each sale — distributors average 60 percent, wholesalers 50 percent, and bookstores more than 40 percent.
- The average direct-mail response rate is below one percent.
- Trade buyers take an average of 104 days to pay an invoice.

- All books sold to the book trade are fully refundable for cash or credit — if they can't sell your book, you can expect to be flooded with returns.

- Most chain bookstores and superstores will rely on one decision maker for new acquisitions. If he or she decides not to take your book, the doors of all stores in that chain will be closed to you.

- It takes time, money, and dedication to continue promoting a book. If you lose momentum, it will be difficult and expensive to regain.

- More and more bookstores are now refusing to buy directly from publishers. They insist on placing orders with wholesalers and distributors, who, in turn, are reluctant to buy from single-title authors and publishers.

Long waits for payment, unconditional returns, cutthroat competition, low percentages — is it beginning to sound impossible to sell your book? There are ways to overcome these obstacles. The first step is to be aware of these drawbacks and find ways to avoid them. Also, you can avoid selling to bookstores and the book trade in general, and concentrate on nontraditional markets and direct sales to consumers.

In order to build the kind of momentum and experience that will allow you to sell exclusively to the lucrative, non book markets and/or directly to consumers, you will probably have to begin your efforts along traditional routes.

Therefore, it is necessary for you to set up distribution channels, find markets for your title, and effectively promote the title to your target audience. All three of these goals must be met in order to achieve success, and if any one is neglected, your books will not sell. For this reason, it is necessary to find markets and outlets that will buy books from you in bulk, at wholesale discounts, and then resell them to the consumer.

Once you have successfully secured distribution channels and found markets for your books, you will not have finished selling those books. You will still need to promote your title in order to get consumers to buy the books.

To make matters more complicated, this process is time-sensitive and must be carried out in the proper order. You cannot begin stocking retail outlets until you've secured distribution channels, and you should not begin promotions until you have gotten your title into some retail outlets. In the book trade, a title is considered to have a six month lifespan as a new or "frontlist" title. Self-published titles can remain in the marketplace for longer than this, but only for as long as there is noticeable consumer demand.

The Marketing Plan

In order to help you accomplish these goals, and accomplish them in order, it is necessary to first devise a *marketing plan*. A good marketing plan specifies clear overall goals, identifies individual objectives that will lead to those goals, identifies the tools that will support your marketing and promotion efforts, and provides a clear time frame.

Without a clear marketing plan, you are going to have a very difficult time trying to sell books, no matter how good your book is. With a good marketing plan, even if you are not successful in all your efforts, you will still sell an adequate number of books.

Marketing Plan Goals

Your marketing plan must: 1) identify your target audience, the people most likely to buy your book; 2) determine the retail markets most likely to buy your title; 3) provide a method of distribution that will make the book easily available to the most outlets in the widest geographical area; 4) promote the title to the largest segments of your target audience to get them into retail outlets; 5) provide a time frame that ensures that these steps occur in the proper sequence, avoiding missed opportunities or premature efforts; and 6) list marketing and promotional tools that will help you reach these goals.

The "W" Questions

To build a marketing plan you need to start by asking yourself five questions: *Who* is my target audience? *Where* do I find this audience? *Why* do they want or need my book? *What* can I do to provoke a response from them? *When* should I begin each phase of my marketing plan so that it runs smoothly and opportunities are not missed?

To help you generate the best and most thorough answers to these questions, use the following steps to guide you:

Setting Up the Marketing Plan

1. *Identify your target audience.*

   For whom are you writing this book? Who is going to find this information interesting, valuable, and exciting? Be as specific as you possibly can. Write down everyone who you think is in your primary target market and why. There are two basic categories of your target market: *broad* and *niche.* A broad market is an interest-defined group such as car owners, parents, or computer users. A niche market is a group with a highly specific common interest. Niche markets tend to be subcategories of broad markets, such as car owners (broad market) who own Porsches (niche market). Similarly, within the broad market of parents exists the niche containing parents of children with Down Syndrome. Broad markets are less limited than niches in terms of potential sales (a broad market is usually larger in population), but niche marketing is the fastest growing and most successful form of marketing among self-publishers and small presses. The more specifically you can define the interests, attitudes, character, and needs of your target market, as well as the outlets they rely on for goods and information, the easier it will be to reach them,

2. *Figure out where to find your audience and how to reach them.*

   If you've penned the ultimate surfing guide, you are not going to find your audience through the *Oklahoma Tribune,* nor is a book on crop subsidy reinvestment strategies going to provoke a lot of interest among subscribers to *Surfing Times* magazine. Using key words related to your book's subject matter, search through directories of associations, organizations, businesses, bookstores and media outlets for appropriate promotional and sales outlets.

3. *Determine the specific reasons why your book will be of specific interest to your target market.*

   What are your title's specific features? What does it offer on the subject that other books do not? What problems does it solve? What benefits does it promise? Make a list of reasons why your audience will be interested in your book.

4. *What will be the theme of your marketing campaign?*

   Choose the message that you want to get across to your audience. Make it clear, simple, and compelling. Try to condense your message into a hook of just one line of copy. You don't have to say everything in that line, just enough to get the attention of your target audience.

5. *When is your message going to be most effective?*

   The publishing industry has two major selling seasons, fall and spring. If seasons, weather, a holiday, or time of year are going to be a major factor in the promoting of your book, plan accordingly. Set a publication date for your book. This is the month by which you expect to have "covered your bases," established distribution channels, launched your initial publicity campaign, and have books in a few bookstores. If your book offers low budget summer vacation alternatives, you will want to set a March publication date so you can take advantage of the spring buying season, have the book on store shelves by April, in the media, and available by early summer when the book's subject is on people's minds. For a March publication date, you need to begin your promotions no later than November.

Researching Your Markets

Your next step will be to begin researching your markets. These are the commercial outlets that will purchase your book at wholesale prices in order to sell them to the consumer for a profit. In the book trade, the most obvious markets are bookstores. Not all bookstores are the same, however. Aside from ranging widely in size, bookstores also vary according to subject matter, customer base, price range, quality of materials, corporate or private ownership, and many other factors that will influence whether they will be interested in your title. Other markets include gift shops, book clubs, catalogs, libraries, schools, and nontraditional markets and customers. To find these markets, you will be relying on the phone book, commercially available mailing lists, reference books, targeted publications, Internet listings, and other reference sources. *(See Chapter 15 for a listing of markets and distribution sources.)*

In order to reach this wide range of markets, you will want to secure a national distributor, regional or specialized wholesalers, or even a simple fulfillment source. These are companies that will take orders, provide processing, ship orders, bill and collect from accounts, and remit money on each sale. Distributors employ a sales force to actively sell your title to book trade markets. Other sources simply stock and list your titles, filling orders that come in, but not actively soliciting them. The larger and more recognized your distribution channels are, the easier it will be for your markets to obtain your title. To find these distribution channels, you will have to do research, including asking the managers of your targeted markets which channels they rely on.

Identifying Media Outlets

Next, you will want to identify the media outlets that will pick up information about your title and carry it to the consumer. Media typically include newspapers, magazines, newsletters, television and radio programs, and the Internet. Most media are targeted to a specific audience, usually defined by age, income, interests, and location. The idea is to find media targeted to your audience. There are many ways to find appropriate media outlets, though the most concentrated sources of this information are in the reference section of your local library.

Final Step is Timeline

Once you have outlined the essentials of your marketing plan, you will need to draft a timeline to put the plan on track. A timeline will help you make sure that everything is accomplished in the proper sequence and meet advance deadlines, making the most of time-sensitive opportunities. On page 181 there is a template for a timeline that lists common time frames and deadlines. This will provide you with a general framework for your own timeline, which you can tailor to fit your specific needs.

The Hook

A good marketing plan is essential to meeting all of these goals and will also help to eliminate unnecessary and redundant efforts. It should also provide a *hook* for your title — a refined sales pitch that makes it possible to communicate the unique qualities of your title powerfully and quickly. Your hook should be used in media releases, sell sheets, Q & A sheets, cover letters, sales calls, and advertising. It should be compelling and explain what the book contains (the *features*), what the book does for the reader (the *benefits*), and for whom it is written (the *audience*). Note that you will develop different hooks for different situations; however, you should have one very strong, main hook or sales pitch.

A Sample Marketing Plan

The following example should give you an idea of how a marketing plan is researched, planned, and executed:

Jonathon Hacker has written a book, *The Electronic Lifeguard: A User's Guide to Safe Surfing on the Internet.* The book examines the dangers Internet explorers face, such as picking up a virus from downloaded files, getting ripped off by scam artists selling on-line investments, children being offered inappropriate material, and other pertinent problems. The book provides information, preventive measures, remedies for common problems, and resources for more information and assistance.

Benefits

In the preceding paragraphs, note how *strong verbs* (examines, ripped off, and offered) are used to describe the work. When marketing a book, using a strong verb to describe how the book can be of value to the reader constitutes a *benefit*. For example, stating the book will "help you get on the Internet in record time" is promoting a benefit the book offers. Author Jonathon Hacker has made up a long list of such benefits by rereading his own book, looking for information that can be applied to solve a problem or improve a skill. He will keep this list handy and return to it again to find appropriate benefits to use in his letters, promotions, and marketing tools.

Research

Hacker already had a rough profile of his audience. They are personal computer owners, people with Internet accounts, and computer professionals. But a little more research at the library, reading computer trade magazines, and quizzing professionals revealed even more specific information: the majority of computer owners are middle income and have a median age of 31; of those owners, 80 percent are men and 20 percent women; and most Internet users are college or graduate students. Hacker discovered that viruses, surveillance, and the security of Internet money transfers concerned the members of

Marketing Plan for *The Electronic Lifeguard*

Publication Date: July, 1996 (Fall Season Release)
Press Run: 10,000 copies, first printing
Distribution: National distribution by Quantum Distributors
Concept: An easy-to-use guide that will protect Internet explorers from a wide range of problems, scams, viruses, and other potential on-line dangers.
Target Audiences: People with Internet accounts, computer owners, Internet and World Wide Web site managers, subscribers and readers of Internet- and computer-related magazines, college students, computer professionals, businesses considering an on-line presence, organizations with on-line presence, or capabilities
Target Markets: General bookstores, computer and electronics outlets, computer and general book clubs, libraries, university bookstores, on-line organizations, Internet service providers, electronics mail-order catalogs, foreign markets (Japan, Germany, UK), Internet seminar leaders, and sales direct to consumer (see Target Audiences)

Overall Strategies:

- Use print, broadcast, and on-line media outlets to increase public awareness of on-line dangers and present this title as the remedy
- Establish an on-line site (Internet and WWW) and hot links to promote and sell title, host chats, receive inquiries and E-mail, and provide information and marketing materials 24 hours a day
- Contact seminar leaders, service providers, Internet software and hardware outlets, and other related businesses to secure cross-marketing and bulk sales
- Set up book event tour, at major bookstores and on-line bookstores. These events will be designed to quickly inform beginners of the most common on-line dangers and simple solutions/preventive measures. Q & A sessions will follow
- Advertise directly to consumers through computer-specific card decks
- Create a dialog on various on-line newsgroups and URL's on the subject of Internet safety/dangers in order to raise awareness and encourage discussion of book/topic
- Offer to submit articles to computer, electronics, Internet, and consumer watchdog magazines, journals, and newsletters on the subject of on-line security and prevention
- Use free newsletter "On-Line Protection Today" as a promotional tool and to build a qualified mailing list

- Investigate co-op exhibiting opportunities for book fairs, electronics expositions, Internet exhibitions and other public exposure opportunities
- Submit title for book awards — complete list forthcoming

Advance Review Media:

Choice Public
Computing
Electronics Today
Internet Magazine
Insider Magazine
Library Journal
L.A. Times Book Review
Modern Electronics
N.Y. Times Book Review
PC Magazine
Library Quarterly
Publishers Weekly
S.F. Chronicle Review
Small Press
The Acquisitions Librarian
The Village Voice
Urban Academic Librarian
Wired Magazine

Targeted Media (specific breakdowns forthcoming):

Computer and electronics editors of all major urban newspapers
UPI, Reuters, and other national & international newswires
Daytime TV talk shows, morning and evening "television magazines"
All media (magazines, newspapers, etc.) with an on-line presence
Talk radio programs, and specialty (computers & electronics) programs
Scientific journals devoted to computing, electronics, and Internet concerns
In-house newsletters at major corporations with on-line presences

Promotional Strategies & Special Events

- Title to be offered as incentive to join America Online (2,500 copies presold)
- Book release event through Internet Bookstore (July 1, 7:00-9:00 P.M. EST)
- Featured speaker at Pacific Northwest Electronics Exhibition, Seattle (July 22, 3:00-4:30 A.M.)
- 15 city book event and promotions tour (Seattle, Portland, Los Angeles, San Francisco, Las Vegas, Santa Fe, Dallas, Louisville, Chicago, Bloomington, Toledo, New York, Boston, Charleston, Atlanta) July–August 1996
- Half-page advertisement in *Radio & TV Interview Report* run four times (July-Oct) to stimulate media attention and exposure
- Set up "Safe Surfing" Web Site — with hot links to various general interest sites
- Submit articles to *Internet World, Modern Electronics, Electronic Age,* and other major computer/electronics magazines and journals about Internet dangers and protecting your data
- Explore selling CD-ROM and electronic rights to software developer or "bundle" publisher

- Develop "Safe Surfing" Newsletter (electronic) to post on Internet URLs (Uniform Resource Locators) and newsgroups
- Contact foreign distributors and publishers to explore foreign rights sales possibilities
- Display at 1996 Consumer Electronics Show (Dallas) in order to reach companies going on-line for the first time
- Offer free presentations at local libraries, schools, colleges, and businesses in exchange for permission to sell books to crowd
- Submit book for awards & honors — *PC Magazine Editor's Choice* et al. (full list forthcoming)
- Have publication date (6/1) declared "Electronics Awareness Day" by local, regional, or state officials
- Begin working on updates for second edition

his target audience the most. Hacker also took the time to find out which magazines, Internet sites, and service providers were the most popular among them.

Hook

With enough research done to get started, Hacker began to put together a marketing plan. Based on what he knew his audience would respond to, he chose his hook: *"Don't risk getting mugged, bugged or spied on! Read this book before you surf the Net!"* This hook is simple, informative, and compelling, providing a basic theme for his book releases, advertising, media leads, talk show topics, and other marketing tools.

Hacker identified the kinds of people who are likely to buy his book, and then researched this target market so that he knew more about them. Next he had to find channels that would get information about his book to this target audience. At the same time he had to find ways to get the book into bookstores and other sales outlets. His primary concern, due to time constraints, was securing testimonial and prepublication reviews.

Uncorrected Proofs

As soon as his manuscript was in its final, rough form, and before he began any other steps in the book's production and promotion, Hacker had the manuscript photocopied and bound with a plastic comb at his local copy shop. He sent these uncorrected proofs to friends, colleagues, and (after calling first for permission) top names associated with the Internet, along with a letter asking for their comments on the book. Hacker was fishing for *testimonials,* or blurbs of praise, to be used on the book covers and in his marketing to promote the work. He knew that a testimonial is one of the most effective forms of ad copy, and that he had to begin his efforts very early in the production process if he wanted strong endorsements to appear on the book's cover. Without enough lead time, his book would be printed before the replies to his testimonial letters started coming back.

Distribution Channels

Hacker knew that without the proper distribution channels, it would be impossible to get his book picked up by the most important sales outlets. Major bookstores, book superstores, and other retail outlets order from distributors and wholesalers, as opposed to directly from the publisher, so Hacker approached wholesalers and distributors before beginning marketing to retail outlets. Several months before the book's publication date, the title was picked up by a national wholesaler. Hacker knew that this company had accounts with most of the book trade outlets, but that it would only fill incoming orders for his title and not actively sell the title.

Hacker continued to approach wholesalers and distributors until he found a national distributor that not only was interested in carrying his title, but also specialized in books on computers and electronics. After scrutinizing the terms set forth in the distribution agreement, Hacker signed the agreement and turned over the exclusive right to sell his title. In return, the distributor would actively sell the title through its book representatives to exactly the markets Hacker was trying to reach and remit a percentage of these sales to Hacker in the form of a monthly check.

Because Hacker had granted the distributor the exclusive right to sell his title to the book trade, his account with the wholesaler was taken over by the distributor. Now that he had a distributor who would sell his title to U. S. book outlets, Hacker could concentrate on selling to individuals, foreign markets, non-traditional outlets, and rights buyers. Most importantly, he could concentrate on promoting his title to consumers to stimulate sales at the bookstores and other outlets.

If Hacker had not been able to secure a distributor with a sales force, he would have begun contacting sales outlets himself, through phone calls, postcard mailings, and other methods. Without a professional sales force, the job of selling the books to book trade outlets is left to the self-publisher. Since Hacker did find a full-service distributor, the distributor stipulated that any retail orders Hacker solicits be directed to their ordering department for processing.

Review Outlets

Next, Hacker chose the outlets to initially target for reviews and other forms of media exposure and promotion. This list contained a mix of traditional book trade magazines, computer and electronics publications, newsletters, a few magazines devoted to the Internet, and selected national columnists and editors with an interest in computers, the Internet, and electronics. He decided to advertise in *Radio & TV Interview Report,* a trade magazine read by the program directors of television and radio shows when shopping for guests and current issues. In addition, he booked himself as a guest on the *Internet Magazine,* an on-line interview forum posted on the World Wide Web of the Internet, which would bring his message directly to his target audience. He found listings and contact names for these publications using *Ulrich's Periodical Directory* and other resources in his local library's reference section. After making contact with everyone on his initial list, Hacker continued researching and contacting new media as part of his continuing efforts.

Cross Marketing

Because Hacker knew that cross-marketing deals were lucrative in terms of large volume sales, reasonable discounts, and promotional potential, he started approaching the appropriate companies early. After making several dozen proposals to various companies, Hacker was contacted by America Online, an Internet account server, which was interested in offering his book as an incentive for new accounts. Before the book reached its publication date, Hacker had agreed to supply this company with large quantities of his title at half the cover price. Hacker knew that this deal would also bring with it promotional exposure, considering America Online's extensive advertising budget and campaigns. Because it is a company that falls outside the realm of the book trade, the distributor's exclusive arrangement does not apply to this situation, and Hacker can sell these books without giving a cut to the distributor.

Book Release Mailings

Once these deals were in the works and his camera-ready manuscript was headed for the press, Hacker set up a book-release and signing party at his local large chain bookstore, then drew up a list of friends, family, clients, and business associates — his "nepotism" list — to whom he mailed invitations. This invitation included a coupon on the back that allowed each person to receive a signed copy of the book by mail at 10 percent off the cover price if he or she could not attend the party.

Hacker also rented, from a mailing list broker, a list of several thousand Internet users across the country to whom he sent direct mail advertisements. Next he began calling individual bookstores to let them know about the book, what was being done to promote it, and which distributor and wholesalers were carrying it.

Because Internet users were his primary market, Hacker paid the small fees required to have his title listed and available through several on-line bookstores. He even posted files containing a sample chapter from his book, with ordering information tacked on at the end, to news groups with an interest in Internet security.

At this point, he was ready to start filling orders as soon as his book came off the press. Following his marketing plan provided him with media exposure, advance sales, and momentum. His message was broadcast, it reached a portion of his target audience, and there were books available to those who responded. His next step was to begin looking for new ways to get his message out to more of his audience, to get the book into more bookstores so that it would be available to a wider market, and to find new opportunities for bulk sales and cross-marketing.

Your Own Marketing Plan

Because Jonathon Hacker's book was a how-to book, it was a fairly simple and straightforward process to create a marketing plan for it, but not all books are how-to books. You might be publishing a novel, poetry, a cookbook, a biography, or a children's book. Each requires a unique and individually tailored marketing plan.

The fictional Jonathon Hacker's marketing plan is, necessarily, oversimplified. It does not address the wide range of contacts and efforts necessary to get the kind of results Hacker ultimately secured. Nor does this idealized model of a marketing plan account for continuing promotions. Your marketing plan probably will be more extensive and involve more effort than this model.

In the following chapters, you will be introduced to more detailed information and more specific examples of promotion and marketing, which will allow you to build a comprehensive, continuing marketing plan tailored to your particular title.

10

DEVELOPING YOUR MARKETING TOOLS

Chapter 10

Marketing tools are the promotional devices that support the goals of your marketing plan. They are designed to send a message: to get a radio producer to call for more information, to ask for a mention in an alumni bulletin, to stimulate book sales, and much more. Each marketing tool has a specific purpose, and should be used only for that purpose. If you hold a book signing event, the invitations you send out in order to attract an audience are a marketing tool. When seeking a guest spot on a TV show, you would send a cover letter, media release, and a question and answer sheet, because these tools contain the information best suited to a talk show producer's needs and interests.

Overall Marketing and Promotion Goals

Before you begin marketing your book, it is important to familiarize yourself with marketing tools. Though each marketing tool has a specific function, in practice they span a wide range of formats, designs, and layouts. It is up to you to tailor each to reflect the style and character of your book and the aims of your marketing plan.

There are two basic types of marketing tools — sales tools and promotional tools. The difference between the two lies in the response each is designed to evoke. A *sales tool* is designed to elicit a sale or demonstrate sales potential. A *promotional tool* is designed to gain media exposure or otherwise bring information about your book to the attention of the public.

In order to market and promote your book effectively, you will need to send individualized marketing and promotional kits, designed to elicit a specific response from each specific contact, to all of your intended markets. You will send sales tools to distribution channels, to impress upon them the sales potential of your title and the effectiveness of your marketing campaign. You will also want to send sales tools to your targeted outlets, in order to get them to carry the book and to let them know which distribution channels carry it. Then you will need to send promotional tools to the media, in order to get the exposure and publicity that will send buyers into the stores.

Marketing Tools

The following is a description of some of the marketing tools available to you, an explanation of various ways to use each one most effectively, and some tips on how to get the most out of each tool.

THE BOOK RELEASE

The book release is your all-purpose marketing tool. You should include a book release in the kits you send to just about every sales or media contact. You cannot effectively market a title without a book release, and it is the single most universal vehicle for information about your book.

There are two kinds of book releases, the *media release* and the *sell sheet.*

The Media Release

Description: The media release is primarily used to pitch a story angle to media contacts and to elicit a phone call for more information. You will be sending a media release to every promotional contact, so it should be the best source of information about your book. Try to keep your media release to one page with a single, pointed message. You may wish to modify the release to fit the interests of specific media outlets, to capitalize on a special event or occasion, or to announce an award or other promotional development.

Features: The release should contain a strong headline, two to three paragraphs of two to three sentences each of body copy; a release date, contact name and phone number; the book title,

MAX BAUD PRESS

1234 MICROCHIP LN • SILICON VALLEY CA 90301

FOR IMMEDIATE RELEASE CONTACT: BEVERLY BOOKINGS
MARCH 1, 1996 CALL: 1-800-SAFENET

THE ELECTRONIC LIFEGUARD

by Jonathon Hacker

Price: $19.95
Pub. Date: March, 1996
Publisher: Max Baud Press
ISBN: 0-924773-90-8
Format: Trade Paper, 320 pps.
Subject: Computers/How-To

Distributed to the trade by Quantum Distributors, Inc. • Los Angeles, CA

WARNING! TRAVELING THE INFORMATION SUPERHIGHWAY MAY BE HAZARDOUS!

Today, an estimated 35 million people around the world have access to the Internet's information superhighway and, with the introduction of the World Wide Web graphic interface, the number of users and the size of the 'Net itself are growing explosively. But, because this is new and ungoverned technology, the potential for abuse is very real, and the unexperienced user may find the Internet a very dangerous place indeed. The unwary 'Net surfer is prone to surveillance, fraud, destructive viruses, and outright theft. To help protect new users, author and Internet veteran Jonathon Hacker now offers ***The Electronic Lifeguard***.

Don't Get Mugged, Bugged, or Spied On!

Let ***The Electronic Lifeguard*** Protect You Online!

The Electronic Lifeguard protects computer users from on-line dangers by alerting them to vulnerabilities and warning signs, as well as providing damage prevention measures. From issues of privacy and access, to on line fraud and credit card hijacking, ***The Electronic Lifeguard*** provides the cutting edge of on-line protection against:

- Viruses and intrusive software
- Credit card hijacking, on-line fraud, and scams
- Inappropriate materials and inexperienced users
- Service provider gouging and hidden costs
- Issues of privacy and security measures
- Encryption, decoding, and the government

Author Jonathon Hacker has been involved with the Internet since 1976, when he helped develop the original UNIX protocol as an MIT graduate student. His writing been featured in *Popular Electronics,* the *New York Times,* and *PC World* magazine. Mr. Hacker is available for radio, television, print, and on-line interviews.

Contact Beverly Bookings, Publicist at ***1-800-SAFENET*** *for information, or to set up an interview.*

# # #

media release

Put A Headline Here That Will Grab Their Attention!

graphic placed here

NAME OF YOUR BOOK:

Your Descriptive or Compelling Subtitle

By (Author Name)

Publisher: Your publishing company ***Pub Date:*** Your date
Format: Binding type, no. of pgs. ***Subject:*** Your subject
ISBN: Your ISBN number ***Price:*** Your Price

"Expert Testimonial Really Helps Sell Books — And This is the Place for It!"
— Prof. Expert Celebrity, Ph. D., Author of *My Famous Book*

What would draw you in to a sell sheet? A question? A promise? A benefit that was *too good* to be true? These paragraphs should be used to convey your primary message — what is exciting, new, valuable, entertaining, outrageous, or compelling about your book. In three or four short sentences, make a promise and back it up. These sentences should support and develop the headline without being overly repetitive.

Use these paragraphs to build on your first paragraph; reinforce, and qualify your promises. Do not tell everything though. You want to leave them with a reason to call you. Do give a sample of what kind of important information, entertainment, or helpful benefits your book is packed with. If possible, show how they can directly improves their lives:

- USE Bullets to compel and sell
- NAME everyone who can benefit
- IMAGINE the uses they can find
- QUOTE statistics to indicate a growing trend
- MOTIVATE with fear, desire, need, or greed
- LIST the photos, worksheets, maps & more!

About the Author *Establish yourself as an expert on the subject you are covering. Use your education, past publications, jobs, life experiences, or anything relating to the subject matter. Remember that people will read a lot into everything you put here. They already want to believe you are an expert, so now give them some specifics. Avoid hobbies and unrelated personal information and focus on future projects. Give them one last compelling tidbit to wonder, marvel, and call about.*

YOUR LOGO

NAME OF YOUR PUBLISHING CO.
Street Address • City State Zip
Phone Number • Fax Number

Contact: Contact's Name, *and Job Title*
1-800-555-1234

generic sell sheet

WARNING! TRAVELING THE INFORMATION SUPERHIGHWAY MAY BE HAZARDOUS!

THE ELECTRONIC LIFEGUARD

by Jonathon Hacker

Price: $19.95
Pub. Date: March, 1996
Publisher: Max Baud Press
ISBN: 0-924773-90-8
Format: Trade Paper, 320 pps.
Subject: Computers/How-To

Distributed to the trade by Quantum Distributors, Inc.

Don't Get Mugged, Bugged, or Spied On!

Let The Electronic Lifeguard Protect You On-Line!

Today, an estimated 35 million people around the world have access to the Internet's information superhighway and, with the introduction of the World Wide Web graphic interface, the number of users and the size of the 'Net itself are growing explosively. But, as the Internet grows, so do concerns over on-line security, possible fraud and scams, and protecting sensitive users from inappropriate material. To help protect new users from these dangers, author and Internet veteran Jonathan Hacker offers ***The Electronic Lifeguard***.

The Electronic Lifeguard provides protection from on-line dangers by alerting you to vulnerabilities and warning signs, as well as revealing damage prevention measures. From issues of privacy and access, to on-line fraud and credit card hijacking, ***The Electronic Lifeguard*** provides you with the cutting edge of on-line protection against:

- ☑ Viruses and intrusive software
- ☑ Credit card hijacking, on-line fraud, and scams
- ☑ Inappropriate materials and inexperienced users
- ☑ Service provider gouging and hidden costs
- ☑ Issues of privacy and security measures
- ☑ Encryption, decoding, and the government

Author Jonathon Hacker has been involved with the Internet since 1976, when he helped develop the original UNIX protocol as an MIT graduate student. Mr. Hacker holds a master's degree in electronic engineering from MIT. His writing been featured in *Popular Electronics*, the *New York Times*, and *PC World* magazine. Mr. Hacker is available for radio, television, print, and on-line interviews.

Call **1-800-SAFENET** for ordering information, or to set up a booksigning.

MAX BAUD PRESS
1234 MICROCHIP LN • SILICON VALLEY CA 90301 PHONE: 864-555-1234

Jonathon Hacker's sell sheet

author, and publisher; the publication date, book dimensions (size, pages, binding); the subject matter and price.

Optional: The author's biography, cover art, testimonials, and bulleted lists are optional additions.

Send to: All review, promotional, and media contacts

Tip: Vary your media release to fit specific situations by shifting emphasis, headlines, and other material. Your headline should make a bold "promise," which the rest of the press release supports and builds on. Provide enough information so the recipient can write a mini review or mention, but withhold enough so that there are still interesting questions to answer.

The Sell Sheet

Description: The sell sheet is your primary sales tool, which will present the basic benefits and features of your title. You will be sending a sell sheet everywhere you wish to sell books, so it should contain ordering information and distribution channels; a page count and release date; and a book category and type of binding. Try to keep your sell sheet to one page and use a single, pointed sales pitch. You may wish to modify the sheet to fit the interests of specific retail outlets, to capitalize on a special event or occasion, or to announce an award or other marketing development.

Features: Like the release, the sell sheet should have a strong headline; two to three paragraphs of two to three sentences each of body copy; a release date, contact name and phone number; the book title, author, and publisher; the publication date, book dimensions (size, pages, binding); the subject matter and price.

Optional: You can also include an author's biography, cover art, testimonials, bulleted lists of benefits and features, and a sample of the book's contents (usually, the chapter headings from the table of contents).

Send To: All marketing contacts

Tip: Vary your sell sheet to fit specific situations by shifting emphasis, headlines, and other material. Your headline should make a bold "promise," which the rest of the sell sheet supports and builds on. When selling to commercial outlets, stress sales potential, consumer interest, or cite a need for the title. When selling to consumers, stress benefits and features.

REVIEW COPIES

(F & Gs, Advance Copies, Uncorrected Proofs)

Description: A review copy is the final draft of the manuscript, bound with a plastic comb on the spine. The cover is usually index card stock printed with the book and contact information.

Features: The review copy is the complete book, which can be uncorrected and unedited, along with certain information: the author's name, book title, publisher, contact name and phone number, publication date, ISBN number, price, book dimensions, subject matter, distribution channels, and format.

Optional: A brief synopsis and relevant background information can be included on the inside front cover, along with a brief author's biography.

Send to: Reviewers, wholesalers, distributors, testimonial targets, book clubs, mail order catalogs, and, upon request, media contacts.

Tip: Have review copies made up early and send them to major review outlets months in advance. You can request F & Gs (unbound folded and gathered signatures) from the printer and make them into review copies. Do not send review copies to trade buyers, librarians, individuals or anyone else who does not require the entire manuscript.

TESTIMONIALS

Description: Testimonials are what other people have to say about your book. The more famous, respected, and well-known your testimonial writer is, the more impressive and believable the testimonial will seem.

Features: Use the testimonial quote, name of person being quoted, and his or her title and position. If the person being quoted is an author, list the name of his or her best known book or books.

Send to: Use testimonials in other tools (such as a media release, cover letter, and return mailer) as well as on the book's front cover, back cover, and dustjacket book flap.

Tip: Get testimonial quotes very early by sending review copies to potential testimonial sources at least a month before cover art is finished. Use testimonials to support claims you make about the book or author.

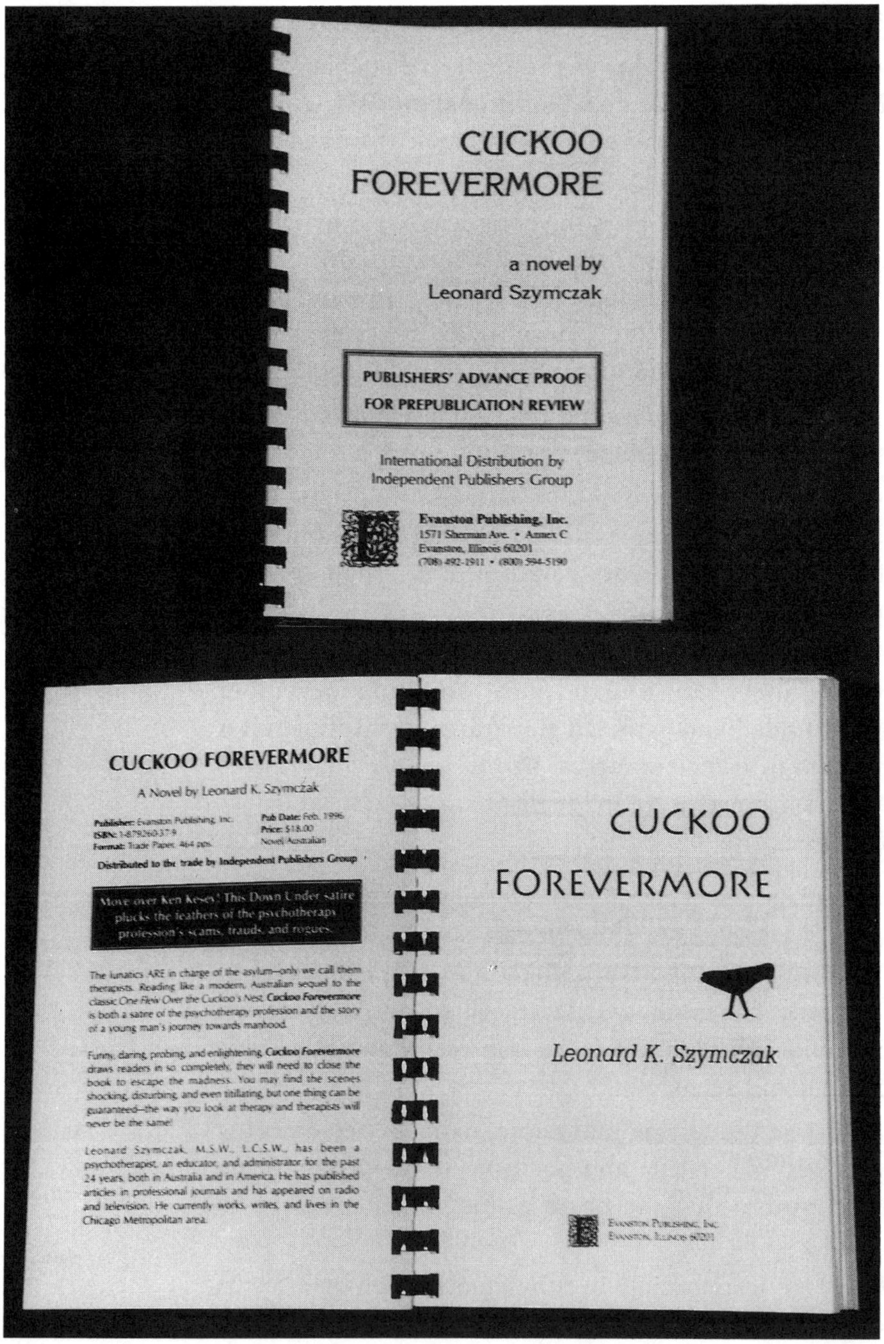

note that the inside cover of the review copy includes a synopsis of the book – if this information were just included in a separate cover letter, editors probably would not forward the letter to their reviewers

BOOK COVERS

Description: Order extra book covers from the printer or use color photocopies from original cover art.

Features: The front cover, spine and back cover give basic information about the book as well as show the cover design.

Send to: Everyone.

Tip: The book's cover is its single most important selling point, as far as most trade buyers are concerned. Covers are an excellent way to promote your book to all sales contacts. At minimum, ask your printer for at least 50 extra covers.

BLADS

Description: A blad is an abbreviated version of the review copy. Media contacts especially appreciate a blad over a review copy.

Features: A blad is made up of cover art, a press release, the book's table of contents, and sample pages or a sample chapter.

Send to: Wholesalers, distributors, and media contacts.

Tip: Blads cost less to make and send than review copies, and are appreciated more by radio, television, and print contacts. Tailor the blad components to specific contact needs or interests .

COVER LETTER

Description: A cover letter is your letter of introduction, telling your contacts who you are, what you have sent them, and why. It should be brief and upbeat.

Features: A cover letter presents your name, address, and title; has a strong opening, a reason why you are sending this material, a list of enclosures, and the name of a contact.

Optional: Use a strong post script (People read a P.S. before any other part of a letter.)

Send to: Any contact.

Tip: This is your opportunity to make a strong, pointed sales pitch, drop the name of a mutual contact, and/or prove that you have a good reason for contacting the recipient. This letter automatically separates your kit from mass-mailed kits that will end up in the trash.

MAX BAUD PRESS
1234 MICROCHIP LN • SILICON VALLEY CA 90 301 PHONE: 864-555-1234

Abigail Bailey
Producer/Host, "Keeping Pace"
KLNR-FM Radio
1234 Clear St.
Seattle, WA 55555

Dear Ms. Bailey:

It was a pleasure speaking with you on the phone last Friday (4/12/96); thank you for giving me so much of your time. Please find enclosed the materials we discussed, including the review copy of ***The Electronic Lifeguard*** you requested.

I have been involved with the Internet since 1976, when I helped develop the original UNIX protocol as an MIT graduate student. Over the years, I've worked closely with many major on-line projects and ventures, and I have seen the damage caused by 'Net hackers, hustlers, spies, and vandals. Millions of Internet explorers are going online every month with no protection and no clue as to the risks they are taking.

I would certainly appreciate the opportunity to share with your listeners, many of whom are already online, the hazards they face on the Internet and the precautions they can take. I am sure that they will, in turn, be thankful for the opportunity to protect themselves.

Please call me at 1-800-555-1234 if you have any further questions, or to set up an interview date. I look forward to hearing from you.

Sincerely

Jonathon Hacker

JH/dh
encl.

P.S. I will be in the Seattle area May 5 to May 8 for an electronics expo. If you are interested, I will able to come in for a live studio interview.

cover letter

GRABBER SHEET

Description: A playful, exciting, or creative presentation of facts and information about your book designed to catch the attention of media contacts, buyers, and consumers. Focus on a quirky, popular, or interesting aspect of your book in order to spark interest.

Features: A grabber sheet has a strong headline or theme, information and facts from the book, information about the author, the book title, publisher, and a contact name.

Optional: Keep in mind this tool can take on just about any format.

Send to: Radio, television, and print media contacts, as well as book buyers.

Tip: This is an opportunity to play up selected aspects of your book, yourself as an author, and upcoming events, as well as anything else that could draw attention to your work.

THE Q & A SHEET

Description: A one-page sampling of provocative questions and exciting answers that provides a demonstration interview for media contacts.

Features: The Q & A sheet contains sample questions and answers, the book title, the author's and publisher's names, and a contact name and phone number.

Optional: There can be a short introductory paragraph, a listing of previous radio, television, and print interviews, appearances, and stories. You might also include a brief author's biography.

Send to: Radio, television, and print media contacts.

Tip: Keep your questions and answers closely related if possible. Build to a particularly interesting or controversial point. Make sure to include only the strongest, most exciting aspects of your book.

MEDIA CLIPPINGS

Description: This is a collection of photocopied reproductions of any article, book review, or mention about you or your book that appears in print. This classification also applies to

MAX BAUD PRESS

1234 MICROCHIP LN • SILICON VALLEY CA 90 301 PHONE: 864-555-1234

Attention Internet Surfers: Beware of Shark Infested Waters!

Don't Put Yourself at Risk! Rely on ***The Electronic Lifeguard*** for Safe Surfing!

Today's Internet is a haven for hackers, scammers, and pranksters. If you thought it was safe to go online, think again! Here are the risks:

- On-line scams and unsecured transactions have cost casual users millions of dollars. On-line businesses ventures are even more vulnerable.
- No transaction is 100 percent safe from hackers — even the most advanced encryption systems have proven to be beatable.
- Viruses, "prank" files, and intrusion methods can destroy valuable data.
- Your children may have full access to inappropriate materials, including pornography, hate-based literature, recipes for bombs, and more!
- A growing number of cases of abduction, rape, and harassment have been linked to Internet chats with strangers — who traced their victims electronically.
- Even service providers can — and will — intrude on your on-line privacy.

How can you protect yourself, your family, and your files from these dangers?

CONTACT: BEVERLY BOOKINGS CALL: 1-800-SAFENET

for the most up-to-date resource for on-line protective measures

THE ELECTRONIC LIFEGUARD

The User's Guide to Safe Surfing on the Internet

by Jonathon Hacker

Price: $19.95 ISBN: 0-924773-90-8 Pub. Date: March, 1996

Format: Trade Paper, 320 pps. Publisher: Max Baud Press

Subject: Computers/How-To

Distributed to the trade by Quantum Distributors, Inc. • Los Angeles, CA

Author Jonathon Hacker is available for radio, TV, and print interviews

grabber sheet

MAX BAUD PRESS

1234 MICROCHIP LN • SILICON VALLEY CA 90 301 PHONE: 864-555-1234

QUESTION:

Can 'Net Surfers Find Themselves in Shark-Infested Waters?

ANSWER:

Just Ask Jonathon Hacker, Author of ***The Electronic Lifeguard!***

Q: *What are the dangers of 'Net surfing today, and who is at risk?*

A: The dangers are many and varied. The least that can happen is that your privacy is invaded, or you pick up a computer virus downloading a file. But on-line scams can cost users thousands of dollars, and on-line business can be taken for much more than that.

Q: *What about anti-virus programs and encrypted "secure transactions?"*

A: These offer some levels of protection, but even the most advanced encryption methods have been shown to be vulnerable. Most on-line activities are not secure, and anyone who knows the Internet programming language, HTML, can intercept — and alter — any information sent via the 'Net.

Q: *What about users who simply "browse" the 'Net, looking for information?*

A: If they have children, they could be allowing them access to inappropriate materials. Worse yet, rape, abduction, harassment and other crimes have been linked to innocent online interactions. Any time you log on to the 'Net, you make yourself a target.

Q: *What can one do to protect himself or herself?*

A: There are many, proven protective measures, some general, some specific to various online activities. The average user can get protection with antiviral software, by choosing a secure service provider, and by using *The Internet Yellow Pages* to confirm the authenticity of a given site. There are many new ways of conducting business online that maximize protection. Of course, knowing the warning signs to look out for is the best form of protection.

Q: *Is there any one source for this information?*

A: My new book, ***The Electronic Lifeguard***, discusses all aspects of on-line risk, and offers the most secure and up-to-date protective measures.

Q: *How do I get more information about* ***The Electronic Lifeguard?***

A: Contact Jonathon Hacker at 1-800-555-1234 to set up an interview or receive a media kit. We also have a fact sheet and newsletter available free to anyone who calls.

# # #

q & a sheet

audio and video cassettes of previous interviews on radio and TV.

Features: Media clippings include articles, and reviews reduced or enlarged for maximum convenience of reading, mailing, and reproducing. When sending more than one example, group the clippings onto a single sheet of paper, or clip or staple pages neatly together. The most prestigious examples should stand out or come first.

Optional: Call station producers and ask if they would like to receive an audio or video cassette of a previously aired interview. More than any other tool, this will tell them instantly whether or not they will want you on their show.

Send to: Radio, television, and print media contacts. Clippings may also be included in mailings to wholesalers, distributors, and catalogs, to show that the book is being widely publicized.

Tip: Media clippings can get out of hand. Keep a morgue of all media exposure of you, your book, and related subjects. Send only the most important and impressive clips. Always put them into a neat, easy to read format.

ADVERTISING

Description: This includes paid and free advertising in magazines, newspapers, book catalogs, newsletters, on the radio, television, and in direct mail card packs.

Features: A good advertisement contains a strong headline, a graphic element (such as the cover art), minimal body copy, and complete ordering information (title, ISBN, price, shipping cost, forms of payment, publisher, address, and phone number).

Optional: Radio and television advertising can take on just about any format.

Send to: Advertising is used primarily to stimulate consumer sales.

Tip: Do not pay for advertising unless you have a very specific reason for doing so, or you are certain of an exceptionally high return of books sold. If you do pay for advertising, in the ad include an 800 number where books can be ordered.

RETURN MAILER

Description: This is a modified press release or other one-page sell sheet, with a three-panel second side.

Features: A mailer contains a strong headline, body copy, graphics, and ordering information on one side. Three equal-sized panels on the second side include: a teaser flap; mailing label, return address, and stamp (or bulk mailing indicia); and a return mail coupon with ordering information, the book's price, and an 800 number.

Optional: If there is room, a return mailer can also include a discount announcement, author's biography, and bulleted items.

Send to: Consumers, especially those with an interest in the subject of your book.

Tip: Although by no means the most cost-effective or productive form of marketing, a successful direct mail campaign depends on the immediate interest of the contacts to whom you are mailing. This includes friends, family, associates, or groups interested in you or the subject of your book.

POSTCARD MAILERS

Description: This is a cheap, effective way of announcing the book and providing ordering information. It is a 3 by 5 inch or other standard-sized postcard with cover art or other graphic on the front, ad copy and ordering information on the back, to be mass-mailed to a large list of contacts, including trade buyers, librarians, consumers, and educators.

Features: Mailers contain a graphic on the front (usually the book cover), often in full color, ordering information, mailing address, return address, postage and ad copy on the back.

Optional: If there is room, the mailer can include graphics and/or ad copy on the front, as well as a graphic, extra copy, and discount announcement on the back.

Send to: Consumers, independent bookstores, libraries, educators, and nontraditional markets.

Tip: Make sure that the size of the postcard qualifies for a reduced postcard postal rate. Apply for a bulk mail permit to keep costs down. The better the mailing list, the better the return. Make sure all information needed to order the book is clear and will not be obscured by postal processing.

BOOK SIGNING INVITATION

Description: This is a personal invitation to be mailed out to friends, family, associates and others with an interest in you, your book, or any other aspect of the signing.

Features: Invitations can be postcards, greeting cards, or letters inviting the recipient to a book signing. Book, author, bookstore, date, time, perks (refreshments, music, readings), and ordering information should be included. Also include information to reserve a signed copy of the book if the recipient cannot attend the signing.

Optional: You can use engraved stationery, a handwritten post script, graphic elements, a discount announcement, or other incentives on the invitation.

Send to: Consumers, especially friends, family, and associates.

Tip: Bookstores often have a list of their own customers and regulars. Offer to do a joint mailing, with a special activity to lure an audience to your book signing. Always call the people you know on your own list and remind them to come. Empty chairs at book signings are no fun, and a handful of friends can often attract a crowd to a signing.

VENDOR UPDATE

Description: An update is an announcement to outlets that sell your book, detailing special media attention or other events that are likely to significantly boost sales of your book in a particular region and/or timeframe. A vendor update is designed to stimulate orders from vendors.

Features: The update should include book, author, publisher, and ordering information, as well as a few short, succinct paragraphs describing recent or upcoming publicity activity and forecasting an increased or upcoming demand for the book.

Optional: The update can include press clippings, graphic elements, sales figures, or anything else relevant to your announcement.

Send to: Wholesalers, distributors, trade buyers, and independent bookstores.

Tip: Vendor updates are most effective when used as part of a planned media and publicity blitz, especially when built around

Your Average Book Event Doesn't
Include Lessons on Safe Surfing
From an MIT Professor
in the Middle of December....

Obviously, This Isn't
Your Average Book Event...

...It's an Electronic Beach Party!

Jonathon Hacker, author of
The Electronic Lifeguard
will be your host

Saturday, December 14
3:00 pm - 6:00 pm
The Cove Bookstore
831 Main St., Spokane WA

Grab your Hawiian shirt, shades, and sunscreen and get down to The Cove. Internet expert Jonathon Hacker will be there to teach you how to surf the Internet—safely—for pleasure and profit. Admission is free and refreshments will be provided.

Call The Cove Bookstore at (555) 732-7662 for more information.

front and inside of book signing invitation

MAX BAUD PRESS

1234 MICROCHIP LN • SILICON VALLEY CA 90 301 PHONE: 864-555-1234

VENDOR UPDATE

Please be aware of the following developments in the promotion of *The Electronic Lifeguard*:

- *Time* magazine will run a feature article discussing Internet safety and mentioning ***The Electronic Lifeguard*** in its 7/14/96 issue.

- Author Jonathon Hacker will appear on "Good Day USA" (ABC-TV) on 8/2/96.

- Author Jonathon Hacker will be making regional promotional appearances on the following dates:

7/21/96 Seattle, WA KTEL-FM "The Bud & Linda Show"
7/26/96 Portland OR KSME-AM "Consumer Digest"
7/28/96 Portland OR KCTC-TV (local cable) "Book Round-Up"
8/5/96 San Diego, CA KRIP-FM "The Morning Show"
8/6/96 Dana Point, CA KQED-AM "Businessman's Lunch"
8/12/96 Reno, NV KWIN-FM "The Mike Drennon Show"

These appearances will coincide with book signings, author appearances, and speaking engagements at regional trade shows.

- ***The Electronic Lifeguard*** has been nominated for *PC Magazine*'s "Editor's Choice Award." Winners of this prestigious award will be announced 9/1/96.

Please make sure that you have adequate stock levels to meet the growing demand for this title

Contact Quantum Distributors, Inc. at 1-800-555-1111 to order additional copies.

For more information, contact Beverly Bookings, *Marketing Director* for Max Baud Press at 1-800-555-1234

vendor update

a specific event or date. Use vendor updates to ensure that books are available widely when consumer awareness is at a peak. Do not use vendor updates frivolously — remember the boy who cried wolf.

Putting Together Your Own Book Releases

When you start putting together your marketing tools, begin with your book releases, the most important tools you will use. The two book releases are the *media release* and the *sell sheet*.

A media release should stress a newsworthy aspect of the book and a sell sheet should stress sales potential. *Do not* try to use a sell sheet for media contacts, as it will only alienate them. In your media release, always stress the news or, in the case of talk shows and other "info-tainment" vehicles, the entertainment value of your book and author. Both kinds of releases should supply anyone interested in the book with enough specific information to order a copy, contact the publisher, print a mini review, or list the title in a catalog. However, book releases are not appropriate to send to individual consumers.

Both kinds of book releases have several essential components: the headline, body copy, ordering information, release date, and contact name. Optional information includes an author's biography, a graphic element such as a picture of the cover, testimonials, bulleted lists, and even a listing of the table of contents.

The Headline

The headline should make a strong, interesting claim that would make the average reader curious enough to read a little further. A newspaper headline is a good model for this type of writing. If the headline is not clear and exciting enough to grab your recipients' attention, they will rarely read further, and you will only be wasting time, postage, and opportunity.

One strategy for building effective headlines is to use action verbs in the present tense. "New diet kills pounds, saves lives!" is a lot more exciting than "This new diet plan could help you to lose weight and become healthier" and "Don't get mugged, bugged, or spied on!" sparks the imagination more than "Important safety tips for Internet explorers revealed." Tantalize the reader with a compelling issue, preferably of an immediate nature. Working sex, death, or wealth into the headline, citing specific quantities, and implying urgency are all proven techniques for successful book release headline writing.

Media outlets rely on book releases to generate leads for news and feature stories. They require information and story leads to fill out their columns, pages, and air time. Your objective should be to provide a headline that will catch their attention, timely information, and an appropriate angle for a story.

With the exception of book reviewers, most media contacts are not going to write as much about the book as they are going to write about the author, issues the book is tied to, events celebrating the book's publication, and trends the book inspired or is inspired by. The point here is that only reviewers care about the actual contents of the book. To all other media contacts, your book is the garnish on a larger dish, which is "the issue" or "the story" surrounding the book. It is up to you to furnish exciting leads upon which that story can be built.

The sell sheet has a different objective. If it is going out to a distributor, wholesaler, bookstore, or other resale outlet, your objective is to promote the book's sales potential and audience appeal. The sell sheet should include the features that make the book unique and the benefits the book offers the consumer, as well as the methods being employed to bring the book to the consumer's attention.

The Copy

When writing the copy for a book release, it is important to focus on what exactly the end-user (either the consumer in the case of a sell sheet, or the media audience for a media release) will gain by reading the book. *Benefits* and *features* clearly and quickly define the unique, and valuable qualities of your book. *Benefits* are specific ways in which readers can use the information in the book to improve their lives. *Features* are information, tables, illustrations, and other aspects of the book that are worth bragging about. Take for example a book designed to quickly teach the reader conversational French. The fact that the book allows the reader to learn French quickly is a *benefit*. If the book has a tear-out sheet with handy French phrases listed for quick reference, that is a *feature*.

Benefits and features command the reader's attention by revealing what is in the book for them. *Bulleted lists* (bullets are periods or "dingbats" placed before items in a list) are a good way to present the benefits and features your book offers. You can take this one step further by showing how a specific benefit or feature can solve a problem, especially a problem the reader was not considering. For example, "The book's handy, tear-out list of special French phrases will help you stay on top of opportunities, emergencies, and unfamiliar situations."

Keep the body copy to no more than three paragraphs of approximately three to four sentences each, which should build from the headline. Do not stray too far from the main topic of your book, or include too much information, or you run the risk of confusing or boring your reader. Whenever you make promises or claims, use facts and information to back them up.

Target your writing directly to the readers to get them involved. Words like "unique," "fantastic," "comprehensive," "lavishly illustrated," and other inflated adjectives are weak, because they do not explain what the book will do for the reader. It is a better idea to use concrete verbs and describe the book in terms of its benefits and features.

Claims

Specific, bold claims also work, if you can back them up properly. A claim such as "What keeps brokers reaping millions is all that stands between you and financial success — simple investment secrets that anyone can follow! Highly successful broker and author Tom Cashman breaks the silence and reveals how being your own broker can make you rich!" immediately identifies for consumers exactly what they stand to gain from buying the book.

Do not make claims you are not prepared to back up. However, if you can make strong claims and back them up authoritatively, you will have people calling you just to challenge your assertions. This is exactly what you want.

Testimonials

To add credibility and emphasis to the statements in your book release, use a strong quote or testimonial. The idea behind testimonials is to use a credible source to make a sales pitch for your book. You'll want to find an author, expert in your field, well-known personality, or perhaps just a typical customer to make a statement such as: "No matter who you are, or how much you are investing, Tom's book will make you more money," or "These are the make-it or break-it secrets that hold investment fortunes together and — until now — were out of your reach!" Testimonials need to be followed by the name of person quoted and at least one of his or her credentials (Ph.D., author of..., Nobel Prize winner). It is very important that if you quote anyone, that you do so with written permission.

Statistics also make credible testimonials, especially when the sources cited are well-known or authoritative, such as the *New York Times* or the World Health Organization. Testimonial is especially effective in a book release when the credentials and/or the quote directly and strongly support your claims and credibility. If you quote a famous basketball star as saying that the author knows the game of basketball better than anyone else, this testimonial will generate interest and sell books. If you quote an unknown college professor's comment that your poetry shows potential, it will not stimulate interest or sales.

Necessary Information

In both the sell sheet and the media release, it is essential that you provide the following information, grouped together for easy access: the book's title and subtitle, the author's name, publication date, ISBN number, price, format, subject, and length. These should appear at the top of the release, just above the headline. The name, address, and phone number of the publisher should also be used for the letterhead. The name and title of the contact person along with a contact phone number must also be clearly visible. On the media release, the words "For Immediate Release" or "Release by [date]" are an indication of the timeliness of the information, and should be placed above the contact person's name.

A photograph of the author or the cover of the book makes a strong graphic addition to any release. Anyone who will be purchasing the book will want to see the cover, and reviewers usually need a graphic of the cover for their articles about the book.

End the book release with a compelling reason why the reader should call immediately to find out more. One way to elicit a response from a media release is to offer something free to anyone who calls, such as a sample newsletter, or information kit. Reporters and editors understand the value of offering their readers something for free and may print a short mention about your book in order to put their readers in touch with a free resource.

Notes on Other Marketing Tools

- You should write a general-purpose cover letter and keep it on file. When you need to send a media kit to a contact, customize your cover letter to fit the specific person and situation. Do not try to "pump up" a cover letter; only include information that must be brought to the contact's attention and is not contained in the book release. Make sure your cover letter doesn't try to do the work of your book release. Keep it short and to the point.
- A grabber sheet can follow almost any format, including top ten lists, five-minute quizzes, bizarre-but-true facts, "mug shot" descriptions of your characters, and outrageous gag news stories. Grabber sheets that pertain to specific occasions such as Halloween, Valentine's Day, or the Super Bowl are particularly effective, as editors and producers are always looking for clever and timely news leads.
- A good Q & A sheet accomplishes two goals: it provides interviewers with an angle that you know is effective, and it indicates to media contacts that you are familiar and comfortable with the interview process.
- Any media attention that you receive can be translated into credibility for you and your book. For this reason, keep a record of any mention made in the media about you, your book, or related events, issues, and topics. Most book reviewers will send you a *tear sheet* (sample) of any article they publish, provided they have been in contact with you. Always request two copies of any article or review in your cover letter.
- Radio and television stations usually provide an audio or video tape of your appearance. These are valuable tools. Sending producers a tape allows them to see or hear you and judge your media skills.
- You can use clippings as part of other marketing tools, or as stand-alone sell sheets by putting ordering information on the back of a copy of an outstanding article (or a collage of articles) about you or your book. People trust the media and believe what they see, hear, and read. What the media reports about your book carries a credibility that outweighs anything you can write about yourself.
- The return mailer is the key tool for direct mail marketing. The idea is to find your target audience, reach them with

your message, and provide them with an easy way to respond. Even with a heavily targeted audience, you will be fortunate if two percent to five percent respond. If you mail to people who are outside your target market, that already small percentage will drop significantly.

- *Teasers* used in direct mail can be thought of as lead-ins to your hook, or bait. The best example of a teaser is the phrase "You may have already won..." This is the true spirit of the teaser — a promise of something too good or too strange to be true, so that you have to open the letter to further investigate. Always keep the teaser relevant to headlines or copy inside the return mailer.

- If you have a scheduled radio or television interview, use it to publicize your book signing. Before the interview date, call around to bookstores in the broadcasting area and let them know that you are doing a local radio interview and that you are also available for booksignings. Tell them that if they sponsor the signing, you will mention their store on the air. This is a very difficult offer for bookstore managers to turn down. It is one example of how momentum can be manipulated to get the most out of an opportunity.

- If you do not have the proper wholesale or distribution outlets, superstores will not be able to order your book for a book signing because they cannot get approval to open a new account for a single-title publishing company or small press. One way self-publishers have gotten around this problem is through a policy of "instant consignment." On the night of the signing, the author brings a specified number of books. After the signing, a tally is made of the amount sold, including any copies the store wishes to keep for its shelves. An invoice is then issued to the bookstore for the number of books sold, as if it had been a straight sale. This method may not always work, but it is a good example of the kind of creative solution which can get you around unfavorable conditions within the book trade.

- There are several ways of conducting promotional giveaways and contests. Offer important information, excerpts, reports, lists or other data, or enclose a small, clever, or whimsical item in the press kits you send to media contacts. This item should tie in with the spirit of your book. For example, the author of a book attacking health care reform recently enclosed a large plastic pill in each media kit he sent out, along with a note reading: "Before you swallow Congress' health care bill, we wanted you to see what they really had in mind..." The pill opened to reveal a pen, and was imprinted with the book's title, author, and publisher.

- Promotional giveaways are items that can be imprinted with your book title or cover artwork, such as T-shirts, keychains, mugs, pens, and hats. Promotional manufacturers make and customize every manner of product. Some products, such as bookmarks, notepads, calendars, and booklets, you can make yourself. With any promotional giveaway, you should set a cut-off date or use the phrase "while supplies last."

More about Paid Advertising

When one of the publishing giants brings out a new title, thousands of dollars are spent advertising the book. This is how best sellers are created. For small and self-publishers, paid advertising usually does not pay off. Unless you can be sure that the publication in which you are advertising is going to reach and motivate a significant portion of your target market to immediately buy the book, you will usually lose money by advertising. The fact is that your time is much better spent trying to elicit free advertising through reviews, articles, radio and television interviews, and other media opportunities. These promotional vehicles are more visible, more compelling, and more credible than a paid advertisement.

There are two easily identifiable reasons for this. When readers come across an ad, they know that the message and language of the ad were written and paid for by the person selling the product or service. Also, it has been proven that the average consumer must see the same ad seven times before he or she will respond to it.

Once you have established yourself as a press, you will begin to receive advertising rate sheets and special offers from major publishing trade magazines and other advertising outlets. A significantly sized ad in a major trade publication can easily cost more than $2,000. If your book is priced at $12.95, you will have to sell more than 100 copies of your book, at full price, just to break even for buying such an ad. In reality, it is unusual to sell more than a few copies of a book through a single print ad of any kind.

For years, targeted print advertising offered a very promising way to sell books, especially through mail order, and many self-publishers made a fortune with this technique. Today the rules have changed. Newcomers to publishing should avoid advertising so they can concentrate on getting free publicity through reviewers and the media.

There are exceptions to this rule. If you are doing a major book signing, purchase a listing in the literary events section of the most widely read local paper. For a major fall or spring release with the potential for strong, nationwide sales, a cooperative ad in *Publishers Weekly* has the potential to get your book noticed. However, do not purchase ad space to accompany a review or article about your book.

Tips on Writing Copy and Headlines

When using ad copy to sell your book, you have between five and ten seconds to get your readers' attention. Do not try to fit everything about your book on to one page, hoping the sheer weight of your argument will be convincing. Keep your language direct, and the amount of copy to a minimum.

- *Headlines*

  Use your headline to make a *promise* that will draw in readers. One way to do this is to tempt them with a benefit your book offers, such as increased wealth, longer life, better sex, losing weight, or an easier job.

  Another approach is to make a *claim* in the headline that seems impossible, and then qualify it in the body copy. In a recent TV advertisement for the U.S. Army, it was stated that "By the year 2000 there will be more computers than people!" Although, technically speaking, there already are more computers than people, the point of the commercial was to stress the need for computer and electronics training by implying that the world will be run by computers within the next few years.

  If your book is how-to or technical, it may not call for a "screaming" headline. However, you still need to find a benefit for the headline. Point out a fear, danger, or disaster from which your book may save a potential reader and you have the *life-saver* benefit for a headline. You can also calculate how much money the reader will save or make from information in your book, and put it into a *fantasy gold mine* headline.

If you've written a biography, there may not seem to be any benefits. Yet, the study of any successful person's life lends itself to the phrase *Learn how...*, even if the book isn't specifically a how-to book. If the subject is not famous, but is an incredible achiever, the *It's a Wonderful Life* headline can be used to portray what life would be like without him or her. Another technique is to pick two contrasting aspects of the subject's character and play them off each other for the *Nuclear Physicist by Day, Mob Hitman by Night* headline.

HEADLINE EXAMPLES

Promise: WITH ***THE ELECTRONIC LIFEGUARD***, YOU WILL NEVER SURF INTO THE "SHARK INFESTED WATERS" OF THE INTERNET

Claim: BY THE YEAR 2000, MORE THAN 100 MILLION PEOPLE WILL BE ON THE INTERNET —INCLUDING CYBERTHIEVES, HACKERS, AND INTERNET PIRATES

Screaming: IF YOU PLAN ON GOING ON-LINE WITHOUT ***THE ELECTRONIC LIFEGUARD***, YOU NEED TO HAVE YOUR MOTHER BOARD EXAMINED!

Lifesaver: READ ***THE ELECTRONIC LIFEGUARD*** TODAY — THE ASSETS, DATA, AND FAMILY YOU PROTECT MAY BE YOUR OWN!

It's A Wonderful Life: WHAT'S THE WORST THING THAT COULD HAPPEN IF YOU GO ONLINE WITHOUT ***THE ELECTRONIC LIFEGUARD***? WE'LL GIVE YOU THE *SHORT* LIST!

Nuclear Physicist By Day...: AS A YOUNG COMPUTER ENGINEER AT MIT, JONATHON HACKER NEVER DREAMED HE WOULD WIND UP AS THE LIFEGUARD FOR THE WORLD'S LARGEST SURFING CROWD

• *Sales Copy*

The function of copy in your sales and marketing tools should be to (1) directly develop and qualify the headline, (2) list the benefits and features the book offers, (3) establish the author's credibility, (4) offer an incentive for ordering immediately, and (5) provide ordering information. Break complex ideas into short, simple sentences. Do not list every detail about the book. The elements of mystery and withheld information are powerful motivators.

• *Promotional Copy*

Promotional copy is different from ad or sales copy in that you are not trying to sell a product, but trying to get a reporter, reviewer, producer, or other information broker interested in the entertainment or information value of your book. Instead of selling yourself and your book to your contact, you want to shift the emphasis to illustrate what you can offer their audiences. Look for the universal appeal: more, better, better for you, sex, money, love, security, a secret, or controversy.

Your promotional copy must convince the contact that you can entertain, intrigue or engage an audience. The reward for doing so is that you get to put in a sales pitch for your book when you are interviewed. This is true for all media contacts, from hometown reporters to Oprah Winfrey's program producers.

11

THE MARKETING TIMELINE

Chapter 11

Large publishing houses generally take one to two years to develop a manuscript into a finished book. With all of their resources and marketing experience, it may seem surprising that traditional publishers take more than twice as long as the average self-publisher to bring a book to market. It takes that long because big press production teams take months developing just the title and cover artwork. Meanwhile, their marketing teams do the majority of their planning, materials development, and pre-publication marketing work well before the book is released. These people know that the longer they take to build a solid promotional and marketing base for their titles, the better the book will sell.

Self-Publishing Marketing Mistakes

Most self-published authors take a different approach, tackling production, promotion, and marketing one at a time, and in that order. Many self-publishers do not even think about marketing until they have a finished book in their hands. Furthermore, most feel an immense sense of pressure to develop their manuscript into a finished book in as little time as possible. Thus prepublication sales opportunities are missed; major book reviewers ignore the work because it arrives in their office less than three months prior to its publication date; and the time spent plotting a marketing plan after the book is finished is time taken away from actual marketing.

It is difficult to stay on course in the ever shifting currents of publishing and book selling, even when you have your course mapped out. Contacts change, companies move, and policies and terms change. Without a good sense of timing, it is easy to make mistakes and miss opportunities.

If your new book is the focus of a feature article in a major paper, and the books are not widely available, you are going to lose out on the sales potential of that exposure. The biggest and best opportunities in the book business are highly time-sensitive. You cannot take advantage of the Christmas shopping season unless you begin your efforts early in the summer.

Your promotional efforts can also be helped or hurt significantly by the planning you invest in marketing prior to the book's production. Testimonials can be a very powerful factor in sales and promotion, but without enough lead time, they will not arrive in time to appear on the book's cover. Prepublication reviews, advance sales, event tie-ins, award deadlines, and library buying cycles are just a few of the sources dependent on preparation and timing.

The Timeline

One of the most valuable tools in your marketing tool kit is the timeline. This is a list of promotional and marketing goals and deadlines which are set up in chronological order to forecast your activities for four to six months before and after the book's *publication date.* It offers a blueprint for scheduling the production, marketing, and promotional goals of a self-published book. Many self-published authors mistake the publication date for the date that they receive finished copies of the book. Actually, the publication date is the month in which you expect to introduce the book to the book trade and when you have set up the proper sales channels to make the book available to the end-user. It would do very little good to have a major book review or article appear about your book and then not have the book in the stores available to the public. A good rule of thumb is to set your publication date at least three to four months after you expect to have the finished books delivered.

Setting Up Your Own Timeline

Using a large desk calendar, begin dividing each month into weekly and daily objectives and goals. Feel free to adjust your publication date if you need more time or the press schedule is moved back. Remember that your timeline is a flexible guide. Up until the time you begin sending out review copies for pre-publication reviews, your publication date can be flexible. It is more important that you set specific goals, anticipate time-sensitive opportunities, and coordinate your efforts to build sustainable

MARKETING GOALS

6 MONTHS

- Create uncorrected review copies for testimonials and major magazine/TV coverage • Research competitive books • Draft press release, cover letter • Decide on primary audience, key media, and publicity angles • Prepare author's biography • Send manuscripts for testimonials

5 MONTHS

- Contact national and local TV shows • Call distributors and wholesalers • Create lists and materials needed for review and publicity mailings

4 MONTHS

- Assemble BLADS • Send review copies to trade reviewers • Obtain testimonials • Send BLADS to wholesalers and distributors • Prepare press kits • Send review copies to major magazines, catalogs, and book clubs

3 MONTHS

- Contact major bookstores for signings • Write direct mail letters • Make travel reservations for author tour • Send review copies to radio, print media, and other contacts

2 MONTHS

- Bind F & Gs for final review copies• Research deadlines for trade display, book awards, and listings • Plan publication date activities and events • Arrange local book signings • Prepare Q & A, grabber sheets, etc. • Begin mailing covers

1 MONTH

- Confirm all interviews, appearances, book signings in writing • Make sure books are in as many stores as possible • Begin mailing invitations, direct mail, etc. • Review overall plan

PUBLICATION DATE

book marketing timeline before publication date

PUBLICATION DATE

IMMEDIATELY

- Launch author tour and media blitz (radio, TV, book signings, etc.) • Keep scheduling interviews • Draft and send vendor updates • Stage publication day events • Make sure books are in the stores

1 MONTH

- Keep sending review copies to small magazines and newsletters • Keep scheduling interviews and book signings • Write new and updated press releases and other marketing tools

2 MONTHS

- Review goals and evaluate responses received • Begin direct marketing, advertising, and postcard mailing (if desired) • Review wholesaler, distributor, and bookstore sales and encourage reorders

3 MONTHS

- Compile promotional sheet with reviews and press clippings • Begin second round of media contact, radio and TV bookings • Offer to excerpt chapters to small and mid-sized periodicals

4 MONTHS

- Explore cross-marketing possibilities • Shop foreign and subsidiary rights • Send review copies to smaller magazines and newspapers • Book author appearances, talk shows, and book store signings • Implement new campaign • Plan campaign for second edition

book marketing timeline after publication date

momentum with your promotions and marketing than it is to have a set-in-concrete publication date.

Marketing Momentum

Momentum is the force that builds up around your book as it begins to get noticed, reviewed, and sold. This force draws attention and credibility to your title; it attracts buyers and catches the attention of industry participants. Momentum inspires a contagious enthusiasm in the author and anyone else who is working to promote the book, and it spreads as the book is promoted.

Let us go back to our hypothetical title, *The Electronic Lifeguard.* The book's author, Jonathon Hacker, sent a manuscript off to the well-known Internet author Barry Baud, in the hopes of receiving a testimonial. Because the manuscript was sent months before the book's production date, the testimonial arrived in plenty of time to be used on the back cover of Hacker's book. In fact, the testimonial was so strong, Hacker included it in a letter to an online bookstore to convince them to set up an online "meet the author" event. The bookstore, impressed by Baud's praise for the title, agreed to do so.

One of the people who then logged on to the online author event was the editor of an important Internet magazine. He was impressed by Hacker's information about Internet security and his advice to inexperienced Internet users. Later, when this same editor received a media release about the book and a review copy, he immediately followed up by calling Hacker and asking more questions. Impressed with the author and his message, the editor wrote an article on the future of online security, referring to Hacker's book and using some of the quotes from their conversation. When the article was published, not only were sales affected, but Hacker also gained an important new marketing tool (the article), and high-profile exposure that would lead to increased consumer awareness and more media attention.

Momentum builds every time you do a book signing, get a review, do a mailing, or make a large sale. Momentum is sustained with continuing promotional efforts, such as sending out press releases, probing new markets, setting up a book tour, and scouting for cross-marketing partners. Success builds momentum, and persistence sustains it.

To create and sustain momentum, plot your timeline, beginning six months prior to the publication date and stretching to four to six months after the book's release. Begin developing the action items on the timeline early, such as drawing up lists of contacts to whom you will send review copies and verifying their current phone numbers and addresses.

Make sure that you clearly understand which events necessarily preclude others, and which have prerequisites. For example, it is unwise to begin aggressively seeking media exposure until your title is available in bookstores. Before you begin trying to get the book into bookstores, it is important that you have wholesalers and/or a distributor who can fill bookstore orders. Momentum builds when the correct sequence is followed, and is lost when it is not.

Your timeline is crucial to your sales and marketing efforts for many reasons. It provides structure for your marketing plan, keeping you focused and organized. It allows you to prioritize and sequence your efforts for maximum efficiency. Perhaps most importantly, a timeline records your goals, results, and upcoming priorities in an efficient and reliable manner. If you try to market without a timeline, you will most certainly miss out on opportunities.

If you slow down promotional and marketing efforts, it will take much more effort to get anything accomplished when you start up again. Time-sensitive opportunities go by and contacts change.

It takes a considerable effort and a strong belief in yourself to sell yourself as an author, and to promote your book enthusiastically. With momentum, it is much easier to infuse positive energy, thoughts, and emotions into your efforts. And with a well-organized timeline, it is much easier to build momentum.

12

IDENTIFYING AND REACHING YOUR TARGET AUDIENCE

Chapter 12

The mailing lists are printed, your cover letters are signed, and the media kits have been assembled. Now comes the test of your success — making contact. The best way to increase your chances for success is to make direct, personal contact before you send out your materials and then follow-up afterward.

If you send a media kit to 100 potential contacts and do nothing else, you may receive a few responses. If you send those kits and then make follow-up calls two weeks later, you will make some surprising discoveries. Some of your contacts never received the package; some never opened it; many had no idea why it was sent to them; a few were not interested, but could tell you who might be; and some just need more information before making up their minds. Two facts would stand out above all the others: only a tiny portion of any mailing list will respond to a given mailing, and that number grows impressively when follow-up calls are made.

Phone Calls: The Most Important Marketing Tool

A phone call increases your chances of developing a sale or media exposure in three ways: 1) it allows you to determine that the contact name and address is correct; 2) it alerts the contact to be on the lookout for your materials; and 3) it gives those materials a context and a purpose. Sometimes, when you call ahead, you will discover that there is no reason to send the information to that particular contact, which can save you shipping and materials costs. Sometimes, information you exchange over the phone will help you to sell the book before your media kit arrives.

After your mailing goes out, wait two weeks and then call to make sure the materials were received. By following up, you increase your chances of receiving a positive response. You will come across as a professional, bring your book to the forefront of your contact's attention, and provide an opportunity to clear up any confusion or make a stronger sales pitch. And, should there be a circumstance that might prevent a positive response, you can identify the problem and work it through.

Calling Protocol

When making telephone contact, there are a few basic steps that you can take to make sure your calling is done efficiently. First, make a *contact log* — write down the contact name, company name, phone number, date you are calling, and your reason for calling, along with notes about the conversation. This will help you stay focused and provide a dated record of all contact efforts and results.

Before making phone calls, line up all relevant materials — a copy of the book, press releases, news clippings, reviews, author's biography—that you may need to refer to for information, and keep them within reach. Know exactly what your objective is in making the call: whether you are trying to get a book review, solicit an interview, follow up on materials sent, or check a contact name. Be prepared to get right to the point of the call.

Calling Hook

Before calling, determine your hook, which is usually the answer to the contact's questions: "Why are you calling me? Why should I be interested?" Although most contacts will not ask these questions directly, this is what is on their minds. Business calls, especially unsolicited, or *cold* calls, tend to dance around these questions. Try to answer these questions before your contact is forced to ask them.

Your strategies should include getting the contact to identify a need by asking simple, qualifying questions, and then demonstrating how your book addresses that need. Another strategy is to lead in with a strong bit of news, such as a major book award, a related media story, or a shocking statistic related to your book, and explain why this news should influence or otherwise be of interest to the contact's customers or audience.

When you get your contact on the other end of the line, do not pounce with your entire marketing pitch all at once. It is often a good approach to introduce and identify yourself, and then ask how the contact is doing. This gives him or her an opportunity to take some initiative in the conversation.

Listen carefully to your contact's responses and think through what you are going to say next. It is easy to get over-anxious and rush to the end of the call, but a lot of opportunities can be missed this way. Being patient, deliberate, and attentive will not waste your time. By asking pointed, relevant questions, and then listening to and building upon your contact's answers, you will make every call a mutually comfortable, if not beneficial, experience.

What to Avoid in Marketing

Never pester or put negative pressure on your contact. Be positive and upbeat, present your case in the strongest and clearest possible manner, without distorting the truth or making claims you cannot back up. Do not be too relaxed or familiar, unless the contact invites you to do so. As an author and a self-publisher you must learn to sell yourself and your book. You are not selling used cars or miracle pills, so avoid hype and the hard sell when dealing directly with individuals. Other things to avoid include:

- *Sloppy packaging:* Do not send out poor reproductions, or marketing tools with spelling errors and other mistakes; handwritten correspondence; damaged review copies; "cute" design elements; and unprotected mailers (use snug, padded mailing envelopes, or boxes and foam pellets).
- *Long Delays:* Do not put off until tomorrow what you can do today. If you must delay, let your contact know why, and stay in touch.
- *Snail Mail:* Do not send any important package or promotional kit through the U.S. Postal Service. Use a next-day delivery system. With regular mail, even if your materials get there on time, there are a surprising number of contacts who will not open a package that was not sent by overnight or next-day delivery. Also, it is impossible to track U.S. mail if something gets lost or is delivered to the wrong person. (UPS, FedEx, and other package delivery services do not deliver to post office boxes. If you send to a P.O. box address, use overnight Express Mail.)

- *Industry Bias:* If you are a self-publisher or a single-title press, avoid broadcasting this fact, as it will invite an industry bias against you. Choose a suitable name for your press (preferably not your own name) and a letterhead with a professional logo.
- *Improper Behavior:* You must assume that your contacts are important professionals, and treat them as such. Never approach contacts from a negative position, or act as though you are doing them a favor. Never criticize them for failing to follow up, or chide them for choosing not pick up your title or story. The publishing world is small, and you do not want to give a negative impression to anyone with whom you come in contact.
- *Improper Appearance:* If you are working out of your home, be careful not to let your home life intrude on your workspace. Establishing a separate phone line with voice mail is essential. You may want to use an assumed name or invent a ghost name to use as your marketing director or administrative assistant. If you choose to put up a business front, be consistent. Remember that the business world expects your office to be open during regular business hours, staffed by responsible employees, and responsive to calls and messages. Always answer your business line with the name of your press.
- *Inadequate Organization:* If you are going to be handling your own publicity and marketing, invest in a contact manager program for your computer. This is software that combines database, spreadsheet, and calendar functions. It is specifically designed to help salespeople track, analyze, and record customer contacts, and remind them of appointments.

The Target Audience

The foundation of successful book marketing is your ability to identify and reach your target audience. Your target audience is people who are ultimately going to buy your book. At the same time you are identifying your audience, it is equally important to determine which media those people rely on for information and entertainment, as well as the outlets from which they are likely to buy books.

Do not confuse your target audience, who represent the end-user of your book, with your target markets, which are the outlets you rely upon to get your books to the target audience.

Identify Your Audience

In today's glutted book market, the decision to stock or carry a title often depends more on marketing considerations than on the contents of the book itself. A title whose audience is confined to a regional area, such as a book of local history, will generally be confined to regional markets, and it will be a difficult task to find a national distributor, bookstore chain, book club, or other large retail outlet to carry it. On the other hand, a book aimed at IBM computer users will be targeted to a national audience whose demographics include disposable income and a history of buying similar books.

If you know your target audience before you go into production, you can design the book and promotional materials to appeal specifically to its interests. In addition, you can adapt your promotions to the media that your audience is most likely to read, listen to, or view.

If you cannot define your target audience, you may be wasting time and resources by promoting your book to relatively small concentrations of potential customers. You are likely to miss out on nontraditional orders, the most lucrative market, because you will not be able to effectively demonstrate your book's sales or alternative market potential. Know the audience for whom you are writing. Identify your target audience and break it down into very specific categories.

Suppose you have a book about cosmetics and earth-friendly beauty supplies. You might assume that your target audience would be "Women." This is not the case. "Women" is not a specific target market. Women have such varied interests, needs, and backgrounds that no single book could appeal to all of them. Your audience would be "Women Who Use Cosmetics," or even "Environmentally Conscious Women." These are helpful restrictions because they allow you to focus on a specific interest or need. "Environmentally Conscious Women" is not only an excellent target audience, but it also represents a *niche,* which is an audience clearly defined by a specific, shared interest, trait, or need.

Because you can make assumptions about the interests, needs, and habits of the members of tightly targeted audiences, it is easier to reach the individual members of that audience. Niche audiences are easier to reach and usually easier to sell to than other markets due to the strong focus on shared interests. When your customers are easy to find and easy to interest, they are easier to sell to.

Target Markets

Once you have identified and researched your target audience, you should begin to focus on your target markets. These are the outlets that would have the greatest interest in selling your title. A good strategy for identifying target markets is to work from the bottom up. Start with the places you would expect your target audience to shop — the bookstores, common retail outlets (in the case of a children's book, stores that sell children's toys or clothing), mail-order catalogs, and other venues — and work your way up the distribution chain.

If you want to know where specific outlets get their merchandise, call and ask. Many sales outlets advertise in magazines directed at target audiences. *Ulrich's Periodical Directory,* as well as your local library's periodical section, and even newsstands, are places to begin your research.

Getting the Details

Your next step is to ask yourself precisely why your audience will be interested in your book. The answers to this question are crucial, as they form the skeleton of your sales and promotional efforts. You will need to point out these reasons to consumers, wholesalers and retailers, as well as how audiences will learn of the book, what will motivate them to go and get it, and how it is superior to related materials on the market.

1. Identify your "typical" customers. Write out 20 questions that will more narrowly define their profiles, interests, and habits. Some examples are: Where do they live? What do they read? What organizations do they belong to? What common traits do they share? How are they different from one another?

2. Name 20 reasons someone in your target audience would want your book. These can be based on a need the book fills, original or hard-to-find information it contains, the popularity of the topic, or anything that will set your book apart. It will be easier to sell your book to retailers if you can tell them why their customers will be attracted to it. Try

to separate the particular motivations of your target audience from those of the general population when making this list.

3. Name 20 benefits and rewards the reader will receive by purchasing your book. Go through the book, page by page, looking for ways the information can be turned into concrete benefits for the reader. Remember that benefits are things that your book will do for the reader rather than everything the book contains. For example, a list of suppliers in your book "puts the reader in touch with" those sellers. Tell people how the information in your book is going to make their lives better. Think in terms of best-case scenarios — what is the biggest reward someone could get from this information?

4. Think of 10 occasions, holidays, or upcoming events that could relate to your book. What can you do to tie your book in with the occasion? What media outlets might carry stories related to these events or holidays? How can your book be an appropriate gift?

5. Name at least 10 nontraditional markets in which to sell your book. A book on yo-yos, for example, can be sold in toy stores, hobby shops, sports equipment stores, nostalgia boutiques, toy catalogs, and directly to a company that makes yo-yos.

6. Go to the library and search the *Directory of Associations* for 20 clubs, organizations, associations, and other groups that would have an interest in your book. A book listing all the marathon races in the United States could be sold through local running associations and health clubs.

7. Does this book make you an expert on its subject? Are you an expert already? Name 10 ways this information can get you a speaking engagement (on the radio, on television, before a group, addressing schoolchildren, at a city hall meeting). Focus on who is interested in an expert's opinion on this subject and why. For example, journalists, talk show hosts, and event planners often rely on experts.

8. Write an article and a review about your book. This will help you understand what kind of information is valuable to journalists, as well as provide you with a ready-to-print feature article, headline, grabber ideas, and valuable media copy.

10. Will your book yield a special report? Write a short (two to ten pages) article offering a quick study of an important aspect of your book. For example, a book on child care for the 21st Century might yield a special report on planning early for a college education.

11. What activities, entertainment outlets, or displays would enhance a book signing or author appearance? Any activity or presentation you can work into an author appearance will help draw a crowd and prompt them to buy your book. These events also help to liven up television and radio appearances, and can make you seem a more attractive and promising guest in to a producer.

Research

Research is a crucial part of building a marketing plan and carrying it out. What you do not know about your customers, media contacts, and competition will only limit your marketing efforts. Mistakes such as pricing your book far beyond your direct competition, entering a glutted market, ignoring a large segment of your market, or missing out on important review opportunities detract from the overall effectiveness of your marketing efforts and undermine your momentum. Good research can have the exact opposite effect, yielding unexpected opportunities, allowing you to make bigger sales to important customers, and allowing you to parlay your momentum into sales.

Research pays off at all levels of marketing and at every stage in the development and promotion of your book. When choosing a title for your book, reading the latest copy of *Books in Print* will not only protect you from using a title that is already taken, but will also help you to develop a title that competes with related books. Researching prices of books similar to your own will help you find a price that is both competitive and profitable. Research at your local library can provide you with reader demographics, new customer bases, hard-to-find media contacts, and nontraditional marketing possibilities, as well as establishing good ideas for a hook. In addition, research will almost always turn up unexpected information or opportunities.

In addition to research at the library, you go to your local bookstores to get a feel for the look, price, availability, and special features of your competition. Look for trends in packaging and marketing of all books. Visiting bookstores in your area will help you to understand their preferences and customers. It will also give you a chance to talk with their owners or managers, which may yield valuable information, as well as test the waters for your own title.

Other forms of research include locating and reading newsletters, magazines, and journals that focus on your subject, audience, and other topics related to your book. Listening to local radio shows, keeping up with national and local newspapers and magazines, watching targeted television talk shows, and checking the Internet for related groups and sites will keep the doors of opportunity wide open for you.

13

DISTRIBUTORS, WHOLESALERS, AND OTHER OUTLETS

Chapter 13

Before you can begin putting together your marketing plans, you will need to familiarize yourself with the markets that are available to you. Not all markets are appropriate for all books. A children's book distributor, for example, will have very little interest in a book on health tips for seniors. It is a wise idea to study your markets before you begin promoting.

The following is a profile of some of the more general market categories. Please note that these descriptions are by no means exhaustive. In addition, you may run across companies that identify themselves as belonging to one market, when they do not. An example of this are the many businesses who call themselves "distribution companies" when, in fact, they are wholesalers. Do your research before you send out kits in order to get the most from your efforts.

Distributors

Distributors service publishers and book trade buyers ordering copies of a title in bulk, warehousing the books, listing them in their catalogs, and employing sales representatives to aggressively sell to buyers across the country. They also provide fulfillment and process accounts receivable and payable, remitting checks to the publisher 30 to 90 days after their invoices are paid. The distributor's sales team will call on everyone from head buyers for the major bookstore chains and wholesalers, as well as owners of small bookstores, gift shops, and museum stores. They get the respect and attention that a small press publisher does not often receive.

Distribution Agreements

Full-service distributors will deduct on average 20 percent to 27 percent of the payment on each book they sell, in addition to the discount they must offer to their customers. The distributor's cut can average out to as much as 60 percent to 67 percent of the book's cover price. Distributors usually require an exclusive marketing agreement, under which only they can sell your title to the book trade. The book trade is generally understood to include all businesses that generate more than half their income from book sales. An exclusive agreement will prevent you from selling directly to the trade, but it also frees you to promote your titles and sell to other, more lucrative markets. The term of a contract with a distributor is usually for a minimum of one year or more, after which time either party may terminate the contract 60 days after providing written notice.

Working with a Distributor

Distributors offer three major incentives for the small press publisher. First, they employ a team of sales representatives who actively sell your book to the book trade. Sales reps are an extremely valuable commodity to a publisher, because they can generate big sales and open the doors to difficult-to-access buyers. Buyers trust reps and follow their recommendations, often letting the reps' suggestions dictate their entire orders. Another advantage of working with a distributor is visibility. Your title will be listed in a catalog, promoted at trade shows, and made available to a much wider range of buyers and media contacts than you could reach on your own. The third advantage is the credibility your book gains when it is listed with a distributor. Head, regional, and national buyers for large bookstore chains rarely buy books not represented by a distributor. At the same time, everyone in the book trade will be positively influenced by the fact that your book is being handled by a major distributor.

In order to ensure that you find the right distributor and get the best results, it is very important to research prospective distributors early on in the book's production. Search for distributors who specialize in books like yours *(see Chapter 15 for distributor and wholesaler lists)*. Call and find out which types of books consistently sell well for them, how many sales representatives they have, and which major accounts they service. Obtain a list of publishers who have worked with the distributor, and call to verify that they were satisfied with the service they received. If you belong to a publisher's organization, ask members for information about prospective distributors.

Try to secure a distributor before your book is finished. This will allow you to advertise your distribution source in all of your pre-publication marketing materials. This is also important because major book reviewers will not consider your book for review unless they have several months' lead time before the publication date to review the title, *and* the book has a national distributor or wholesaler.

What is a distributor looking for in your book? A strong title, an attractive, attention-getting cover, a well-written text, a marketable topic, quality workmanship, strong author support for the book's promotion, harmony with the rest of the distributor's book list, a clear, coherent marketing plan, and a compelling hook.

Warnings

Signing with a distributor is a big commitment. If the distributor does a poor job of selling your book, you are still legally bound to continue with that company for the specified time period, and you cannot go after those missed sales. Another potential danger is selling too many books at too large a discount. With the high percentages of each sale that are consumed by the trade discount and the distributor's cut, there is a possibility of only a tiny profit margin, or even a loss. Do your math before signing a contract to make sure that you can make a profit if you sell to your distributor at its terms.

Also watch out for hidden costs and unreasonable restraints within the distributor's contract. Some distributors charge seemingly incidental fees for storage, processing, returns, catalog listings, credit card sales, and other services that are a normal part of the distribution process. These fees can, however, quickly add up to burdensome figures that will send your bottom line into the red. If a distribution company seems to put an emphasis on monthly maintenance or recurring fees other than a fixed percentage of the sales, it could be an indication that this company is taking advantage of you. Always have a lawyer evaluate any contract before you sign it.

Another danger is a distributor who is in financial trouble. Such a company is likely to look for new titles and let outstanding publisher payments mount in an attempt to boost their bottom line and stave off bankruptcy. If you sign a contract with such a distributor, your books are almost certain to fail with them. A few phone calls to some of the distributor's publishers and creditors should be able to confirm any financial problems. You are entitled to a list of creditors from any distributor who wishes to carry your title.

The Contract

It is imperative that you bring any distribution contract to a lawyer to have it evaluated before you sign it. This will allow you to find any hidden restrictions and fees. It will also help you to completely understand your obligations. When working with your lawyer, use your imagination to come up with some worst-case scenarios and examine the contract to see how it might restrict or aid you in these situations.

Publicizing and Promoting the Book

Although the distributor's representatives can be counted on for direct sales to trade buyers, unless there are consumers buying your books from the stores, those books ultimately are going to be returned to you, the publisher, for a full refund. So it is essential that while the reps handle the trade sales, you undertake the critical task of publicizing and promoting the book to the public in order to encourage consumer sales.

To work most effectively with a distributor, you must promote and market your own book aggressively, making sure that the buyers know which distributor carries your title. Make sure you list your distributor on every marketing piece you send out. Whenever an article, interview, or media event promoting your book appears in a particular city or region, call area bookstores, tell them of the publicity, and indicate which distributor (and/or wholesaler) carries the title. This will, at best, prompt orders for the book, or, at least, alert buyers as to how they can order the book.

Wholesalers

Wholesalers usually identify themselves as such, although some also call themselves distributors. Wholesalers, like distributors, warehouse your books, fill orders from the book trade, handle all of the accounting, and take a cut of each sale. However, there is a tremendous difference between wholesalers and distributors: wholesalers do not have a sales force and, outside of a catalog listing, do nothing to promote the sale of your book. Wholesalers merely fill orders for your book that come their way.

This difference, coupled with the fact that distributors service wholesaler accounts for you, makes the wholesaler a poor substitute for a distributor. But if you cannot secure a distributor, or are not willing to enter an exclusive agreement, you are going to need not just one wholesaler, but several. The reason for this is that trade buyers are reluctant to buy directly from small publishers, preferring the bulk discounts and reduced paperwork that accompanies wholesale orders. Most wholesalers are regional, servicing a limited geographical area, and bookstores must depend upon a variety of wholesalers in order to get a full range of quality titles. The bottom line is that for each wholesaler with whom you do not have an account, there will probably be orders for your book going unfilled.

Generally, wholesalers order books in quantity (though usually not more than 100 at a time); fill orders as they come in; take 40 percent to 55 percent of the cover price of each book; and then reorder to keep stock levels constant. They pay on consignment, in monthly installments, returning the leftover stock when orders appear to be drying up. Wholesalers do not require an exclusive agreement, and if they ask for one, make sure that they not only have an adequate sales force, but one that has a reputation for results. Do not easily give up the right to sell your own book.

Wholesaler Requirements

What are wholesalers looking for? Marketable books that fit their regional or subject profile, a strong marketing plan that addresses their territory, and/or orders already placed for your book before they have even heard of it through their regular channels. Wholesalers, like distributors, should be approached before your book's publication date, so that all of your promotions and marketing pieces list the widest variety of outlets for ordering. Remember, if the book trade can not buy a book easily, they probably will not purchase it at all.

Jobbers

Jobbers are similar to wholesalers, except for two main differences. Jobbers generally service the library trade more than the book trade, which means smaller orders, and they usually seek out the publisher themselves. Jobbers find books for librarians and other book buyers, place orders with the publisher and forward the books to their customer. Jobbers take discounts according to the same schedule as bookstores, which usually means that the publisher sets the terms.

Even though jobbers will eventually find you, it is still a good idea to send a sell sheet or book catalog to a number of jobbers to ensure that they know where you are and what books you publish.

Alternative Distributors

Alternative distributors sell magazines, periodicals, mass-market paperbacks, and speciality books and products to grocery stores, malls, mini marts, newsstands, gift shops, and other retail outlets. These distributors usually limit their titles to romances, best sellers, and magazines, but may be open to such publications as cookbooks, maps and travel guides, as well as books that have a strong regional theme. Keep in mind that these companies tend to be limited in their sales territory to a regional area.

Libraries

Libraries will generally order only one copy of your book per branch or collection. For this reason, you should never spend your day making phone calls to librarians, trying to persuade them to carry your title.

The best way to reach the library market is to be aware of the sources librarians depend upon for their information, and get your book into those places to be noticed. The *Library Journal* is a good place to start, though reviews in the *School Library Journal* or *Urban Academic Librarian* are other good choices, depending on your subject matter and market. Regional library associations are organized by region, state, or subject matter. For every library association there is an annual exhibition or convention, the largest of which is the American Library Association Convention, where new titles are displayed for the nation's librarians. You can display your book there through exhibition companies, as well as through some small press organizations, often for less than $50 per book.

Libraries themselves offer an excellent forum for promotion and book sales, as most library visitors are already book lovers. Setting up readings and special presentations are a good way of not only reaching people directly, but also of getting publicity in local papers, or at least in library circulars. In addition, there are many newsletters, library reviews, event calendars, and library-centered groups and publications that can review your book, invite you to be a speaker, or ask you to write articles for their member newsletters.

Independent Bookstores

Independent bookstores come in all shapes and sizes. Some independents are bigger than the largest superstore outlets, while some are not much bigger than a walk-in closet. Some cater to general interest titles, and some only carry books for a very specific range of interests or clientele. All independent bookstores do their buying out of the store itself, usually through a manager or the owner. This means that you can call the store, sell the buyer on your book, and fill that order, all on the same day.

It is easier to sell to independent book stores over the phone than it is to get them to respond to mailed promotions, and it is always more effective to represent the book in person. For this reason, always carry marketing tools with you when you travel and make a point of visiting independent bookstores. You will be surprised at how receptive these outlets are to travelling authors. Many will even schedule a book signing if you give them enough notice.

Bookstore Chains and Superstores

The growth of corporate-owned bookstore chains and superstores, such as Barnes & Noble, Crown Books, and Borders Books & Music, has been dramatic in the past few years. They put intense competitive pressure on local independent bookstores and, at the same time, provide a fantastic opportunity for book sales and author events. With hundreds of outlets to fill with books of all kinds, the regional and national buyers for these companies can put a real dent in your inventory if you can get a purchase order from them. However, there is a lot of competition to get their orders.

The best method is to go through an established sales representative, either through your distributor, as part of a co-op effort, or by contacting independent book representatives until you can find one willing to take on your title. If you decide to work cooperatively with other small publishers, arrange to meet with a book rep who will sell all of the co-op publishers' books together as a "line" of books.

Book Appeal for Superstores

What are superstores looking for in a title? Nationwide appeal. If the interest in your book is restricted to a specific region, or the target audience is a very limited group, these stores will not be interested. To get a sale, you must convince the buyers that your book has national appeal, a broad target market, weak competition, or a tie-in with a current trend. It is also important to tell them what you are doing to promote the title across the country. It helps to have solid plans for signings, events, interviews, media campaigns, advertising, and/or exhibiting. The more specifics you can provide, the more convinced they will be that you are working hard to create a demand for your book on the national level. These buyers will not accept books that fall below professional aesthetic standards. A strong, vibrant, professionally designed cover, trade or case binding, bar code, compelling jacket copy, and a strong, catchy title are some of the elements they are looking for.

Superstore Discounting

Like all bookstores, superstores will generally follow the discount schedule you dictate. If they do buy in quantity, be sure to give them at least a 50 percent discount. And remember, if you are unable to get consumers into the stores to buy your title, your books will be sent back to you for refund. It is very important that you follow up such large sales with focused publicity efforts.

Approaching Book Clubs

For those readers who cannot get out to the bookstores as often as they would like, the bookstores will come to them, in the mail. Book clubs are an excellent source of bulk sales and offer an advantage the superstores cannot hope to match — no book returns. If a book club selects your work as a feature or an alternate, you can count on selling thousands of your books. Unlike most bookstores and other book outlets, book clubs have a captive audience because their members are obligated to buy a certain number of books a year; the question is simply which titles they want to purchase.

Book clubs are not easy to break into. Some of the larger clubs will only buy books through literary agents. The clubs require a long lead time, which often can be a year or more. Of course, such a lucrative opportunity attracts intense competition, and calls for your best custom sales pitch.

Sometimes it is more economical for book clubs to reprint a title themselves, and then sell that edition to their customers. Always consult with a lawyer experienced with publishing contracts before signing any agreement. Your deal with the book club should be limited to a one-time reprint permission in exchange for payment.

The best way to approach a book club is to be selective. Find the clubs that cater to your audience or that carry titles on a subject related to your own. Call and ask what they are specifically looking for, how best to send in a book, and when in a book's production they want to see it. The best place to find listings for book clubs is in *The Encyclopedia of Associations*.

Book clubs generally prefer case bindings, illustrated books, famous names, topical and timely themes, controversy, sex, and books with universal appeal. It is important that the price of the book be high enough for the book club to make an adequate profit.

Mail Order Catalogs

There are enough mail order catalogs in circulation in the United States to fill a small library. From toys to lingerie, to gourmet foods and surplus scientific equipment, just about anything you can buy in a store you can order through a catalog, and that includes books. There are catalogs that feature only books, but, more importantly, many of the non-book catalogs also feature a few titles. How can you locate your market in this sea of mail-order opportunities? Fortunately, they have been grouped together for your convenience in the *Catalog of Catalogs*, which contains more than 12,000 listings, and can be found in the reference room of your local library.

Catalog Requirements

Catalogs operate in much the same way as book clubs in terms of long lead times, comfortable discounts, no returns, and their appeal to specific interests. However, catalogs do not focus on books, and often use them as a tangent to their main line of consumer items. A perfume, bath soap, and massage oil catalog might, for example, be interested in a book on aromatherapy, herbal massage, or how to make fragrances. A wilderness outfitter might like a guide to state parks, a backpacker's cookbook, or a children's wilderness activity book. Matching your book to the interests of a given catalog becomes much easier and more realistic once you have actually seen the catalog, if only in an annotated form.

Museum Stores and Other Outlets

A store does not have to be bookstore in order to sell books. Museum stores, cultural and historical society stores, gift shops, art galleries, and even restaurants sometimes sell books. Of course you are a lot more likely to see books in a museum store than you are in a restaurant, but if you use the restaurant's well-known recipes in your volume, or discuss its special architecture, that restaurant might sell a few copies of your book for you. Use your imagination, back it up with persuasion, and just about any retail outlet can become part of your sales territory.

There are no limits to targeting retail stores as a prime market, but museum stores and gift shops are a good place to start. Next, begin approaching outlets that offer goods or services related to your book's topic. A sporting goods store would be a good place to market a book on how to form a soccer team, and truck stops would probably be interested in regional travel guides. These markets are also attractive because they do not expect large discounts. Of course you will have to modify your sales pitch to fit their needs and interests, but again the objective is finding retailers who service your audience or market.

Non-Traditional Markets

The key to making bulk sales of books to non-traditional markets is in matching what you are offering in your book with an organization or company that offers the same sort of product or service.

The publisher of a book that teaches children the basics and benefits of recycling recently made a lucrative deal with Commonwealth Edison, Chicago's privately owned electric company. The energy giant, ever mindful of public relations, has linked itself with children's issues, recycling, and the environment. These books were bought in bulk and distributed as part of an ongoing promotional campaign. Another good example would be a deal between the publishers of *The Internet Yellow Pages* and Internet service providers, such as Prodigy and America Online, to provide this book as part of an introductory package for new accounts.

Other examples of non-traditional bulk sales include motivational books for employee consumption; companies purchasing books that profile their founders, products, or history; and a political party purchasing a lampoon of their rivals or a book praising their candidate. The examples, like the opportunities, are endless.

When soliciting bulk sales and approaching non-traditional markets, you have to abandon your usual sales approach and customize your promotion to fit each opportunity. It may take a considerable amount of work to go after even one such lead, but the rewards are also considerable. The average discount for bulk sales is only 25 percent, payment is usually upon receipt of the books, and there are no returns. Plus, once you have made a bulk sale to a non-traditional market, you do not have to worry about following up with promotions — these are direct-to-consumer sales.

Foreign Rights Sales

Foreign rights, especially German, Japanese, and Spanish language rights, are a way to benefit financially from your work without actually selling books.

Foreign publishers are always on the lookout for quality titles from other countries, especially from the United States. These publishers will pay you for the exclusive right to translate, print, and sell your book to markets in their own country. This arrangement really benefits both parties. The foreign publisher is purchasing a title that has already been fully developed and brought to market. There are no author's royalties, development fees, or other considerations involved. The book will simply be translated, repackaged, and run through the presses. You are getting paid to allow someone to sell your book to a market you probably would not have been able to reach. Furthermore, there is no risk and no investment necessary on your part.

In addition to these advantages, you can boost your promotion efforts by sending out press releases announcing any successful rights sales. Major book trade magazines (most notably *Publishers Weekly)* and smaller publications servicing the trade run announcements of rights sales, which, in turn, stimulate trade sales.

Aside from books and resource lists that specifically feature foreign rights buyers and agents, the best source for these contacts is the *Literary Market Place* and the *International Literary Market Place.* These books are available in the reference section of any library.

Reprint Rights

Reprint rights are exactly what the name implies, the right for other publishers to reprint your title and sell the books themselves. These publishers are buying the right to print and sell a single press run of a predetermined amount. You are not selling the copyright, nor are you giving them permission to reprint the book again later. This is a good way to keep your title profitable after you have exhausted your means to tap the book's market on your own.

Film Rights

If your title has what it takes to carry over into television, film, the stage, or animation, you will want to begin selling the rights to develop the book in another format. If you have little or no experience in this area, it is a good idea to find an agent who can help you. Reference books such as the *Literary Market Place* and *Book Publishing Resource Guide* offer listings for some of these agents. Write a sell sheet outlining why and how "performance rights" buyers would be interested in your book, and what advantages your title has over any competition in this area. Present an exciting vision of your book. Compare elements of your work to currently popular shows, trends, themes, personalities, and characters. By comparing what you have to offer with something proven to be popular and successful, you retain greater control over how rights buyers will interpret your work and keep the buyer's mind on the positive potential of your title.

Just how much you can expect to receive for entertainment rights has a lot to do with who is buying them and how much money will be spent on the production as a whole. Your best bet is to settle for royalties, with an advance based on projected returns. You will receive less money for an *option* — a script that is rented until a studio decides whether o produce it — than you will for the sale of the rights, but it still should be a comfortable sum.

It is a good idea to work through an agent when soliciting a rights offer. They have the contacts, know how to talk the industry jargon, and will most likely get you the fairest market price, less their commission, for any rights sold or optioned.

Serial Rights

Serial rights have traditionally offered authors a way of getting paid for their writing without actually securing a book contract. Many magazines and periodicals, such as *Reader's Digest*, publish book excerpts or serialize whole books and pay the author a fee for the right to do so. This will not interfere with your ability to sell your book, and in fact, the exposure will help you to sell more copies. Serial rights are marketed in the same way as any other rights, although you can scout out magazines that serialize and contact them directly.

Cooperative Marketing

The independent publishing world can be a friendly place when it comes to interacting with the competition. When two small presses with similar interests and target audiences realize that they are converging on the same market, they are likely to shake hands. Cooperative marketing is a consequence of this competition. These marketing ventures involve two or more publishers who are trying to reach the same audience with news of their products. The idea is to use a single mailing to promote the presses' titles collectively, sharing resource lists and production and mailing costs in order to make direct-mail marketing more viable and profitable. A co-op mailing can involve as little as two publishers, each with a closely related title, to 30 or more publishers.

There are other forms of co-op marketing, such as group-purchased ad space in major trade magazines, events coordinated to showcase local publishers, co-op booths at trade shows and conventions, and more.

The best way to solicit co-op marketing opportunities is to join a local, national, and/or international independent publishers' association. As a member of these groups, through phone calls, mailings, and newsletter notices, you should be able to find a co-op venture to fit your needs.

Card Decks

One kind of cooperative marketing mailer is the card deck. These are the plastic-wrapped packages of preprinted postcards that arrive in your mail marked "resident." They contain coupon mailers, free send-aways, and products of every description. Advertising in a card deck involves producing a catchy, attractive 3 by 5 inch card, usually in two or more colors, with an ad for the book on the front and a return mailer on the back. The card deck company is paid to print up vast quantities of the card and mail the decks out to entire ZIP Code areas.

This method can be very effective with the right type of book or product, but remember, there is really not much targeted marketing in card deck mailings. You will be reaching a lot of people with a wide and varied range of needs and interests, as opposed to a tightly targeted group of people likely to have a direct interest in your book.

Remainders

Remainders dealers are the last stop on the line for books that have ceased to be profitable. These companies buy books by the hundreds, paying only pennies on each dollar of the books' cover prices.

Traditionally, once a title reaches the point at which it costs more to market than it is earning in sales, the remaining stock is sold to a remainders dealer. Because these buyers pay considerably less per book that the production costs, there is no way to make a profit selling to them. When this type of sale is undertaken, it is to get a quick infusion of cash, to liquidate an outdated edition, or to make sure that a title stays on the market after all other sales outlets have dried up.

As an independent publisher, you do not have the restrictive window of opportunity that the large publishers have when it comes to selling your title. It is possible to stretch book sales out for years without incurring significant marketing costs. Avoid remainders dealers for as long as possible. If you do decide to remainder your title, shop around to find the highest price and try to negotiate a higher price than is offered. Do not give up after only a few tries, because you are bound to find an interested remainder buyer for just about any book.

A Diagram Outlining Sales Channels and Book Vendor Relationships

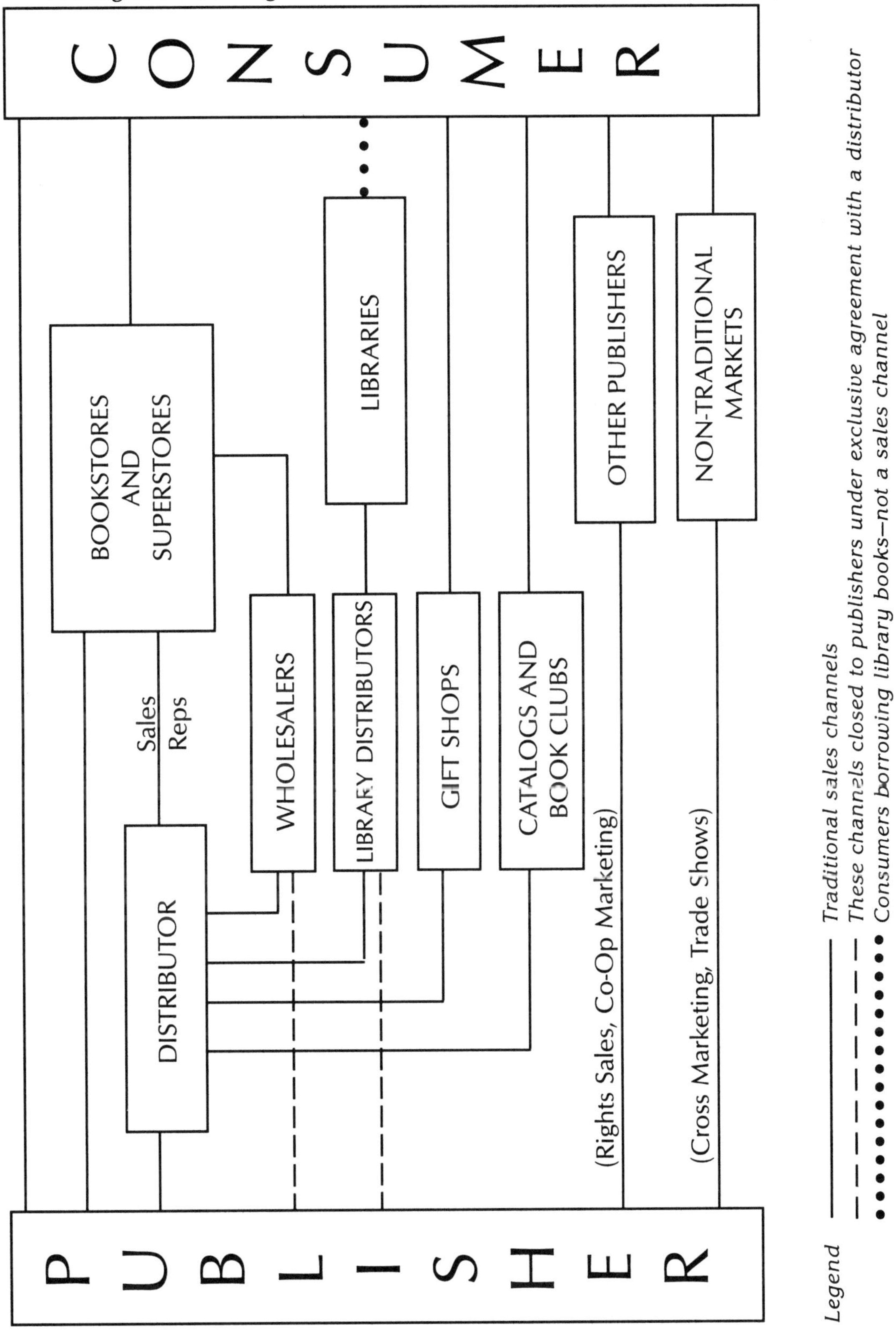

14

THE INTERNET AND OTHER LESS-KNOWN MARKETS & RESOURCES

Chapter 14

The Internet is the foundation of the "information superhighway" we all hear so much about. It is made up of a network of computers, linked together globally, that allows millions of computer users to post, retrieve, and access information, as well as communicate and conduct commerce. While the Internet promises new opportunities for sales and marketing, at the present time it remains an uncertain source of direct retail sales. Even so, the Internet allows you to post information, veiled advertising, and calls for submissions, assistance, cooperative ventures, and much more. Although it is important to familiarize yourself with this medium, getting "on the Internet" should not be your first priority as a self-publisher. You should also be wary of committing significant amounts of time and resources to selling through the Internet.

The Internet as an Information Source

The Internet was initiated as a military project in 1969. It was designed to create a communications network that could continue to function even in the event of nuclear war or global catastrophe. Most functions on the Internet were originally carried out in UNIX, a language developed specifically for computer networks. As the Internet became more popular, more complex and powerful protocols were developed. The *World Wide Web* is a recent development of the Internet and consists of a large number of interlinked Internet sites that support a graphical interface. This means that complex color graphics as well as text can be incorporated into a web site.

With the development of HTML (Hypertext Markup Language), and the World Wide Web, the Internet became a dynamic environment, complete with online graphics, sound, video, and jump-off points that lead to other "sites." Complex programs like Netscape Navigator and Global Network Navigator were developed to allow users to just point and click with a mouse. With these programs running, all of the technical language and complex UNIX commands are carried out in the background, allowing the user to carry out complex functions just by clicking on a single word or command. The UNIX shell still can be very useful for quick, efficient navigation and use of resources, once you have a basic understanding of how it works.

Getting on the Internet

In order to get on the Internet, you will need access to a personal computer and a modem capable of 9600 baud or more. You will also need to contact a *service provider* in your area. A service provider is a business that operates a computer network directly linked to others on the Internet. When you call your local service provider (via modem), your computer "links up" with its mainframe computer on the other end of the telephone line. Through the mainframe your computer becomes linked to every other computer on the Internet.

Service Accounts

There are three levels of service available on the Internet: a UNIX shell account, a PPP account, and a SLIP account. The *UNIX shell* is the least expensive and comes with the fewest features. It is text only, and you will have to know a few UNIX commands to use it. It will give you access to the Internet, and you will be able to send and retrieve E-mail, perform searches, join newsgroups, and post and download all manner of files. The major advantages of a UNIX account are speed and efficiency — commands and file transfers occur quickly.

The next level of service on the Internet is a *PPP account,* which uses Point-to-Point Protocol to carry out functions too complex for UNIX. A PPP account will allow you to run a full-service Internet browser. You do not have to learn UNIX commands and you will have complete access to the graphics of the World Wide Web. This level of service is more expensive and slower than using a UNIX shell, but also less complicated.

One step beyond PPP is the *SLIP account.* In addition to faster operating time than PPP accounts, SLIP accounts can handle almost any Internet-related activity, turning your personal computer into a "virtual mainframe." SLIP requires the protocol contained in a program called TCP/IP (Transmission

Control Protocol/Internet Protocol), which must be installed on your computer to use the account.

On-Line Services

Online services such as America Online, Prodigy, and CompuServe offer a lower level of Internet access than a traditional service provider. When you use these services, most of the surfing you will do will occur within a slower network that they operate and control. It is comparable to sailing around in an enclosed bay with a small river that leads out into the ocean. However, it might not be a bad idea to learn in a sheltered environment before taking on the high seas alone.

E-Mail

How can self-publishers make use of the Internet's resources and capabilities to promote their titles and themselves? One of the most powerful and useful aspects of the Internet is *E-mail* (electronic mail) capabilities. E-mail acts as an online postal system, sending and receiving computer files, such as business letters, help files, and registration forms. This feature allows you to send and receive computer-generated sales tools, sample chapters, letters, and other information instantaneously and cost-effectively, anywhere in the world.

E-mail is a standard feature offered by online service providers, and as a result, anyone who has an Internet account will usually have an E-mail box address, and capabilities. Businesses, online services, and promotional sites can publish their E-mail addresses in all of their promotional literature and use this service to directly interact with their targeted markets. E-mail allows you to build an electronic mailing list and instantaneously broadcast a promotion to every address on a given list. It provides an inexpensive and flexible vehicle for interacting with your customers and markets.

Commercial Aspects of the Internet

The Internet has a growing commercial population that can be used for sales, and promotion. More and more private users, commercial interests, and private organizations have established presences on the Internet, and private users are exploring the 'Net from their home computers. The number of users on the World Wide Web is expected to quadruple between 1996 and the year 2000. However, surveys report widely different assessments of how many people actually make use of their access accounts.

Although there has been a rush of commercial sites going up on the Internet, actual sales volume has not been growing nearly as fast as the Internet itself. It is true that some vendors have been successful, but they are few, specialized, and experienced in the unique rules of online marketing. Many more businesses are using the Internet to support and expand their marketing and promotional efforts in the "real" world. However, until they can overcome the problems of online commerce, and until the consumer comes to accept Internet shopping as routine, sales for the average vendor on the Internet will continue to be unpredictable.

Online Bookstores

There are also a growing number of companies that offer to promote books to Internet browsers. One service currently being offered is a listing of a title on a site that acts as an online bookstore. These services can be affordable and require little work on your part. Most of them take orders and forward them to you for fulfillment. If you decide to take advantage of this type of marketing, make sure that you are dealing with a well-known, well-established Internet presence. Some, like BookZone and the MAPA Web Site, have a proven track record.

Your Own Internet Site

With enough experience and planning, you will be able to open your own site on the Internet, providing information, sales opportunities, and an interactive forum for anyone interested in your book. There are generally two ways of going about setting up a site on the Internet — low cost home pages and more expensive web sites. A private home page will allow you to post information in such a way that anyone who is on the Internet can access it, but you will be limited in scope and content because most services will not allow commercial postings or transactions on a noncommercial web page. A commercial web site can be expensive to maintain, but will allow you greater freedom in promoting and selling your book.

For the economy-minded, setting up a noncommercial home page will allow you to reach large segments of your target audience. That includes anyone online with an interest in information and activities related to your book's subject. You can use your home page to post articles, events, a question and answer forum, and other devices to catch the interest of your target audience and let them know that your book exists. Even if you cannot sell or directly advertise on a noncommercial site, you can create a high-profile environment from which to broadcast information, including press releases or how interested parties can directly contact you. Your audience can also use your page as an electronic "bulletin board," posting information of related interest for other Internet users. Furthermore, your site can be an *access point*, providing links to other sites of related interest, such as an online bookstore carrying your book.

If you establish a commercial site, you can openly advertise and even sell your book and related products. This is advantageous only if you know that you have a large, general target audience.

Selling on the Internet

One of the problems of doing business on the Internet is the transfer of money to complete a sale. Currently, there are four basic ways of getting money from a customer for a product or service sold through the Internet:

> *Forwarded Orders:* Several of the online bookstores will take orders from online customers and then forward them to you by mail, E-mail, or fax. Even though the sale is made online, payment and fulfillment take place in the real world.
>
> *Credit Accounts:* Customers must set up an account with an online vendor or mall. This is outside of the Internet environment — by mail, fax, or phone — and the customer receives a line of credit to be used for online purchases.
>
> *Tokens:* The customer invests in tokens or virtual money. These are only accepted by certain Internet vendors, but are more flexible than credit accounts, which are only honored by the vendor who issued the credit line.
>
> *Encryption*: Sophisticated encryption programs allow customers to encode sensitive information, such as credit card numbers and account codes, so that it can only be decoded by a vendor with an electronic key. This is a secure form of handling virtual currency, as it allows existing

accounts and payment methods to be used safely on the Internet.

Other Promotional Strategies

You do not need to pay a vendor in order to use the Internet to market your book. Currently, most people use the Internet as more of a library than a shopping mall. Begin by promoting your book for free on the Internet and wait until you have learned the rules of the superhighway before investing money in marketing this way. You can post press releases and other sales tools to *newsgroups*. Newsgroups are bundles of posted files on a related subject that are automatically forwarded from computer to computer along the whole network. Internet surfers specify which lists they are interested in and receive postings automatically.

Internet Etiquette

If you have written a book on skiing, you may reach a potential buyers by posting an ad to the alt.snow.skiing newsgroup. However, you may also get a nasty reply from the readers of the newsgroup if *all* you do is leave an ad on their forum. Be aware that serious Internet users do not take kindly to unabashed promotion and commercialism. Commercial sites on the Internet are a recent phenomenon, and those Internet surfers who have been online for years have established protocol for individuals using noncommercial sites and broadcast E-mailings for advertising. If you are using this medium for flat-out free advertising for your book, or if you broadcast commercial E-mail, you may be *flamed.* This involves clogging up your computer mailbox with nasty letters and exposing you throughout the Internet as an electronic heretic.

If you want to advertise directly, you have to use a commercially sponsored site or be very subtle about self-promotion. An example of proper Internet etiquette would be leaving a useful sample chapter of a book, such as *The Fly-Casting Bible*, on a fishing newsgroup with a short note at the end explaining how to get more information about the book. This way only those interested in your information will see your ad, and they will have gotten more than just a commercial.

Your best approach to the Internet is to explore it first as a tourist, then work on using it as an information resource to support your marketing efforts, just as you would use the library. Once you have a basic idea of how it all works, you can begin to do low-level promotion and marketing for free. Join discussions and news groups, either on publishing or a subject closely related to your book. Look for questions you can answer on these topics or ask questions yourself. When you receive an answer, send an electronic thank you note, along with information on your book and your publishing company. If you are answering a question, you can also slip in a little bit of promotional information.

Keep self-promotion subtle and discuss any promotional ideas you have with an experienced Internet user before carrying them out. The reaction and insight you get can help you to gauge the reaction of the online community.

The Internet is the future of information brokering, electronic publishing, and promotion. This does not mean that you must dedicate a lot of time or resources to using it. The rules are still being written, protocol is being established, and the rewards and drawbacks are still being discovered. Become familiar with the Internet as a browser before committing time to using it as a marketing and promotional vehicle.

Trade Shows

From the Frankfurt Book Fair, the largest book fair in the world, down to a conference for regional history enthusiasts, wherever people gather for the purpose of buying, selling, and discussing books, there are opportunities to promote and market. Even if you have only one title to market, you can still take advantage of these gatherings.

Traditionally, trade shows offer companies servicing the book trade an opportunity to showcase their goods and services. Publishers set up booths stocked with their most recent titles for the buyers to see. Book designers and manufacturers also turn up to solicit accounts from publishers and show off their newest materials and techniques. Rights buyers are there looking for titles that will travel well, either to foreign markets or to movies, TV, audio tapes, and electronic books. Trade buyers collect catalogs, looking for attention-catching covers, and meet with reps.

Cooperative Exhibits

Even if you have only one book to market, you can take advantage of trade shows. Many companies and organizations sponsor cooperative exhibits, either as a service to their members, or for profit. These include regional publishers' associations, national publishers associations, and private companies. Also, small presses sometimes band together for co-op booths at trade shows. You can find calls for co-op partners in trade magazines and newsletters, or you can solicit for partners yourself.

Setting Up an Exhibit

If you are planning to set up a booth at a trade show, do your homework beforehand. If possible, try to attend a similar trade show before setting up your own exhibit. Design and plan your exhibit to be attractive, comfortable, and accessible. Make a list of your goals, such as finding a national distributor or selling foreign rights. Have your most outgoing and knowledgeable staff or friends on hand to help work the booth.

If you are cooperating with another publisher or through an association or exhibit service, try to volunteer to work the booth yourself. This way you can steer buyers in the direction of your book when they show an interest in you, your books, or a subject your books deal with. Be subtly aggressive in approaching passersby with assistance.

Bring all the materials with you to the show, including extra copies of your book, media kits, and media clippings, and stow them someplace out of the way. Bring plenty of business cards, order forms, and book catalogs, if you have them.

The Booth

If you plan to exhibit on your own, or if you will be responsible for the design and setup of the booth, there are a few things you should know. The first is that it can be very expensive to set up even a simple display. There are companies that design and rent convention equipment, from the basic furniture, to signs, shelving, display units, and even entertainment, telecommunications hook-ups, and computer equipment. Because of union rules at trade shows, you will be paying top dollar to employ these services, but the outcome is almost certain to be of professional quality.

If you choose to do it all yourself, you can save a lot of money, but you also run the risk of creating an unprofessional-looking booth. To avoid this, do some advance planning. Find out the dimensions of the booth space, draw up diagrams until you find a good arrangement, and set up the booth beforehand to test its appearance. If you can afford it, it helps to set a theme with color,

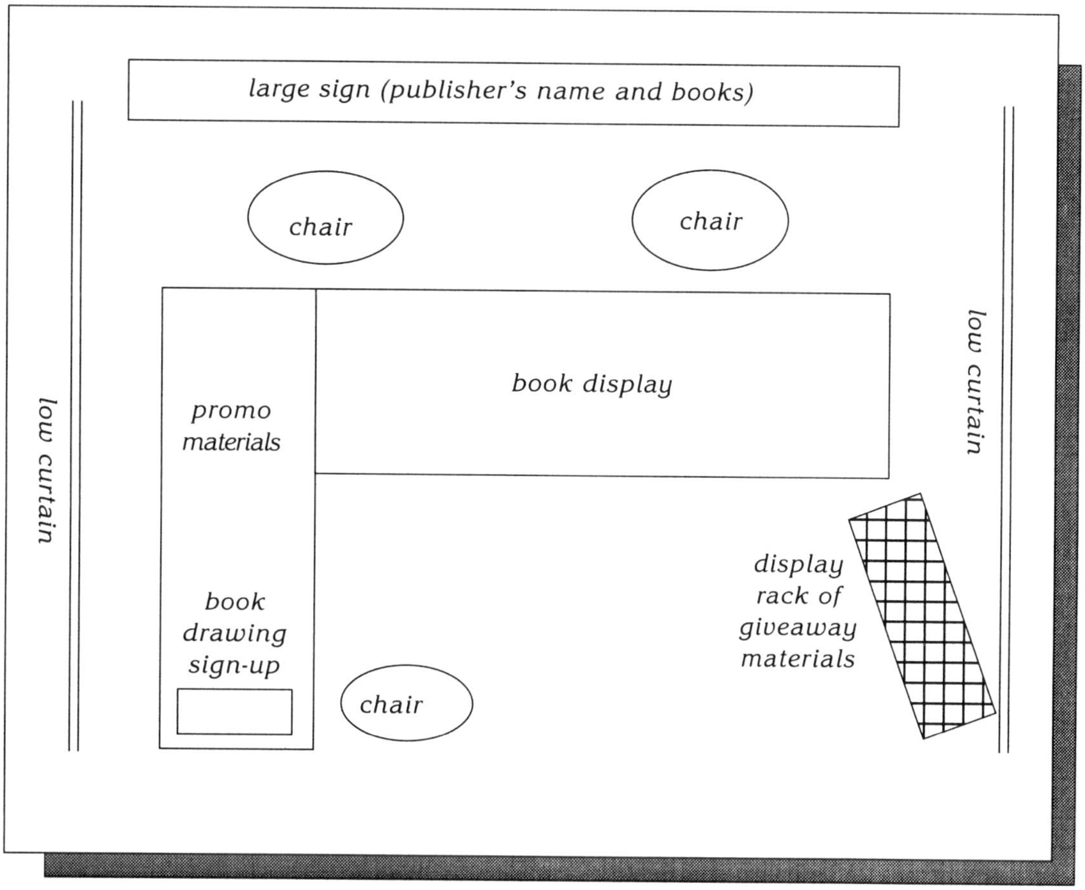

diagram for a basic book show booth

decorations, costumes, or other devices. However, with attention to detail, a bare-minimum display can also be very effective.

The basic requirements are a long, folding table with a fabric covering that reaches the floor on three sides; two to three chairs (convention goers will really appreciate the chance to sit down); a large, neat, well-crafted sign with a stand; display copies of your book; any other relevant merchandise, catalogs, brochures, or handouts that identify you and your book and provide ordering information; and a giveaway item or gimmick to lure people to your display. Make sure you have at least two people at your booth, so that someone is always available to greet browsers if you have an important meeting with a buyer or need to take a food break.

Keep in mind that union rules may limit what you do yourself in the world of conventions and trade shows. Most convention centers require you to hire union workers at union wages for certain tasks, such as carrying anything weighing more than 40 pounds into the display area. Check with the convention organizers as to what you can and cannot do yourself.

Working the Show

Before the convention, try to contact distributors, wholesalers, rights buyers, foreign agents, magazine editors, and anyone else you would like to meet at the event. Explain to them that you will be at the show and try to set up a time to get together. While you are at the convention, take time out to browse the booths — it is a good way to get to know what your colleagues and competitors are up to. Introduce yourself to distributors, buyers, and editors, and the other exhibitors. This is your opportunity to get to know the book trade and its members the easy way, face-to-face and all in one place.

Pick up the more attractive catalogs, brochures, samples, and other promotional items and use them for ideas for promoting your own book. Always ask questions; the professionals are there to provide information.

Conventions and Other Types of Trade Shows

Outside of the book trade, there is still a wealth of opportunity to be taken advantage of at conventions and trade shows. Once you have defined your target audience, their needs and interests, ask yourself: "Is there a trade show or association that services these people?" From history to computers, recreation to job hunting, you will find shows that cover all interests. If, however, you do not want to get your own booth at the Karate Expo, get in touch with the event sponsors. Chances are you will find exhibitors willing to let you "piggyback" your book with theirs.

The reference section of your library is the best place to research associations, trade shows, and special interest organizations. *The Directory of Associations*, *Chase's Annual Events*, and *Trade Shows Worldwide* should help you find what you're looking for. There are companies, as well as most publisher's associations, that offer inexpensive vehicles for exhibiting your book at trade shows. The drawbacks to these are that you are not staffing the booth yourself so you cannot actively promote your own book, and there will be many other titles displayed along with your own.

Researching Resources

There are countless other resources you can use to find customers, opportunities for bulk sales, public relations and marketing ideas, media contacts, cooperative marketing opportunities, supportive author/publisher's associations, contests, exhibitions, and other opportunities.

Information brokers such as Gale Research Company, R. R. Bowker, and Reed Reference Publishing issue directories that list decision makers, business leaders, and sales and marketing contacts by gender, age, race, industry, association, and private and professional interests. These publications include *American Men & Women of Science, Corporate Meeting Planners, Who's Who in American Art, The Retirement Sourcebook, Sporting Goods Register, Gardener's Source Guide,* and hundreds more. There are directories of directories, catalogs of catalogs, fax directories, and specialty "yellow pages." These resources contain the most thorough listings of media contacts and buyers that you can find. All of these directories are available in the reference department of your local library.

Do not try to have it all figured out before going to the library — leave yourself open to new discoveries. Take the time to browse and then dig deep. Remember, research equals opportunity. You will get more solid ideas and leads by poring over an open book than you will by relying on your own experience *(see the Appendix for a bibliography of books and resources)*. Do not hesitate to ask the librarians at the reference desk for help; they are there to assist you and they will lead you to specific reference books they think will help you.

Although research is important to putting together an initial marketing strategy, it is also useful in other stages of book promotion and marketing. For example, you are going to want to research a distributor before signing an exclusive contract. Researching a talk show host by listening to the program and talking to the show's producers will allow you to get the most out of any appearance you make.

Phone research can save you time, money, and frustration if you use it to qualify and verify contacts, names, and addresses before sending materials. "Look before you leap" may be the most important advice you can get as a self-publisher.

15

NAMES, ADDRESSES, AND PUBLICATIONS YOU NEED TO KNOW

Chapter 15

The following lists identify the most important, best known, or the most accessible contacts and companies for each category listed. These contacts are intended to give you a starting point in your marketing and to be used as a basis for further research. They are in no way a complete listing of book trade contacts, and a company's inclusion in this book is not an endorsement of its services. These lists were updated at the time of publication, but are part of a rapidly changing marketplace. All contacts, addresses, and submission protocol should be verified by phone before any materials are sent out.

Distributors

Distributors are companies that contract to sell your book to the book trade and retain a substantial percentage of each sale. They employ sales representatives to sell directly to buyers and typically require the exclusive sales rights to the U.S. book trade.

Associated Publishers Group
1501 County Hospital Road
Nashville, TN 37218
Phone 615-254-2450 Fax 615-254-2456

Atrium Publishing Group
Brenda Plowman, Acquisitions
3356 Coffey Lane
Santa Rosa, CA 95403
Toll Free 800-275-2606 Fax 707-995-1814

NACSCORP
Krista Long, Acquisitions
528 E. Lorain Street
Oberlin, OH 44074-1298
Phone 216-775-7777

Consortium Book Sales & Distribution
Attn: Randall Beek
1045 Westgate Drive
Saint Paul, MN 55114-1065
Phone 612-221-9035

Inbook Distributors
David Wilk, President
140 Commerce Street
East Haven, CT 06512
Phone 203-467-4257 Fax 203-469-7697

Independent Publishers Group
Curt Matthews, President
814 N. Franklin Avenue
Chicago, IL 60610
Phone 312-337-0747 Fax 312-337-5985

The Talman Company, Inc.
Marilee Talman, President
131 Spring Street, Suite 201 E-N
New York, NY 10012
Phone 212-431-7175

Lifetime Books
Attn: Don Lessne
2131 Hollywood Boulevard
Hollywood, FL 33020
Phone 800-771-3355

Login Publishers Consortium
Dominique Raccah/Mitchell Rogatz
1436 W. Randolph Street, 2nd Floor
Chicago, IL 60607
Phone 312-733-8228 Fax 312-666-2680

National Book Network
Jed Lyons, President
4720 Boston Way #A
Lanham, MD 20706-4310
Phone 301-459-3366 Fax 301-459-2118

Partners Book Distributing
Vicky Lynn Eaves, President
720 E. Shiawassee
Lansing, MI 48912
Phone 517-485-0366

New Product Acquisitions
Publishers Group West
Corporate Offices
4065 Hollis Street
Emeryville, CA 94662
Phone 510-658-3453 Fax 510-658-1834

Samuel French Trade
New Title Acquisitions
7623 Sunset Boulevard
Hollywood, CA 90046
Phone 213-876-0570

SCB Distributors
Aaron Silverman, President
15612 S. New Century Drive
Gardena, CA 90248
Phone 310-532-9400

Seven Hills Book Distributors
Ion Itescu, President
49 Central Avenue, Suite 300
Cincinnati, OH 45202
Phone 513-381-3881

Southern Publishers Group
Tom Moore, Acquisitions Director
147 Corporate Way
Pelham, AL 35124
Phone 800-628-0903 Fax 205-664-6984

Spring Arbor Distributors
Attn: Dick Malone
10885 Textile Road
Belleville, MI 48111
Phone 313-481-0900

Gryphon House, Inc.
Contact: Larry Clapham
PO Box 207
Beltsville, MD 20704-0207
Phone 301-595-9500

Music Book Services
Warren Hicks, General Manager
16295 NW 13th Avenue, Suite B
Miami, FL 33169
Toll Free 800-555-2626

Foreign & International Distributors

These companies distribute books to foreign markets and may be useful in marketing foreign rights.

E.J. Dwyer (Australia) PTY Ltd
Attn: Anthony Dwyer
Unit 13, Perry Park, 33 Maddox Street
Alexandria, Sydney, NSW, Australia 2015
Phone 61-2-5502355

Fastlane Distribution Limited
Attn: Stephen Reiter
Park House, 15-23 Greenhill Crescent
Watford, Herts, UK WD1 8QU
Phone 441-923-211343

Laval Publisher/Distributor, Inc.
1565 Montee Masson
Laval, Quebec, Canada H7E 4P2
Phone 514-661-4242

Limerock Books, Inc.
Attn: Christopher Vaughan
41 Perry Avenue

Norwalk, CT 06850
Phone 203-840-6629

Koch, Neff & Oetinger
Verlagsausliefrung GmbH
Schockenriedstraße 39
D-70565 Stuttgart. Germany
Phone 49-711-78990 Fax: 49-711-7899-1010

Swindon Book Company Ltd.
Ms. Dorothy Hui
13-15 Lock Road
Kowloon, Hong Kong
Phone 8552-2376-2062

China Book Import Centre
PO Box 2825
PRC-Beijing 1000044
Phone 86-1-841-6126

Wholesalers

Wholesalers, like distributors, contract to sell your book to the book trade, but take a smaller percentage of each sale. Wholesalers do not employ sales representatives or require an exclusive agreement and usually service a regional territory. If you cannot secure a distributor, you should rely on several wholesalers to reach markets across the nation.

ASI Distributors
Henry Weingarten,
350 Lexington Avenue
New York, NY 10016
Phone 212-949-7211

Baker & Taylor Company
Julia Quinones, Buyer, Small & New Presses
Susan Tomae, Buyer, Small & New Presses
652 E Main Street
Bridgewater, NJ 08807-0920
Phone 908-218-3803 or 908-685-3006
Fax 908-218-3980

Bookpeople
Sheridan McCarthy, Small Press Titles
7900 Edgewater Drive
Oakland, CA 94621-2004
Phone 510-632-4700 Fax 510-632-1281

The Booksource
Tim Hand, Small Press Acquisitions
1230 Macklind
St. Louis, MO 63108
Phone 314-647-0600 Fax 314-652-1635

The Bookmen
John Kudrle, Paperback Buyer
525 N. Third Street
Minneapolis, MN 55401-1296
Phone 612-341-3333 Fax 612-341-2903

Ingram Book Company
Wanda Smith, Manager of Public Relations
Debbie Pressnel, Division Manager, Children's
Products & Marketing
One Ingram Blvd.
Lavergne, TN 37086-1986
Phone 615-793-5000 ext. 7563
Fax 615-793-3825

New Leaf Distributing
Lisa Rogo, Small Press Buyer
401 Thornton Road
Lithia Springs, GA 30057
Phone 770-948-7845 Fax 800-326-1066

Pacific Pipeline Inc
Troy Ryan, New Title Acquisitions
8030 S. 228th
Kent, WA 98032-1171
Phone 206-872-5523 Fax 206-872-0849

Publishers Distribution Service
Clay Cronin, Vice President, Operations
6893 Sullivan Road

Grawn, MI 49637
Phone 616-276-5196 Fax 800-950-9793

Small Press Distribution Inc
Steve Dickison, Book Buyer
1814 San Pablo Avenue
Berkeley, CA 94702
Phone 510-549-3336 Fax 510-549-2201

Bookazine Book Distributor
Tom DeMarco, Small Press Buyer
75 Hook Road
Bayonne, NJ 07002
Toll Free 800-221-8112

Children's Small Press Collection
Attn: Kathleen Baxter
719 N. Fourth Avenue
Ann Arbor, MI 48104
Toll Free 800-221-8056

Sunbelt Publications
Heather Stevenson, Senior Buyer
1250 Fayette Street
El Cajon, CA 92020
Phone 619-258-4911

Moving Books, Inc.
Allison Radke-Bogen, Acquisitions
948 S. Doris Street
Seattle, WA 98108
Phone 206-762-1750

Golden-Lee
Attn: Manie Barron
1000 Dean Street
Brooklyn, NY 11238-3393
Phone 718-857-6333

DeVorss & Co.
Attn: Hedda Lark
PO Box 550

Marina del Rey, CA 92094-0550
Phone 213-870-7478

Koen Book Distributors, Inc.
Attn: Sheila Kowalsky
10 Twosome Drive
PO Box 600
Moorestown, NJ 08057
Phone 609-235-4444

Non-Traditional Markets

A non-traditional market is generally defined as any outlet that buys your title in bulk, yet makes less than half its income from book sales. These can include gift shops, retail outlets, social, political, and religious organizations, clubs, and bulk product wholesalers.

Advanced Marketing Services
Allen Orso, New Title Acquisition
5880 Oberlin Drive #400
San Diego, CA 92121
Phone 619-457-2500 Fax 619-452-0532

Linda Nelson, Book Buyer
Plan-a-Gram
33 S. Sixth Street
Minneapolis, MN 55240
Phone 612-304-8572

Smithsonian Museum Shops
Norma Ryan, Book Buyer
Capital Gallery Building #295B
600 Maryland Avenue SW, Room 295
Washington, DC 20024
Phone 202-287-3563 x133 Fax 202-287-3080

The Nature Company
Tracy Fortini, Book Buyer
Corporate Offices
750 Hearst Avenue
Berkeley, CA 94710-1927
Phone 510-644-1337 Fax 510-841-8679

Eastern Mountain Sports
Jeana White, Book Buyer
Book Department
One Vose Farm Road
Peterborough, NH 03458
Phone 603-924-7231

Costco Wholesale
Pennie Clark, Book Buyer
999 Lake Drive
Issaquah, WA 98027
Phone 206-313-8524 Fax 206-828-8101

Internet Sources

The following resources include Internet service providers, which connect your computer to the Internet, and Internet sites, including bookstores, publishers' forums, and other relevant services.

BookZone*
PO Box 2228
Scottsdale, AZ 85252
Phone 602-481-9737 Toll-Free 800-536-6162
**Lists your title, forwards orders, charges no discounts or fees*

*Title Net**
Inforonics
550 Newtown Road
Littleton, MA 01460
Phone 508-486-8976 Fax 508-486-0027
E-mail info@ifor.com
**Internet Product Catalog for Publishers*

Online Bookstore
Karen Fuhrman, Editorial, Inc.
Whistlestop Mall, Rockport, ME 01966
Phone 508-546-7346 Fax 508-546-9807
E-mail Laura@editorial.com

The Online Bookstore — READ USA Inc.
365B Main Street
Center Moriches, NY 11934
Phone 516-878-6675

Bookstacks Unlimited
Charles M Stack, President
200 Public Square #26-4600
Cleveland, OH 44114-2301
Modem 216-861-0469 E-mail Telnet books.com

America Online
Jonathon Bulkeley, Vice President, Advertising & Shopping
8619 Westwood Center Drive
Vienna, VA 22182-2285
Phone 703-448-8700 Toll free 800-827-6364

Author Book Net *
Bestsellers Online**
Gaughen Public Relations Agency
Mike Frick
226 East Canon Perdido, Suite B
Santa Barbara, CA 93103
Phone 805-965-8482
Internet http://www.bestsellers.com/bestsellers
**Fax-on-demand information broadcaster*
***Internet display site*

Bibliophile Online*
301 Arizona Avenue #200
Santa Monica, CA 90401
Fax 310-394-9076 Modem 310-394-7710
**Electronic bulletin board service*

BibiloBytes
Glen Hauman, Publisher
1130 Willow Avenue, 3rd Floor
Hoboken, NJ 07030-3222
Phone 201-222-1600
E-mail hauman@bb.com *or* BBytes@aol.com

Smart Pages™ Direct*
Attn: Books Direct Product Manager
Greyden Press
2020 Builders Place
Columbus, OH 43204
Toll Free (800) 881-9421
**MAPA (Mid America Publishers Association) Home Page*

Bookwire*
E-mail jbennett@bookwire.com
Internet http://www.bookwire.com
**Online forum and directory for book trade and publishing professionals*

Library Wholesalers

The following companies function as book wholesalers, stocking titles and filling orders from libraries. While most of these companies will only take a small percentage of each sale, some may expect 50 percent or more.

Quality Books Inc.
Michael Huston, Product Development Specialist
1003 W. Pines Road
Oregon, IL 61061-9680
Phone 815-732-4450 Fax 815-732-4499

Library Book Selection Service
Larry Efaw, Manager
2714 McGraw Drive
PO Box 277
Bloomington, IL 61704-0277
Phone 309-663-1411 Fax 309-664-0059

Murr's Library Service
Jane Murr
4045 E. Palm Lane, Suite #5
Phoenix, AZ 85008
Phone 602-273-1121

Follett Library Book Company
Patti Hall, Director of Purchasing
4506 NW Highway
Route 14 & 31
Crystal Lake, IL 60014
Phone 815-455-1101

Midwest Library Service
Regina Laws, Book Buyer
11443 St. Charles Rock Road
Bridgeton, MO 63044-2789
Phone 314-739-3100

Mumford Library Book Sales
Douglas McNamara, President
7847 Bayberry Road
Jacksonville, FL 32256
Phone 904-737-2649

Major Trade Reviewers

These are the review sources book buyers turn to for recommendation and guidance in their seasonal buying choices. These are the major outlets for *advance reviews*; you must submit titles for consideration at least three to four months in advance of the book's publication date.

Publishers Weekly
Diane Roback, Editor, Children's Books
Dulcey Brainard, Editor, How-To Books
Sybil Steinberg, Editor, Fiction Forecasts
Genevieve Stuttaford, Editor, Nonfiction Hardcover
Maria Simson, Editor, Paperback Forecasts
249 W. 17th Street
New York, NY 10011-5301
Phone 212-463-6758 Fax 212-463-6631

Small Press Magazine
Tom Bodus, Editor
121 E. Front Street, 4th Floor
Traverse City, MI 49684
Phone 616-933-0445

New York Review of Books
Robert Silvers, Editor
Barbara Epstein, Editor
250 W. 57th Sreet #1321
New York, NY 10107-0169
Phone 212-757-8070 Fax 212-333-5374

"Voice Literary Supplement"
The Village Voice
Lee Smith, Editor
36 Cooper Square
New York, NY 10003
Phone 212-475-3300, Ext. 2110

The Bloomsbury Review
Attn: Tom Auer
1028 Bannock Street
Denver, CO 80204-4037
Phone 303-892-0620

American Bookseller
Dan Cullen, Editor
American Booksellers Association
828 S. Broadway
Tarrytown, NY 10591
Phone 914-591-2665

The New York Times Book Review
Attn: Charles McGrath
229 West 43rd Street
New York, NY 10036
Phone 212-556-7088

Booklist
Bill Ott, Editor/Publisher
Bonnie Smothers, Adult Books Editor
Sally Estes, Books for Youth Editor
American Library Association
50 East Huron Street
Chicago, IL 60611-2795
Phone 312-944-6780 Fax 312-440-0901

Choice
Rebecca Bartlett Fischer, Book Editor, Humanities Selections
Helen MacLam, Subject Editor, History & Sociology
Francine Graf, Subject Editor, Business, Economics, Political Science
100 Riverview Center
Middletown, CT 06457
Phone 203-347-6933 Fax 203-346-8586

Current Books Magazine
Edwin S. Grosevenor, Editor
PO Box 34468
Bethesda, MD 20827
Phone 301-530-8200

Feminist Bookstore News
Carol Seejay, Editor
2358 Market Street
San Francisco, CA 94114
Phone 415-626-1556 Fax 415-626-8970

*The Horn Book Magazine**
Anita Silvey, Editor
11 Beacon Street
Boston, MA 02108
Phone 617-227-1555 Fax 617-523-0299
**Children's books only*

Kirkus Reviews
Kimberly Olson Fakih, Editor, Children's Books
Anne Larsen, Editor, Fiction Books
Sarah Gold, Editor, Nonfiction Books
200 Park Avenue S #1118
New York, NY 10003-1543
Phone 212-777-4554 Fax 212-979-1352

Library Journal
Francine Fialkoff, Editor
249 W. 17th Street
New York, NY 10011-5301
Phone 212-463-6819 Fax 212-242-6987

ALA Booklist
"Up Front," Advance Reviews
50 E. Huron Street
Chicago, IL 60611
Phone 312-944-6780

San Francisco Review of Books
Paschal Fowlkes
126 S. Park
San Francisco, CA 94107
Phone 415-543-7372

Utne Reader
Josh Glenn
Book Editor
1624 Harmon Place #330
Minneapolis, MN 55403
Phone 612-338-5040

The Washington Post
Nina King, Book Editor
"Book World"
1150 15th Street NW
Washington, DC 20071
Phone 202-334-7881

USA Today
Attn: Robert Wilson
1000 Wilson Boulevard
Arlington, VA 22229
Phone 703-276-3400

The Boston Book Review
Attn: Theoharis C. Theoharis
30 Brattle Street, 4th Floor
Cambridge,MA 02138
Phone 617-497-0344

Small Press Book Review
Attn: Henry Berry
Greenfield Press
PO Box 176

Southport, CT 06490-0176
Phone 203-268-4878

Los Angeles Times Book Review
Attn: Sonja Bolle
Times Mirror Square
Los Angeles, CA 90053
Phone 213-237-7778

Word: The Literary Magazine
M. Mark, Editor-in-Chief
340 W. Broadway
New York, NY 10012
Phone 212-343-9030

The Bookwatch
Attn: Diane C. Donovan
166 Miramir Avenue
San Francisco, CA 94112
Phone 415-587-7009

Book Clubs

A book club contract can help make your book a best-seller. Book clubs buy in bulk, at reasonable discounts, and do not return books. Some book clubs will print their own edition of your title for sale through their mail-order channels. Submit your clean, well-edited manuscript and other relevant materials as far in advance of the book's publication date as possible.

Book-of-the-Month Club
Tracy Brown, Editor-in-Chief
Greg Tobin, Paperback Editor
Time-Life Building
1271 Avenue of the Americas
New York, NY 10020-1368
Phone 212-522-4200

Children's Choice Book Club
Vita Jimenez, Editor-in-Chief
Newbridge Book Clubs
333 E. 38th Street
New York, NY 10016-2745
Phone 212-455-5000

Doubleday Book Club
Sam Blum, Editor
1540 Broadway, 23rd Floor
New York, NY 10036
Phone 212-782-7200 Fax 212-984-7450

History Book Club
Kathleen McDermott, Assistant Editor
BOMC/Time-Life Building
1271 Avenue of the Americas
New York, NY 10020-1368
Phone 212-522-4200

How-To Book Club
Kate Hertzog, Manager
McGraw-Hill/Tab Book Clubs
PO Box 40
Blue Ridge Summit, PA 17294-0850
Phone 717-794-2191

Quality Paperback Book Club
Judith Estrin, Small Press Buyer
BOMC/Time-Life Building
1271 Avenue of the Americas
New York, NY 10020-1368
Phone 212-522-4200

College Bookstores

These companies operate chains of bookstores on college campuses across the United States. Like other chain stores, all the buying for college bookstore chains is done centrally. These stores cater to a specific target markets of college and university students and professors.

College Bookstores of America*
Robert Iverson, President
Matthews & McCoy
11559 Rock Island Court
Maryland Heights, MO 63043
Phone 314-432-1400 Fax 314-432-7044
**These stores buy on an individual basis. Call for a list of locations.*

Follett College Stores
Bill Scharnweber, Trade Books
400 W. Grand Avenue
Elmhurst, IL 60126
Phone 708-279-2330 Fax 708-279-2569

Wallace's College Bookstores
Attn: Dale Sutton
928 Nandino Boulevard
Lexington, KY 40511
Phone 606-254-8861

Mail Order Catalogs

Like book clubs, mail order catalogs contract to sell books to their own customers. They buy in bulk, at relatively low discounts, and do not return books. The earlier you submit your book for consideration, the better, but call ahead for specific submissions policies.

ARE Press
Jon Robertson, Manager of Acquisitions
68th & Atlantic Avenue
Virginia Beach, VA 23451
Phone 804-428-3588 Toll free 800-723-1112

Atlantic Monthly Press
Book Buyer
841 Broadway
New York, NY 10003
Phone 212-614-7850

Barnes & Noble Catalog
Donna Sepkowski, Buyer
1 Pond Road
Rockleigh, NJ 07647
Phone 201-767-8844

Big Books From Small Presses
Amy Crawford, Acquisitions
Upper Access, Inc.
PO Box 457 Upper Access Road
Hinesburg, VT 05461
Phone 802-482-2988 Fax 802-482-3125

Blacklist Mail Order
Attn: Merchandise Director
475 Valencia
San Francisco, CA 94107
Phone 415-255-0388

Opportunities for Learning
Andrew Love, Marketing Manager
941 Hickory Lane
Mansfield, OH 44901-8103
Phone 419-589-1700

A Common Reader
James Mustich Jr., President
The Akadine Press Inc.
141 Tompkins Avenue
Pleasantville, NY 10570
Phone 914-747-0777 Fax 914-747-0778

Entrepreneur's Bookshop
Helen Hecker, Merchandise Director
Twin Peaks Press
PO Box 129
Vancouver, WA 98666
Phone 360-694-2462 Fax 360-696-3210

The Lighter Side
New Product Department
Johnson-Smith Company
4514 19th Street Court East
Bradenton, FL 34203
Phone 813-747-2356 Fax 813-776-1834

Paperback Catalog Service
Rex Coston, Buyer
170 Lake Shore Road
Roaring Brook Lane
Putnam Valley, NY 10579-9729
Phone 914-528-8227

Things You Never Knew Existed
Johnson Smith Co
New Products Division
4514 19th Sreet, Court East
Bradenton, FL 34203-3799
Phone 813-747-5566 Fax 813-746-7896

Uniquity Catalog
Shirley Sing, Buyer
PO Box 10
Galt, CA 95632-0010
Phone 209-745-2111 Fax 209-745-4430

Talk Show Hosts

The best publicity money cannot buy is an author appearance on a nationally syndicated daytime talk show. Oprah Winfrey has made several books into best sellers. Approach the producers for these shows in a professional manner, and sell them on your ability to grab an audience's attention or to create controversy that will be lively and entertaining.

Oprah Winfrey
The Producers
Harpo, Inc.
Box 909715
Chicago, IL 60690
Phone 312-633-0808 Fax 312-633-1515

David Letterman Show
Sheila Rogers, Talent Coordinator
CBS-TV
1697 Broadway
New York, NY 10019
Phone 212-975-5300 Fax 212-975-4780

Phil Donahue
Suzy Stein, Producer
NBC-TV
1 Penn Plaza, Suite 2225-35
New York, NY 10119
Phone 212-664-6501 Fax 212-757-5386

Geraldo Rivera Show
Jose Pretlow, Executive Producer
Investigative News Group
524 W. 57th Street
New York, NY 10019
Phone 212-265-8520 Fax 212-581-8196

Good Morning America
Patti Neger, Segment Producer
ABC-TV
147 Columbus Avenue
New York, NY 10023
Phone 212-456-5900 Fax 212-456-5962

Live With Regis and Kathie Lee
Michael Gilman, Executive Producer
WABC-TV
7 Lincoln Square, 5th Floor
New York, NY 10023
Phone 212-887-3054 Fax 212-469-5249

The Jenny Jones Show
Susan Schreiner, Director of Research
WMAQ-TV
454 N. Columbus Drive, 4th Floor
Chicago, IL 60611
Phone 312-836-9400 Fax 312-836-9473

Sally Jesse Raphael
Amy Rosenblum, Senior Producer
515 W. 57th Street, 3rd Floor
New York, NY 10019
Phone 212-582-1722 Fax 212-265-1953

The Today Show
Andrea Smith, Producer, Authors/Books
NBC-TV
30 Rockefeller Plaza #304
New York, NY 10112
Phone 212-664-4602

The Tonight Show
Todd Yasui, Talent Coordinator
NBC-TV
3000 W. Alameda Avenue
Burbank, CA 91523
Phone 818-840-4444 Fax 818-840-2240

News Services & Major Newspapers

News services write and distribute news stories that are picked up by newspapers around the world. Send media kits to news services regularly. Also contact the book review editors of the following newspapers. Other appropriate section editors should be approached to obtain a mention, feature article, or event listings. Send media releases frequently, stressing news-related and timely aspects of your book.

Associated Press
221 S. Figueroa Avenue
Los Angeles, CA 90012
Phone 213-626-1200

United Press International
2 Penn Plaza, 18th Floor
New York, NY 10121
Phone 212-560-1100

Universal Press Syndicate
4900 Main Street, 9th Floor
Kansas City, MO 64112
Phone 816-932-6600

Tribune Media Service
435 North Michigan Avenue
Suite 1500
Chicago IL 60611
Toll Free 800-245-6536

Newspaper Enterprise Association
200 Madison Avenue
New York, NY 10016-0079
Phone 212-293-8500

New York Daily News
Sherryl Connelly, Book Editor
450 W. 33rd Street
New York, NY 10001
Phone 212-210-2100

Los Angeles Times
Times Mirror Square
Los Angeles, CA 90053
Phone 213-237-5000

San Francisco Examiner
Joan Smith, Book Editor
110 Fifth Street, PO Box 7260
San Francisco, CA 94120
Phone 415-777-2424

Denver Post
Genn Giffin, Book Editor
1560 Broadway, PO Box 1709
Denver, CO 80201
Phone 303-820-1010

Washington Post
Nina King, Book Editor
1150 15th Street NW
Washington, DC 20071-0001
Phone 202-334-6000

Chicago Tribune
Larry Kart, Book Editor
435 N. Michigan Avenue #400
Chicago, IL 60611-4022
Phone 312-222-3232

Boston Globe
Gail Caldwell, Book Editor/Reviewer
135 Morrissey Boulevard, PO Box 2378
Boston, MA 02107-2378
Phone 617-929-2897

Minneapolis Star Tribune
Dave Wood, Book Editor
425 Portland Aveune South
Minneapolis, MN 55488-0001
Phone 612-673-4000

Independent Bookstores

Unlike the chains, these bookstores can order books directly from the publisher, and are independently owned and operated.

Prairie Lights Books*
Paul Ingram, Book Buyer
15 S. Dubuque Street
Iowa City, IA 52240
Phone 319-337-2681
**Ask about appearing on their radio program*

Powell's Books
Attn: Order Office
1005 W. Burnside
Portland, OR 97209
Phone 503-228-4651

A Clean, Well-Lighted Place
Leona Weiss, Owner/Buyer
601 Van Ness Avenue
San Francisco, CA 94102
Phone 415-441-6670

Odegard Books of St. Paul
Lisa Hamnes, Purchasing Manager
857 Grand Avenue
St. Paul, MN 55105-3377
Phone 612-222-2711

Olsson's Books & Records
1239 Wisconsin Avenue NW
Washington, DC 20007
Phone 202-338-9544

Strand Book Stores
Fred Bass
828 Broadway at 12th Street
New York, NY 10003-4805
Phone 212-473-1452

Barbara's Bookstore
Pat Peterson, Buyer
3130 N. Broadway
Chicago, IL 60657
Phone 312-281-2333

The Tattered Cover Bookstore
Gordon Pierce, Buyer
1536 Wynkoop Street
Denver, CO 80202
Phone 303-322-7727

National Bookstore Chains

These companies operate many stores throughout the country, under a single corporate name and ownership. Buying is done through centralized buying offices, with a single buyer often selecting titles (either by subject or category, such as fiction or paperbacks) for a specific region or chain-wide. Some chains will not establish a vendor account for a small press, and will only buy a book through wholesale or distribution channels. Individual stores will usually set up booksignings and events.

B. Dalton/Barnes & Noble
Marcella Smith, Small Press Acquisitions
122 Fifth Avenue
New York, NY 10011-5605
Phone 212-633-3300

B. Dalton/Barnes & Noble*
George Carner, Small Press Assistant
122 Fifth Avenue
New York, NY 10011-5605
Phone 212-675-0413
**Many specialized buyers, call for specific buyers' names and titles*

Crown Books
Book Review Department
Corporate Offices
3300 75th Avenue
Landover, MD 20785
Phone 301-731-1200

Waldenbooks*
New Press Acquisitions
515 E. Liberty Street
Ann Arbor, MI 48104
Phone 313-913-1100
**Call for specific submissions procedures*

American Opinion Bookstores
David Martin, General Manager
770 Westhill Boulevard
PO Box 8040
Appleton, WI 54913
Phone 414-749-3780

B. Dalton Bookseller
Julie Arthur-Sherman, Regional Book Seller
7505 Metro Boulevard
Minneapolis, MN 55435-3990
Phone 612-893-7869 Fax 612-893-7245

B. Dalton Bookseller
Karen Perea, Regional Book Buyer
Century Center Building
26522 Alameda #360
Mission Viejo, CA 92691
Phone 714-582-7556 or 714-364-5232

Coles Bookstores
Helen Babiak, Book Reviewer
90 Ronson Drive
Etobicoke, ON M9W 1C1
Canada
Phone 416-243-3132 Fax 416-243-8964

Crown Books
Jeanne Herrick, Softcover Buyer
Corporate Offices
3300 75th Avenue
Landover, MD 20785
Phone 301-731-1263 or 301-731-1200

Bookland Stores
Sandra Wilson, Hardcover Buyer
Staci Moscovitz, Softcover Buyer
PO Box 19768
Birmingham, AL 35219
Phone 205-942-3737

Publisher's Associations

Designed to support small publishers through information, resources, networking, cooperative efforts, publisher's associations can be great sources of support and opportunity. Each region of the United States has its own publishers' association, complete with local chapters. There are also many specialized interest publishers' groups, servicing publishers of specific materials as well as those who share a common ethnic, religious, gender, or business background. Ask for a listing of your books in the member's newsletter when you join.

COSMEP, Inc.
The International Association of Independent Publishers
PO Box 420703
San Francisco, CA 94142-0703
Phone 415-922-9490

Mid America Publishers Association (MAPA)
Jerry Kromberg, Executive Director
PO Box 30242
Lincoln, NE 68503-0242
Phone 402-421-9666

Publishers Association of The South
Molly Burns, Director
PO Box 43533
Birmingham, AL 35243
Phone 205-967-4387

Book Publishers Northwest
Duse McLean
Thistle Press
13106 NE 38th Place
Bellevue, WA 98005
Phone 206-885-3173

National Association of Independent Publishers
Betsy Lampe, Director
PO Box 430
Highland City, FL 33846-0430
Phone 813-648-4420

Multicultural Publishing and Education Council
Rennie Mau, President
2280 Grass Valley, Highway #181
Auburn, CA 95603
Phone 916-889-4438 Fax 916-888-0690
E-Mail mpec@aol.com

Women's National Book Association
The Bookwoman
160 Fifth Avenue
New York, NY 10010
Phone 212-675-7805

Publishers Marketing Association
Jan Nathan, Director
2401 Pacific Coast Highway #102
Hermosa Beach, CA 92054
Phone 310-372-2732

Small Press Centers

These organizations provide a showcase for authors, self-publishers, and small presses to exhibit and promote their works.

Poets House
72 Spring Street, 2nd Floor
New York, NY 10012
Phone 212-431-7920

PEN American Center
Pamela Pearce
568 Broadway
New York, NY 10012-3225
Phone 212-334-1660

Small Press Center
20 W. 44th Street
New York, NY 10036
Phone 212-764-7021

Direct Marketing, Mail Order, and Mailing List Distributors

These companies sell and rent list of contacts, broken down by demographic criteria, and often provide other marketing or mail order-related service.

Book Publishing Resource Guide
Ad-Lib Publications
51½ W. Adams Street
Fairfield, IA 52556
Phone 515-472-6617 Fax 800-669-0773

Direct Mail List: Rates and Data
Standard Rate and Data Service
1700 W. Higgins Road
Des Plaines, IL 60018
Phone 708-375-5000

Cahners Direct Mail Service
List Manager
249 W. 17th Street
New York, NY 10011
Phone 212-337-7176

Best Mailing Lists, Inc.
888 S. Craycroft Road
Tucson, AZ 85711
Phone 602-745-0200

Publisher's Representatives & Professional Marketing Services

The following companies provide sales and marketing services especially for book publishers. The services provided by these companies can be expensive, and are often geared toward larger presses.

Como Sales Company, Inc.
Attn: Sam Herman
799 Broadway
New York, NY 10003
Phone 212-677-1720

DBP & Associates
Denise Buzy-Pucheu, President
31 Merritt Street
Port Chester, NY 10573
Phone 914-937-5558

Fast Forward Marketing, Inc.
Attn: Steve Wallace
3420 Ocean Park Boulevard #3075
Santa Monica, CA 90405
Phone 310-396-4434

Heinecken & Associates, Ltd.
Ted Heinecken
1733 N. Mohawk Street
Chicago, IL 60614
Phone 312-649-9181

International Publishers Marketing
Azad Ajamian, President
13950 Park Center Road
Herndon, VA 22071
Phone 703-689-0303

KSB Promotions
Kate Bandos, President
55 Honey Creek, NE
Ada, MI 49301-9768
Phone 616-676-0758

National Association of Independent
Publishers' Representatives
Attn: Ralph Woodward
Zackendorf Towers, Suite 157
111 E. 14th Street
New York, NY 10003
Phone 508-877-5328

Rising Star Promotions
Attn: Dan Heise
929 Elmwood Avenue
Evanston, IL 60202
Phone 847-869-6410

Sensible Solutions, Inc.
275 Madison Avenue, Suite 1518
New York, NY 10016
Phone 212-687-1761 Fax 212-986-3218

Cooperative Marketing Programs

These companies offer opportunities for cooperative marketing, in which two or more publishers pool their resources in order to lower the cost of marketing ventures.

Rights from USA Review
Jan Nathan, Director
Publishers Marketing Association
2401 Pacific Coast Highway #102
Hermosa Beach, CA 90254
Phone 310-372-2732

Combined Book Exhibit*
Jon Malinowski, President
277 White Street
Buchanan, NY 10511
Phone 914-739-7500 Fax 914-739-7575
E-mail cbe@interserv.com
**This company provides opportunities to exhibit at major and specialized book-related trade shows.*

Interviews & Reviews Magazine
Saundra Kreeger, Director of Marketing
Media Advocates
2218 Bamboo Street
Mesquite, TX 75150

Midwest Co-op Marketing
Sherry Wells
Lawells Publishing
PO Box 1338
Royal Oaks, MI 48068-1338
Phone 810-543-5297

Research Sources

These companies publish directories, listings, qualified mailing lists, and other information resources. They are the largest providers of information resources to the publishing industry. Some of these companies offer specific marketing services in addition to information and resources. Included after each listing are the most important resources they publish.

Bacon's Information
332 S. Michigan Avenue #900
Chicago, IL 60604-4301
Phone 312-922-2400
Bacon's Radio/TV Directory; Bacon's Publicity Checker

Cahners Direct Mail Service
(R. R. Bowker Mailing Lists)
245 West 17th Street
New York, NY 10011
Phone 212-337-7164

U.S. Industrial Directory
Gale Research Company
835 Penobscot Building
Detroit, MI 48226-4094
Phone 313-961-2242
Publishers Directory, Encyclopedia of Association National, Directory of Special Libraries and Information Centers, Gale Directory of Publications, Regional State and Local Organizations

R. R. Bowker Company
121 Chanlon Road
New Providence, NJ 07974
Phone 908-665-2818
Books in Print, Literary Market Place, Distributors and Wholesalers of the United States, American Book Trade Directory, American Library Directory, Marquis Who's Who Series, Ulrich's International Periodicals Directory

H. W. Wilson Co.
920 University Avenue
Bronx, NY 10452
Phone 212-588-8400
Readers' Guide to Periodical Literature, Cumulative Book Index, Book Review Digest, Business Periodicals Index, Public Library Catalog

Author's and Speaker's Registers/ Bureaus

These registers provide listings of speakers by subject and profession. Journalists, event planners, and producers rely on these registers to find experts, sources, and spokespeople for interviews and background information.

Yearbook of Experts, Authorities & Spokespersons
Mitchell P. Davis
2233 Wisconsin Avenue NW #406-P
Washington, DC 20007-4104

Contemporary Authors
Gale Research Company
835 Penobscot Building
Detroit, MI 48226
Phone 313-961-2242

National Speakers Association
Sara Hayden, Editor
Professional Speaker Magazine
1500 S. Priest Drive
Tempe AZ 85281
Phone 602-968-2552

The Author's Guild
Paul Aiken, Executive Director
Author's Guild Bulletin
330 W. 42nd Street
New York, NY 10036
Phone 212-563-5904

Five Star Speakers Trainers & Consultants
Nancy Lauterbach, President
8685 W. 96th Street
Overland Park, KS 66212
Phone 913-648-6480

National Speakers Bureau
Review Committee
222 Wisconsin Avenue
Lake Forest, IL 60045
Phone 708-295-1122

World Class Resource Management Group
Joseph Kessler, Kessler Management International
10747 Wilshire Boulevard, #807
Los Angeles, CA 90024-4432
Phone 310-824-3333

Reference Bibliography

The following books will assist you in finding contacts, answering specific questions, and developing strategies for selling to specific markets. Titles are available in local bookstores and libraries.

Applebaum, Judith, *How to Get Happily Published,* Fourth Edition, (Harper & Row, 1992) ISBN: 0-0627-1544-5

Applebaum, Judith & Janovic, Florence, *The Writer's Workbook: A Full and Friendly Guide to Boosting Your Book's Sales,* (Pushcart Press, 1991) ISBN: 0-916366-69-3

Bodian, Nat G., *Book Marketing Handbook: Tips and Techniques,* Vols. I & II, (R.R. Bowker, 1980) ISBN: 0-8352-1685-3

Bodian, Nat G., *How to Choose a Winning Title,* (Oryx Press, 1989) ISBN: 0-89774-540-X

Brewer, Annie M, and Brewer, Donald T., *Talk Shows and Hosts on Radio,* (Whitefoord Press, 1993) ISBN: 0-9632341-1-0

Bunnin, Brad and Beren, Peter, *Author Law and Strategies,* (Nolo Press, 1983)

Burgett, Gordon, *Self-Publishing to Tightly Targeted Markets,* (Communication Unlimited, 1989) ISBN: 0-910167-17-6

Chambers, Wicke and Asher, Spring, *TV PR: How to Promote Yourself, Your Product, Your Service, Or Your Organization on Television,* (Prima Publishing, 1987) ISBN: 0-9615565-9-5

Kavka, Dorothy, *Selling Your Book: The Writer's Guide to Publishing and Marketing,* (Evanston Publishing, 1993) ISBN: 0-879260-01-8

Kramer, Felix and Loraas, Maggie, *Desktop Publishing Success,* (Business One Irwin, 1991)

Kremer, John, *Book Marketing Made Easier* 3rd Ed., (Open Horizons Publishing, 1991) ISBN: 0-912411-34-1

Kremer, John, *1001 Ways to Market Your Books — For Authors and Publishers,* (Open Horizons Publishing, 1993) ISBN: 0-912411-42-2

Lant, Dr. Jeffrey, *How to Make a Whole Lot More Than $1,000,000 Writing, Publishing and Selling How-To Information,* (Jeffrey Lant Associates, 1990) ISBN: 0-940374-26-9

Lant, Dr. Jeffrey, *The Unabashed Self-Promoter's Guide,* (Jeffrey Lant Associates, 1992) ISBN: 0-940374-18-8

McHugh, John B., *College Publishing Market,* 3rd. Ed., (McHugh Publishing, 1994)

Mueller, L.W., *How to Publish Your Own Book*, Revised Edition, (Harlo Press, 1978)

Poynter, Dan, *The Self-Publishing Manual*, 8th Rev. Ed., Completely Revised (Para Publishing, Santa Barbara, CA 1995) ISBN: 1-56860-003-8

Raab, Susan, *An Author's Guide to Children's Book Promotion*, (Raab Associates, 1992) ISBN: 0-9621211-2-6

Typesetting, Editing, Design & Production

Beach, Mark, et al, *Getting It Printed: How to Work with Printers and Graphic Arts Services to Assure Quality, Stay on Schedule, and Control Costs*, (Coast to Coast Books, 1992) ISBN: 0-9602664-7-X

The Chicago Manual of Style, The Essential Guide for Writers, Editors, and Publishers, 14th Edition, (University of Chicago Press, 1993) ISBN: 0-226-10389-7

Williams, Robin, *The PC is not a Typewriter*, (Peachpit Press, 1991) ISBN: 0-938151-49-5. Also available, *The Mac is not a Typewriter*, ISBN: 0-938151-31-2

Worcester, Robert L., *In Print: How to Plan, Purchase, and Produce Print*, (Media Associates International, Inc. Bloomingdale, IL 1989) ISBN: 0-9623741-0-5

White, Jan V., *Graphic Design for the Electronic Age*, (Watson-Guptill, 1988) ISBN: 0-8320-2122-X

Directories, Reference, and Resources

Keifer, Marie and Kremer, John, *Book Marketing Profitcenter*, (Ad-Lib Publications, 1993) more than 7,000 contacts on disk, various computer formats.

Chase, Helen and Bill, *Chase's Annual Events, the Day-by-Day Directory to 1995*, (Contemporary Books, annual) ISBN: 0-8092-3732-6

Artz, Joan W., Editor, *Hudson's Subscription Newsletter Directory*, (H and M Publications, 1993) ISBN: 0-9617642-4-4

Palder, Edward, *The Catalog of Catalogs III: The Complete Mail-Order Directory*, (Woodbine House, 1993) ISBN: 0-933-149-59-X

Hahn, Harley and Stout, Richard, *The Internet Yellow Pages*, (Osborne McGraw-Hill, 1995) ISBN: 0-07-882098-7

Colgate, Craig Jr., *National Trade and Professional Associations of the U.S.A.*, (Columbia Books, Inc., 1994)

Grants and Awards Available to American Writers, 18th Ed. (PEN American Center, 1994-95) ISBN: 0-934638-13-6

Standard Periodical Directory, (Oxbridge Communications, 1994) ISBN: 0-917460-49-9

World Guide to Libraries, Expanded 12th Edition, (K.G. Saur, [a division of Reed Reference Publishing Company] 1995) ISBN: 3-598-20721-2

American Library Directory 1995-96, (K.G. Saur, [a division of Reed Reference Publishing Company] 1995) ISBN: 3-598-20721-2

Literary Market Place, (R.R. Bowker Co., 1995) ISBN: 0-8352-3475-4

Books in Print, (R.R. Bowker Co., annual) ISBN: 0-8352-3498-3

Encyclopedia of Associations: Index, (Gale Research Company, 1993) ISBN: 0-8103-8317-9

American Book Trade Directory, 40th Ed., (R.R. Bowker, 1994-95) ISBN: 0-8352-2423-1

Malott, Gene E. and Malott, Adele R., Eds., *Senior Media Directory*, (GEM Publishing Group, 1994) ISBN: 0-9629034-3-4

Reference Companies

The following companies publish, sell, and distribute a wide range of books, reports, resources, and directories on publishing and marketing. Contact them to locate or order books on this list, as well as to request their respective catalogs.

Reed Reference Publishing Co.
121 Chanlon Road
New Providence, NJ 07974
Phone 800-521-8110

Gale Research Company
835 Penobscot Building
Detroit, MI 48226
Phone 305-752-2547

R.R. Bowker
121 Chanlon Road
New Providence, NJ 07974
Phone 800-521-8110

Open Horizons Publishing Company
John Kremer, President
209 S. Main Street #200
Fairfield, IA 52556
Phone 800-796-6130

Para Publishing
Dan Poynter, President
PO Box 2206
Santa Barbara, CA 93118-2206
Phone 800-727-2782

Maverick Mail Order Bookstore
PO Box 1500, Dept. MOBG
Buena Vista, CO 81211

APPENDIX

Proofreading Symbols

Punctuation

- apostrophe
- colon
- comma
- em dash
- hyphen
- period
- parentheses
- question mark
- quotation marks (double)
- quotation marks (single)
- semicolon

Typography

- align horizontially
- boldface
- broken letter
- capitalize
- center
- close up
- delete
- insert (caret)
- italics
- stet let it stand (don't change)
- lc lower case
- move right
- move left
- new paragraph
- no ¶ no paragraph
- small caps
- # space
- sp spell out
- tr transpose
- wf wrong font

Special

- ? query to author
- move copy to indicated place
- AA author's alteration
- PE printer's error

Using Proofreading Symbols

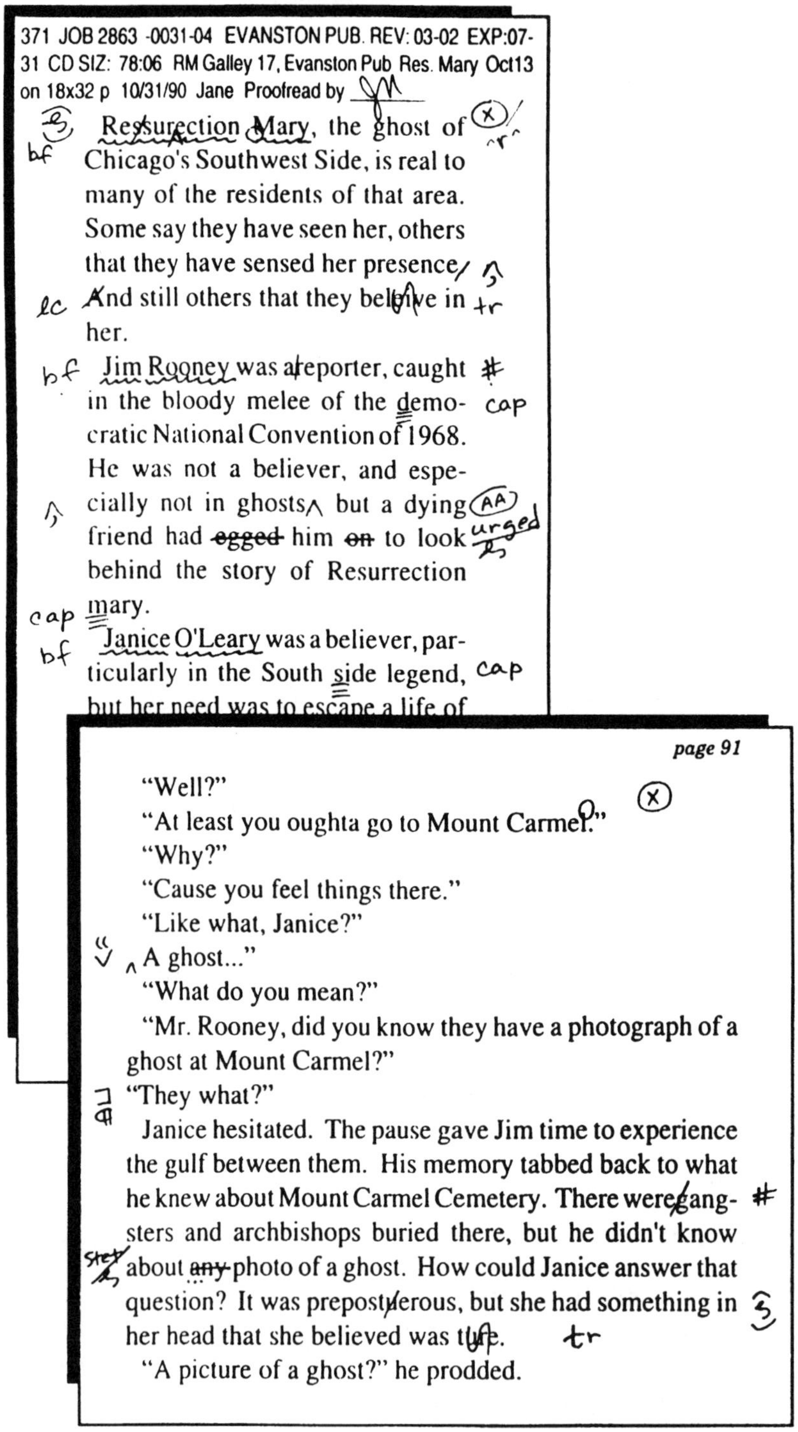

371 JOB 2863 -0031-04 EVANSTON PUB. REV: 03-02 EXP:07-31 CD SIZ: 78:06 RM Galley 17, Evanston Pub Res. Mary Oct13 on 18x32 p 10/31/90 Jane Proofread by

Ressurection Mary, the ghost of Chicago's Southwest Side, is real to many of the residents of that area. Some say they have seen her, others that they have sensed her presence, And still others that they beleive in her.

Jim Rooney was areporter, caught in the bloody melee of the democratic National Convention of 1968. He was not a believer, and especially not in ghosts but a dying friend had egged him on to look behind the story of Resurrection mary.

Janice O'Leary was a believer, particularly in the South side legend, but her need was to escape a life of

page 91

"Well?"

"At least you oughta go to Mount Carmel."

"Why?"

"Cause you feel things there."

"Like what, Janice?"

A ghost..."

"What do you mean?"

"Mr. Rooney, did you know they have a photograph of a ghost at Mount Carmel?"

"They what?"

Janice hesitated. The pause gave Jim time to experience the gulf between them. His memory tabbed back to what he knew about Mount Carmel Cemetery. There weregangsters and archbishops buried there, but he didn't know about any photo of a ghost. How could Janice answer that question? It was preposterous, but she had something in her head that she believed was tuer.

"A picture of a ghost?" he prodded.

galley and page proof with proofreader's and editor's marks

Formatting for WordPerfect in Windows

It is necessary to format your book so it is camera ready for the printer. That means correct margins, binding edges, and no mistakes, if possible.

Helpful Hints:

1. Always write your manuscript before you do any special formatting. If you use editors or proofreaders, they will require an 8½ by 11 inch, double spaced unformatted form. Only when the book is as finished as you think it can be do you actually format the pages.

2. Learn to use "reveal codes." (Alt + F3 or right click + click on reveal codes). Reveal codes allows you to see all the codes that have been entered into the document. This is especially helpful if the computer "insists" on doing something you do not want it to do. By looking in the reveal codes screen you can eliminate extra commands that were entered accidentally.

3. Indents and tabs: Never use the space bar for more than two spaces or to align text. Tabs are used to move a set amount of spaces per line. Indents move a set amount of spaces per sentence, paragraph, or until a hard return.

4. "Em dashes" are used, in place of the hyphen, when showing a break in thought. (Example of em dash: Will you — can you. Example of hyphen: non-entity.) To use the em dash it is necessary to:

 1. Click on Insert ▶Character ▶Typographic Symbols ▶then choose symbol 4,34
 or
 2. Press Ctrl W and enter 4,34 or m- as the code.

5. When quoting another source you need to use "book" or closed quotes instead of the "standard" quote (tick) key on the keyboard. WordPerfect calls them Smart Quotes. There are several ways to insert book quotes.

 1. Click on Insert ▶Character ▶Typographic Symbols ▶then choose symbol 4,32 [“] for double opening quote and symbol 4,31[”] for double closing quote, 4,29 [‘] for single opening quote and 4,28 [’] for single closing quote.
 2. Press Ctrl W, then enter 4,32, 4,31, 4,29 or 4,28 as the code.
 3. This method converts the "standard" tick marks into "SmartQuotes." Choose Tools ▶QuickCorrect ▶ Options ▶Turn on Single and Double SmartQuotes ▶Close.

This lesson was written for "The Complete Publisher Seminar" by Myra Schultz, Vice-President and Director of Operations and Design, RBS Technologies, Inc.

If you need to use a tick mark in the body of your paper you must deselect the SmartQuotes. At the QuickCorrect Options you can also format your paper for "sentence corrections" and "end of sentence corrections", (i.e., spaces after a sentence, capitalize first letter of each sentence, etc.) This is the only formatting that you should do before you even write one word of text.

6. Never underline anything unless for stylistic purposes. In typesetting underlining signifies italics.

7. A book title mentioned within your text is always italicized.

8. As you write your book save each chapter in a different file under the same directory. Call the files Chap1, Chap2, etc.

9. When typing your manuscript use only one space after periods.

10. Use your Spell Checker often!

11. To see how your manuscript looks use View ➤Two Pages. This will change the screen to two pages (a "double page spread") and allow you to view the formatting before printing.

Formatting Steps

1. ***Margins:*** The common size of a page in a book is 5½ by 8½ inches with ¾ inch margins.

Formatting: Format ➤Margins *or* Ctrl + F8.

Define the size of each margin in the appropriate box. Right and left margins should be 2¼ inches, top and bottom 2 inches.

or right click on first row of icons, left click on layout, click on PgMargins icon, set margins as above.

2. ***Binding:*** Books must be bound following printing; therefore, you need a "binding edge". This is an extra ¼ inch margin that alternates right and left depending on the page number.

Formatting: Format ➤Page ➤Binding/Duplex

In binding width box click "left", (this will start the binding edge on the first left page). Enter .25 in the amount box, (this will give each page a ¼ inch binding edge). Click on OK. This will put the extra ¼ inch on the first left page and then alternate it with every page.

3. ***Numbering:*** Page numbering can begin anywhere, be placed anywhere, look any way and say anything you want. There are several steps you must take to accomplish this task.

Formatting: Format ➤Page ➤Numbering.

Step 1: Choose where you want the numbers to be placed on each page at the Position box. "Alternating top" or "alternating bottom" will put numbers on opposite corners of paper.

Step 2: In same screen, click on Font, choose the desired font and type size, click OK. This will bring you back to the original screen.

Step 3: If you want anything other than plain numbers (eg., 1, 2, 3, etc.) click on Options, this allows you to customize the numbers to appear on each page. Choices include upper and lower case letters, upper and lower case roman numerals and plain numbers. If you choose to use text or dashes around the page number, define what you want in the Format and Accompanying Text dialog box (eg., page 1, - 1 - , ~ 1 ~, etc.) Remember the text or symbol is placed around the [pg#] command exactly the way you want it to look. (eg., page [pg#], - [pg#] -, ~ [pg#] ~). Click OK. This will bring you back to the original screen.

Step 4: If you want to begin with any number other than "1" click on Value and enter the appropriate number. You can change page values, styles, fonts, etc. anytime you desire within your document. Click OK. This will bring you back to the original screen. Click OK on main screen. Your numbering requests are now all entered.

4. ***Paragraphs:***There should only be a small difference in the amount of leading or space between paragraphs and between sentences.

Formatting: Format ➤Paragraph ➤Format

1. Paragraph spacing: Define the amount of space you want between paragraphs, (e.g., 1.10, 1.15 etc.). This means you want slightly more than one space between paragraphs.

2. Paragraph indenting: You can also define how much you want the first word of each paragraph to indent in or out from the margin. The standard indentation is 0.3. Using this system, you do not have to do anything when typing; the computer will do it for you.

3. Quotations: Short quotations are defined by book or closed quotes. Long quotations are indented on both sides of the margins. Formatting for this is done separately for each quotation. At the beginning of the quotation to be indented click Format ➤Paragraph ➤Dbl Indent ***or*** press Ctrl, Shift, F7 at the same time.

5. ***Header/Footers:*** Chapter and book titles, or any other text you desire, can be included on each page or alternating pages. There are several steps to use this option properly.

Formatting: Format ➤Header/Footer

Step 1: Choose Header A or B or Footer A or B. Click Create. The computer will automatically bring you to the top or bottom of the page.

Step 2: You now format the text for font and size. This is done through Format ➤Font ***or*** clicking the Font icon and letter size icon. If you want the text to be italic and/or bold, click the appropriate icon.

Step 3: You must also set your Header and Footer margins to correspond to the margins of the book. After you have opened the Header/Footer window click Format ▶Margins, then set the margins to agree with your books margins (2¼ inches right and left).

Step 4: Now decide on which pages you want the text to appear. Click the Pages button and choose either Odd, Even, or Every Page. Then click OK. If you choose Odd your text will appear on all odd numbered pages, Even means the text will appear on even numbered pages and Every means the text will appear on all pages. To have a different header on each double page spread you must use Header A and Header B. One is placed on the Odd page and one is placed on the Even page. Normally the book title is on the even page and the chapter title on the odd page.

Step 5: The distance between the text and the header or footer is optional but the computer has a default setting of setting of 0.167 inches. To change this amount click Distance and enter the spacing you desire.

Step 6: You can make your Headers and Footers fancier by adding lines. Clicking the Insert Line button gives you a single horizontal line. To design a custom line click on Graphics ▶Custom Line. Choose the style, position and length, spacing, thickness and color (if you have a color printer). Click OK.

6. ***Widow/Orphans:*** It is preferable to keep your text together whenever possible. By using the Widow/Orphan option you prevent single words or lines from appearing at the end of a paragraph or the bottom or top of a page. A Widow is defined as the first line of a paragraph appearing on the last line of a page. An Orphan is the last line of a paragraph appearing on the first line of a new page.

Formatting: Format ▶Page ▶Keep Text Together.

Click on the area describing Widows/Orphans to turn this option on. The computer default is two lines of text, while one line is more customary. To change the default number click on Conditional End of Page and change the number to one (1). Click OK. The computer will now automatically move lines of text to prevent single lines from appearing as the last line or the first line on a page.

7. ***Justification:*** The text in books is traditionally fully justified.

Formatting: Format AJustification AFull *or* click on the justification icon (will normally state Left) and choose full.

8. ***Hyphenation:*** Fully justified text will stretch itself to fit across an entire line. Since it is necessary to Fully Justify your text, you need to hyphenate words to prevent blank areas on lines. The computer can do it automatically for you.

Formatting: Format ▶Line ▶Hyphenation

Click Hyphenation On to activate. Click OK. The computer will hyphenate words as you type or change the text. Any word not in its dictionary will appear on the screen with a question of proper hyphenation. You can then change the hyphenation point or tell the computer to ignore the word.

You have now completed the formatting of your document!

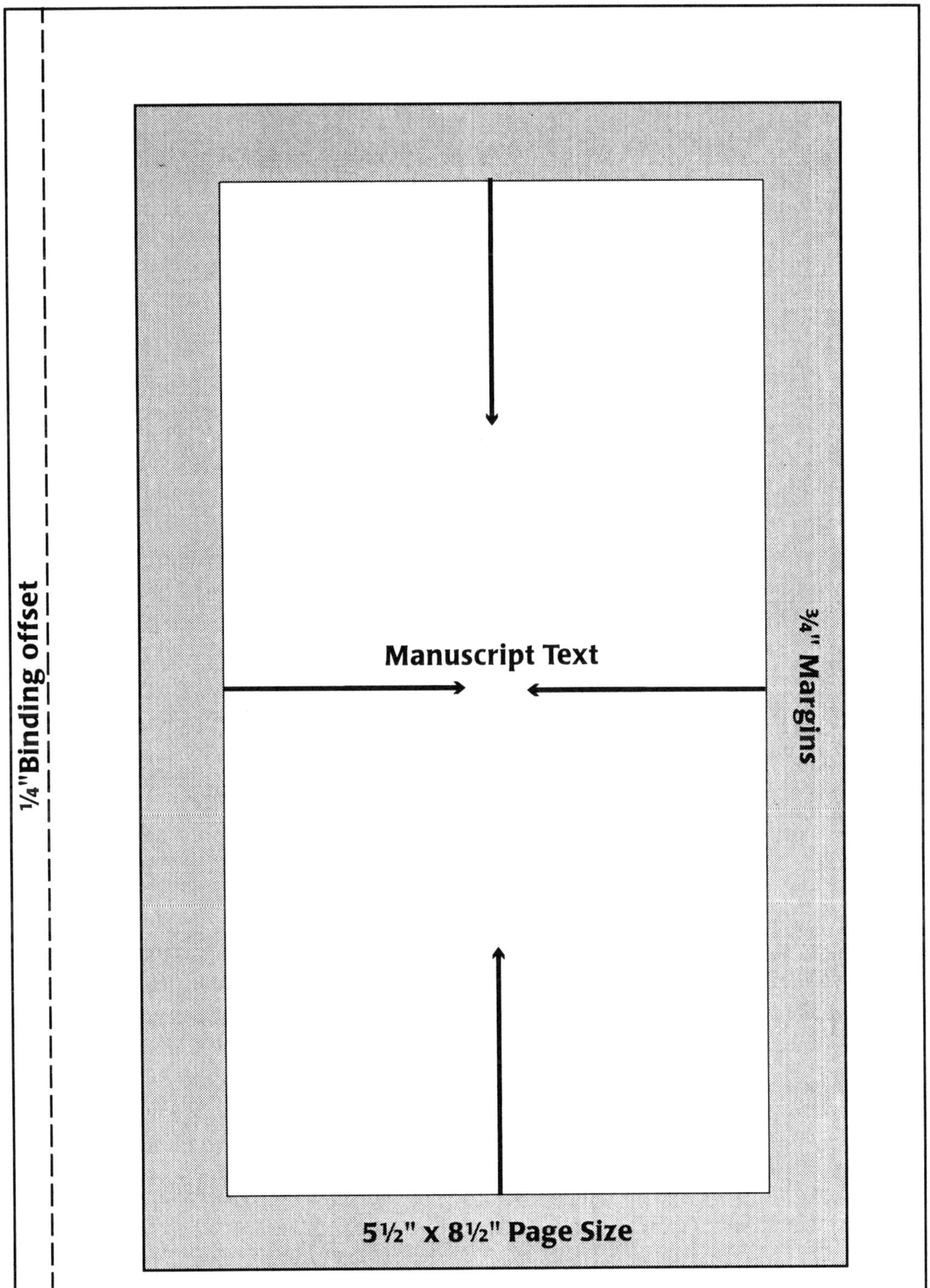

one inch default margins for 8½ by 11 inch sheet of paper

"From time immemorial the academic physicians had despised the barbers, 'army surgeons,' and so called 'bathers' to whom were relegated surgical cures. In fact, the very word 'surgeon' means a 'manual worker'". The status of surgeons changed gradually and by the late 18th century they enjoyed as much prestige as any other physician. However, they were extremely

Page 1

limited in the types of surgical procedures they would perform. Prior to the discovery of anesthetic agents, patients requiring any form of surgical intervention either "screamed in pain or clenched their teeth upon a piece of leather". If the patients did not succumb to the pain, they would die from infection. In the annals of Massachusetts General Hospital there were

Page 2

only forty-three operations performed during the years of 1821 to 1823. Few surgeons braved opposing the prevalent convictions of the medical establishment to perform anything more than amputations on tumorous appendages and repairing fistulas by burning them with red-hot pokers.

– 3 –

Almost forty years before the discovery of anesthesia and some sixty years before antisepsis, the mounted healer of the Kentucky woods [Ephraim McDowell] had dared to oppose the professional opinion of the whole world. Operating on his living room table, he had opened up the abdomen of a living human being, and his

– 4 –

~ 5 ~

patient had not died. The year was 1809, the patient was a female with an abdominal tumor and the prognosis was considered fatal. Other surgical successes were extremely rare or nonexistent.

Thorwald describes a typical operating room of the 1800s. It often consisted of an operating chair, upholstered in red

~ 6 ~

plush, and with an adjustable back. There would be rows of benches for students and other spectators which rose in a semicircle above the operating theater. When the patient entered the room, the surgeon would remove his coat and replace it with an old jacket which was covered with stains and stiff with the dried blood of innumerable

page number placement in Wordperfect

Samples of Book (Closed) Quotes and Double Indents in Wordperfect

This is a sample of a short quotation using book quotes to set it apart. It is part of a longer paragraph and is not indented on both sides.

"The century of modern surgery began in 1846 in the operating room of Massachusetts General Hospital in Boston. October 16 of that year marked the birth of the art of producing insensibility to pain by the inhalation of chemical gases." The advent of anesthetic agents resulted in the first major change within the field of surgery. Speed was no longer a necessity, and patients slept quietly throughout the most painful procedures.

The following is an example of a longer quote. It is set apart from the other text by indenting both margins. This is done with the Double Indent code. Do not use book quotes around an indented quote.

The advent of anesthetic agents resulted in the first major change within the field of surgery. Speed was no longer a necessity, and patients slept quietly throughout the most painful procedures. Ether and chloroform now enabled the surgeons to do more complex surgery, but one important element had not changed. Patients were now surviving the surgical procedure only to die from postsurgical infections.

> ...even with pain defeated, surgery was faced with a second, equally formidable enemy. It, too, was age-old, and had been feared especially in the case of abdominal wounds. But since the spread of anesthesia this particular menace seemed likewise to be growing mysteriously beyond all bounds...It was the same throughout [all] the hospital[s], whether called wound fever, pyemia, septicemia, erysipelas, gangrene, blood poisoning, or...infection.

Top paragraph demonstrates full use of 8½ by 11 inch paper with one inch margins right and left, ¼ inch binding, and full justification.

"From time immemorial the academic physicians had despised the barbers, 'army surgeons,' and so called 'bathers' to whom were relegated surgical cures. In fact, the very word 'surgeon' means a 'manual worker'." The status of surgeons changed gradually and by the late 18th century they enjoyed as much prestige as any other physician. However, they were extremely limited in the types of surgical procedures they would perform. Prior to the discovery of anesthetic agents, patients requiring any form of surgical intervention either "screamed in pain or clenched their teeth upon a piece of leather." If the patients did not succumb to the pain, they would die from infection. In the annals of Massachusetts General Hospital there were only forty-three operations performed during the years of 1821 to 1823. Few surgeons braved opposing the prevalent convictions of the medical establishment to perform anything more than amputations on tumorous appendages and repairing fistulas by burning them with red-hot pokers.

Second paragraph demonstrates reducing text to 5½ BY 8½ inch paper with ¾ inch margins right and left, ¼ inch binding, and full justification.

"From time immemorial the academic physicians had despised the barbers, 'army surgeons,' and so called 'bathers' to whom were relegated surgical cures. In fact, the very word 'surgeon' means a 'manual worker'." The status of surgeons changed gradually and by the late 18th century they enjoyed as much prestige as any other physician. However, they were extremely limited in the types of surgical procedures they would perform. Prior to the discovery of anesthetic agents, patients requiring any form of surgical intervention either "screamed in pain or clenched their teeth upon a piece of leather." If the patient did not succumb to the pain, they would die from infec-

Samples of Paragraph Spacing

1.25 spacing

Almost forty years before the discovery of anesthesia and some sixty years before antisepsis, the mounted healer of the Kentucky woods [Ephraim McDowell] had dared to oppose the professional opinion of the whole world. Operating on his living room table, he had opened up the abdomen of a living human being, and his patient had not died. The year was 1809, the patient was a female with an abdominal tumor and the prognosis was considered fatal. Other surgical successes were extremely rare or non-existent.

Thorwald describes a typical operating room of the 1800s. It often consisted of an operating chair, upholstered in red plush, and with an adjustable back. There would be rows of benches for students and other spectators which rose in a semicircle above the operating theater. When the patient entered the room, the surgeon would remove his coat and replace it with an old jacket which was covered with stains and stiff with the dried blood of innumerable past operations.

1.50 spacing

Almost forty years before the discovery of anesthesia and some sixty years before antisepsis, the mounted healer of the Kentucky woods [Ephraim McDowell] had dared to oppose the professional opinion of the whole world. Operating on his living room table, he had opened up the abdomen of a living human being, and his patient had not died. The year was 1809, the patient was a female with an abdominal tumor and the prognosis was considered fatal. Other surgical successes were extremely rare or non-existent.

Thorwald describes a typical operating room of the 1800s. It often consisted of an operating chair, upholstered in red plush, and with an adjustable back. There would be rows of benches for students and other spectators which rose in a semicircle above the operating theater. When the patient entered the room, the surgeon would remove his coat and replace it with an old jacket which was covered with stains and stiff with the dried blood of innumerable past operations.

1.75 spacing

Almost forty years before the discovery of anesthesia and some sixty years before antisepsis, the mounted healer of the Kentucky woods [Ephraim McDowell] had dared to oppose the professional opinion of the whole world. Operating on his living room table, he had opened up the abdomen of a living human being, and his patient had not died. The year was 1809, the patient was a female with an abdominal tumor and the prognosis was considered fatal. Other surgical successes were extremely rare or non-existent.

Thorwald describes a typical operating room of the 1800s. It often consisted of an operating chair, upholstered in red plush, and with an adjustable back. There would be rows of benches for students and other spectators which rose in a semicircle above the operating theater. When the patient entered the room, the surgeon would remove his coat and replace it with an old jacket which was covered with stains and stiff with the dried blood of innumerable past operations.

Standard Access Chart for Windows Programs

No.	Char	No.	Char	No.	Char	No.	Char	No.	Char	No.	Char	No.	Char
1	—	42	*	83	S	124	|	165	¥	206	Î	247	÷
2	—	43	+	84	T	125	}	166	¦	207	Ï	248	ø
3	—	44	,	85	U	126	~	167	§	208	Ð	249	ù
4	•	45	-	86	V	127	•	168	¨	209	Ñ	250	ú
5	—	46	.	87	W	128	•	169	©	210	Ò	251	û
6	—	47	/	88	X	129	•	170	ª	211	Ó	252	ü
7	—	48	0	89	Y	130	‚	171	«	212	Ô	253	ý
8	—	49	1	90	Z	131	ƒ	172	¬	213	Õ	254	þ
9	—	50	2	91	[	132	„	173	-	214	Ö	255	ÿ
10	“	51	3	92	\	133	…	174	®	215	×		
11	”	52	4	93	]	134	†	175	¯	216	Ø		
12	—	53	5	94	^	135	‡	176	°	217	Ù		
13	—	54	6	95	_	136	ˆ	177	±	218	Ú		
14	—	55	7	96	`	137	‰	178	²	219	Û		
15	/	56	8	97	a	138	Š	179	³	220	Ü		
16	—	57	9	98	b	139	‹	180	´	221	Ý		
17	—	58	:	99	c	140	Œ	181	µ	222	Þ		
18	—	59	;	100	d	141	•	182	¶	223	ß		
19	—	60	<	101	e	142	•	183	·	224	à		
20	—	61	=	102	f	143	•	184	¸	225	á		
21	—	62	>	103	g	144	•	185	¹	226	â		
22	—	63	?	104	h	145	‘	186	º	227	ã		
23	—	64	@	105	i	146	’	187	»	228	ä		
24	—	65	A	106	j	147	“	188	¼	229	å		
25	—	66	B	107	k	148	”	189	½	230	æ		
26	—	67	C	108	l	149	•	190	¾	231	ç		
27	—	68	D	109	m	150	–	191	¿	232	è		
28	—	69	E	110	n	151	—	192	À	233	é		
29	—	70	F	111	o	152	˜	193	Á	234	ê		
30	—	71	G	112	p	153	™	194	Â	235	ë		
31	—	72	H	113	q	154	š	195	Ã	236	ì		
32		73	I	114	r	155	›	196	Ä	237	í		
33	!	74	J	115	s	156	œ	197	Å	238	î		
34	"	75	K	116	t	157	•	198	Æ	239	ï		
35	#	76	L	117	u	158	•	199	Ç	240	ð		
36	$	77	M	118	v	159	Ÿ	200	È	241	ñ		
37	%	78	N	119	w	160		201	É	242	ò		
38	&	79	O	120	x	161	¡	202	Ê	243	ó		
39	'	80	P	121	y	162	¢	203	Ë	244	ô		
40	(	81	Q	122	z	163	£	204	Ì	245	õ		
41	)	82	R	123	{	164	¤	205	Í	246	ö		

Keyboard Shortcuts

C=Control
S=Shift

CS+=	—
C+=	–
CS+[	“
CS+]	”
C+[	‘
C+]	’
CS+8	•
CS+6	§

Most characters between 1 and 31 are not commonly used. A dash has been substituted for such characters. Character 32 is the “Space” character.

sample in Times Roman typeface – access these characters by holding down the alt key + 0 + character number (¼ = alt + 0188)

Sample Page Layouts

Cuckoo Forevermore

Melody leaned forward. "I must reiterate once more. Since you've received your degree and have found employment, our counseling will soon terminate."

As if smacked by an emu's egg, my head reeled. "I... I'm not ready. There's so much to work through. This morning I dreamt a giant wedge-tailed eagle was attacking me. Its razor sharp claws were clenching my testicles."

"Peter, I've been telling you for the past two months that our therapy must end. You're no longer attending the University. The Counseling Department caters for students. I agreed to continue with you only through the transition period. Even now, I shouldn't be counseling you."

I glanced at the honeyeater feeding her chicks. I wasn't strong enough. I desperately needed her encouraging words.

My mouth gaped. "I... I could sign up for a part-time course."

"You know that's merely avoidance."

"So what? I can't make it without you."

"I believe you're more than capable."

"How many more sessions can I have?"

"We've gone over this a number of times, Peter. We have another session in two weeks and then our final session, one month after that. You keep resisting termination. It's time you were weaned from therapy. I'm confident you can fly on your own."

I protested at being pushed out of the nest. It wasn't fair! "What if I have another anxiety attack?"

"If you have any difficulties, you already have several names of private therapists."

-4-

standard 5½ by 8½ inch page verso layout for fiction

❧ *EARLY DAYS*

The astonishing thing about my brother, Edward Dart, is how unlikely he was to succeed. If you had lined up the Dart children when we were growing up, there's no doubt where Ned, as we called him, would have come—last, or more likely not even in the running.

There were four of us who survived infancy. Harry, with his exceptionally brilliant mind, and Ninette, who won the citizenship prize in grade school and was fluent in French, were the two oldest. I was next and according to my teachers (who were, alas, dead wrong), I had a promising career ahead in art or singing. It was these same teachers who shook their heads in despair over Ned. He was a disruptive nuisance, and though they laughed at his antics and loved him for making them laugh, it was clear they thought he would never amount to anything. They were dead wrong about him too.

As it turned out Ned was successful beyond anything they—or we—would have imagined. He was listed in *Who's Who in America,* which none of the rest of us were, and received more honors and awards than anyone can count. His habit seems to have been to stash away the certificates and scrolls in a drawer and forget about them—or more likely throw them away as was his custom with his drawings when he was done with them. But even without an accurate list of his honors, not to mention a complete list of his buildings, it's easy to find dozens of citations and newspaper encomiums about him and his work.

For example, the American Institute of Architects (AIA) alone gave him eighteen awards, one of which was the AIA National Honor Award.

3.

chapter opening with indented large initial cap letter

CHAPTER VI

THE CONSPIRACY OF 1862

The declaration of martial law seems to have affected Camp Douglas only, and not other Northern prisons. Careful guidelines were laid down by Colonel Hoffman. The decree had to be posted outside the camp and published in the local papers. A line of stakes 50 feet apart and close to the camp would mark the boundaries of martial law.

A buffer zone around the camp seemed desirable in view of Southern sympathizers in Chicago. An incident involving a clergyman, who was arrested for talking to a prisoner through the fence, seems to have triggered the idea. A judge in Chicago agreed that this was a restricted zone. That gave Hoffman the idea of pushing Stanton to issue the decree. Colonel Tucker published it onjuly 12, 1862.[1] The notice read: "Any person violating military authority within said line will be subject to punishment by short confinement or trial by court-martial at the discretion of the commanding officer."

Tucker was authorized to impose martial law "for a space of 100 feet outside and around the chain of sentinels." This created a loophole which allowed Tucker to extend the zone as far as he liked by throwing out his picket lines. This way the decree ran as far as State Street six blocks to the west, and probably included the old University of Chicago across the road on the Douglas property. The idea was to keep civilians away from all sides of the camp except Cottage Grove, and Colonel Tucker placed 200 posters around the neighborhood.

the chapter opening of a more heavily designed nonfiction book

THE PHOTOGRAPHER'S WALTZ

Seen at a wedding,
Dancing with his camera
As bride and groom
Ride on heavy chairs
Around the room,
The photographer make
Of his job of remembering
A most graceful dance,
Assumes an erect posture
In his tuxedo,
Back arched like a penguin
One hand holds the camera
To his handsome face,
The other downward,
Fingers glued together,
Like a fish's fin at his side.

The photographer
Moves to the music
As though he has
No need to hide,
He is part of
The dance of the lovers,
And his gliding
Helps them to glide.

Imagine him
Gliding through Europe,
His dance floor
The vast countryside,
The lovers are
All his people,
And in his dream,
Not one of them has died.

18 *The Ladder of Memory*

poetry should not be centered on individual lines, but by the total poem

Romantic Alcove

I wish I had a terraced lot,
    a tree surrounded, country spot
        with flowers, shrubs, a privet hedge,
            and potted ferns on stone-walled ledge;

gazebo as a focal point
    where lovers meet each to anoint
        the other with a word, embrace,
            unhurriedly, at leisure pace.

- 27 -

poetry can look very elegant when set in unusual ways and/or with large margins

Understanding Color Printing

Color comes from an object's ability to reflect or absorb light, which our eyes see as color. When you view a scene, your eyes use three kinds of receptors, each sensitive to one of the primary colors of light — blue, green, and red. The receptors send impulses to the brain that are interpreted as color. Blue, green, and red are called *additive primaries* because they produce white light when added together.

In order to prepare a painting or drawing for the press, it must be separated into these same additive primaries. To get a red negative of the artwork, a red filter is used. The negative subtracts all the red from the image and thus the film will be made up of just blue and green, which together become *cyan*.

In the same manner, the blue negative will use a blue filter, leaving only red and green, which when combined in additive colors produces *yellow.* When the green filter is used, the red and blue will combine to make *magenta.* The three colors of cyan, yellow, and magenta are called *subtractive primaries,* because they are formed by subtracting an additive primary. The subtractive primaries are the basic colors of the process inks used in *process color* (full color) printing. When these three colors are combined on the press, they become a good representation of the original artwork. However, since inks are not as pure as light, just using these three colors will produce a muddy image. Therefore, black is added to increase the contrast and clarity of the colors. These four colors are abbreviated by designers and printers as C (cyan), M (magenta), Y (yellow), and K (black).

Colors are also described by their *hue, value, and saturation.* Hue is simply the name of the color (purple, green, orange). Value is the lightness or darkness of a hue, and saturation is its density.

It is important to understand that a computer monitor, scanner, desktop printer, and a printing press each works with a different kind of color perception and reproduces a different range of color. Therefore, what you see on your computer monitor is different from what you will get from your desktop printer, and the final color print job done on a large commercial press will also have subtle differences. All will probably be slightly different from the color of the original artwork, too. It is almost impossible to recreate the *exact* hue, value, and saturation from one form of color re-creation (such as a chalk drawing) to another (such as the ink on a large commercial press).

Halftones and Color

Most original artwork is made up of solid blocks of color that are blended together. This is called continuous-tone artwork. A photograph is also continuous-tone. Such artwork cannot be printed just as it is on a commercial press, but first must be changed into a halftone screen. This means that the continuous-tone is broken into dots of various sizes. Black and white artwork is converted into black dots and color artwork is changed into cyan, magenta, yellow, and black dots. The smaller the dot the lighter the area and the larger the dot the darker the area. When color dots of cyan, magenta, yellow, and black are overlapped, they "simulate" all the other different colors in the rainbow.

Spot colors are different than process colors in that they are not made up of subtractive primaries, but instead are made from premixed colors. They are usually used for two or three color printing jobs. Spot colors can be overlaid on each other to create new colors (red and yellow produce orange), but are not as flexible as process color. Spot color printing is not used for full color printing, because every color would have to be separately prepared, and presses can handle only from two to six colors at one time.

Often, different values of a hue can be produced with a *tint*, which is an increase or decrease of the number of dots used. In printing, a tint is called a *screen*. A 50 percent screen of a red spot color appears pink, and a 40percent screen of black looks grey. Skillful use of tints can make a two-color spot color printing job look multicolored, without the expense of process color.

Separations

Process color is prepared for the press by separating all the colors in the original artwork into film separations for each ink (C,M,Y,K). Each ink gets a separate piece of film. This film is used to make the printing plates *(see Chapter 7)*.

When separations are made, if you look at the film you will see that on overlapping elements the bottom color is *knocked out*. This means that there is a blank space exactly the size of the top color taken out of the bottom color so that when the printing takes place, the top color is clean and true. If the bottom color was not knocked out, you would get a color that is a combination of both the top and bottom colors. Black usually does not have color knocked out behind it, but overprints the bottom color because other colors cannot be seen behind it.

Other Techniques

Trapping is a technique used to make sure that if the press is slightly *off register* (the colors do not line up exactly), that you will not see any space between different color elements adjacent to each other. Trapping is a slight overprinting of one color over another where the edges touch. It is done with with a minimal overprinting (one or less points in size) so that it is usually imperceptible.

Moiré patterns come from the dots on a halftone screen being lined up incorrectly, so that a pattern of the dots form that look like the waviness of moiré cloth. Halftone dots must be printed at a specified angle so they form into a symmetrical pattern called a "rosette" pattern, which the human eye sees as a continuous-tone.

If you produce your own halftones by scanning in your photographs, your printer may ask you to lighten their value because of *dot gain*. Depending on the type of press used, halftone dots can increase in size as the ink goes through the press. If the dots get too close to one another, images and colors will print darker than you may want. Your printer should tell you how to adjust your scans for the press being used.

Your commercial printer is your best source of information on color printing. If you are unsure of any of the techniques you need to use to make a professional looking book, always ask your printer for his or her advice. Find out what color matching system the printer uses (most use Pantone), the paper that will look best for your color job (usually a coated paper, because an uncoated dulls the color), what prepress preparation you are responsible for, how many colors should you use for the most cost-effect look, and what sort of color information is needed for your book (color layout, desktop color-print, or just a black and white copy marked for color).

If you choose a printer with whom you are comfortable working, if you schedule your work and stick to your schedule, and if you are in constant communication with your printer, you should end up with a color book that will enhance the value and salability of your work.

Preparing Spot Color Separations (Mechanicals)

Supplies:

- artboard a little larger than page size (usually 2-ply bristol board)
- nonreproducing blue pencil or pen
- overlay acetate tracing paper
- glue wax or adhesive (use special glue that allows work to be repositioned)
- color pencils or markers

Because printing requires that each color be separately processed, any part of a book that has two or more colors must be carefully prepared for the press. If you do not know anything about color separation, do your research before you begin preparing the boards. Books on design and printing can be very helpful.

Computer draw programs and some desktop publishing programs prepare separations automatically. Make sure that the program is set for spot color, not process color, and that you include crop mark settings and registration marks when indicating your program preferences.

To prepare separations by hand takes time, patience, and a steady hand. First, rule the art board to the exact size of the page, using a nonreproducing blue pencil. Light blue color is not picked up by the camera.

If you are preparing a cover, make sure the measurements include the size of the spine. First find out the PPI (pages per inch) of the paper to be used for your book. Then use the formula of page count divided by PPI. Thus, if your PPI is 530, that means a 288-page book will require a spine that is .54 inches wide (288 divided by 530).

Crop marks (which tell the printer where to cut the page) are placed exactly at the corners of the page (*Illustration A*). The fold marks of the spine are indicated with dotted lines.

Because mechanicals can be handled by at least six people before they are turned into film, they cannot be fragile. Have original artwork scanned or photostated. Statting is not the same process as photocopying; it is a photographic technique that can be handled with little danger of flaking or smearing.

Never include a photograph in the paste-up of boards. Indicate where the photo goes by drawing a box to the exact size. Using blue pencil, lightly mark the box and the back of the photo with the same letter or number. The printer will turn the photograph into a halftone and place it in position.

Look carefully at the copy and artwork, determining how many colors they contain. Black is considered a color and but white is not because that is the color of the paper for the cover. If your budget only allows two colors, consider using color percentages to get a multicolor effect at no extra cost. For example, grey can be a 10 percent to 80 percent screen of black. A light screen of red appears pink. White, which is the absence of color (called a *reverse*), can add interest to the colors *(Illustration B)*.

Each color (but not the screens which are just shades of the same color) must be pasted down on a separate board. To make it easier to align those separations, most designers use acetate or tracing paper for each color except the main one which is on the artboard. Then the overlays are taped on the artboard.

Each separation contains all the parts of the text and illustrations that are one color, in their exact location in relation to the other colors. This alignment is done with *registration marks,* which are placed on each separation in exactly the same place. When all the registration marks are placed one on another, the picture looks as if it had never been separated *(Illustration C)*.

Using tracing paper, prepare a separate *color layout* by drawing the entire cover to size and filling in the colors with colored pencils or markers. Indicate the Pantone (PMS) numbers so there is no confusion as to the exact color shades. These numbers make up a standard chart that every printer uses and are easy to obtain at an artists' supply store. Also, on this layout, mark the areas that are to have color screens, and what those percentages are. If your color, copy, or artwork runs off the edge of the page (a *bleed)*, show that also.

Keep in mind that the skill of preparing mechanicals is usually left to professionals who have had years of training and experience in this field. If you are unsure of your ability to do precise, clean separations, then you probably should not prepare your own boards.

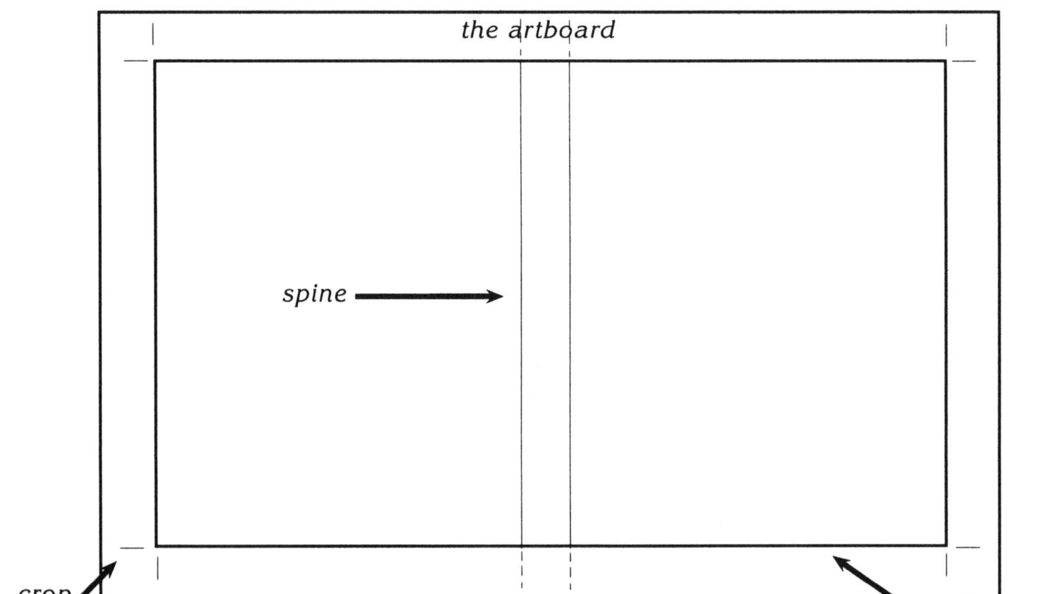

illustration A

illustration B

One color mechanical with 10 percent and 60percent black screens, reversed type, and four-way bleed. (Note: bleeds should always extend at least ¼ inch past edge of page dimensions.)

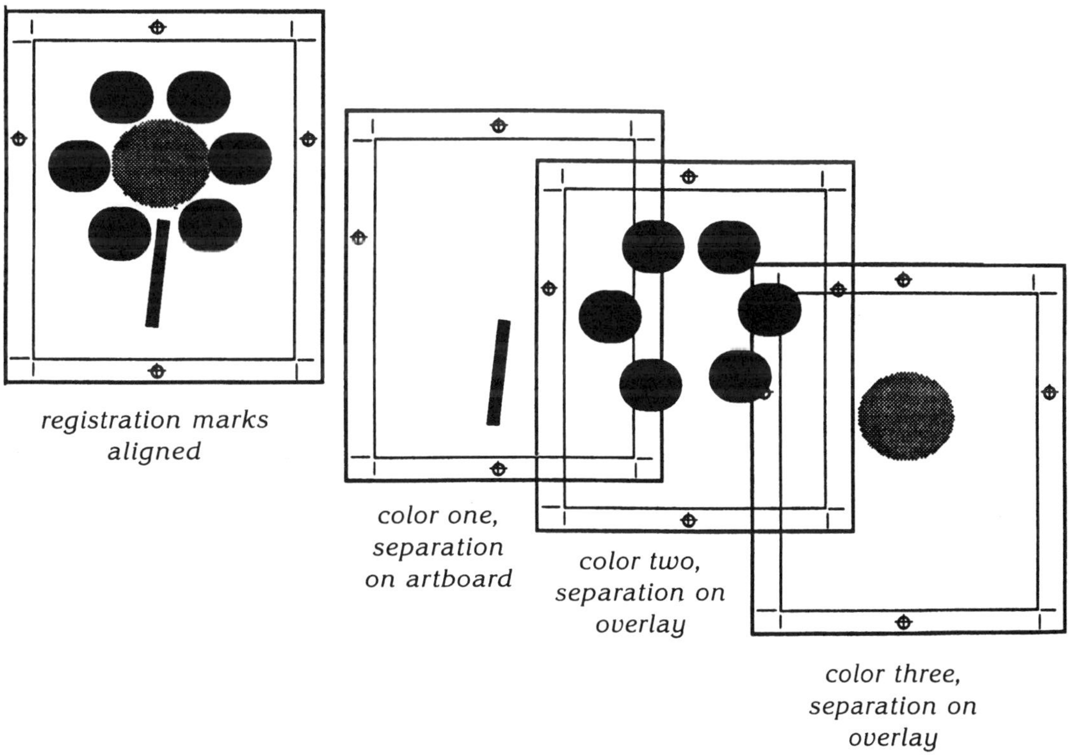

illustration C

The Publisher-Printer Relationship

Choosing and working successfully with any commercial printer comes down to trust and responsibility. If problems arise, and they usually do, solutions should be reached fairly for both sides. That is why you should be in constant contact with your printer from the beginning of your project to make sure that you understand every aspect of the production process. Making a book is a creative process, and like most creative endeavors, has to be flexible to achieve completion.

1. Meet with your printer before you begin production and discuss your specifications and scheduling needs. It is essential that both totally understand what the exact responsibilities are for the printer and the publisher. Discuss how up-to-date the printer's equipment is, what is the usual delivery time, and ask for some names of their other clients as references. Expect to see samples of the company's work; a printer will show the best he or she has produced, so if that work doesn't meet your standards, find another printer. Make sure to find out how wastage will be billed; some printers will quote a very low price, but charge you for everything that comes off the press, including unusable wastage.

2. Find out if the printer offers special prices on in-house paper stock, special trim sizes, or if there are slow times on the press when prices will be less. Keep in mind that special offers now may not be available later when you need a reprint of the book. Standardization of your book size, paper, and run will always be more financially beneficial for you.

3. Your exact specifications for your book should be written up and sent with the camera-ready material. Keep a copy for yourself. Any changes thereafter needed must be written down and given to the printer. Always keep a copy of these communications. Keeping track of a project as large as the production of a book means making sure that both you and printer do not forget or misinterpret any instructions.

4. Keep your printer up to date on the production of the book that you, as publisher, are handling. Once your printer knows that your book is coming in, you will be assigned a press time. If you are running late in preparing your camera-ready materials, you must let your printer know so that your press time can be rescheduled and the delivery time of the books can be recalculated.

5. It is always worth double-checking that your printer has the paper stock you need on hand to get the job done on time. With paper prices

PHONE: 708/492-1911
CONCEPT/COPY/DESIGN/PRINT FACSIMILE: 708/492-1967
EVANSTON PUBLISHING, INC. 1571 SHERMAN AVENUE, ANNEX C EVANSTON, ILLINOIS 60201

PRINTER SPECIFICATIONS

TO: **DATE:** **QUOTE #:**

BOOK TITLE:
PERFECTBOUND CASEBOUND SADDLESTITCHED
SIZE: **RUN:** **NUMBER OF PAGES:**

PAPER: 50# 60# 70# OTHER

COVER:
SPOT COLOR 1 2 3 4 PANTONE ______
FULL COLOR
SEPARATIONS ENCLOSED
FILM ENCLOSED COLOR LAYOUT ENCLOSED BAR CODE ENCLOSED
PRINTER PREPARE SEPARATIONS SEND MATCHPRINT SEND RANDOMS
SPECIAL INSTRUCTIONS

EXTRA COVERS FILM LAMINATE NON-CURL LAMINATE HINGED COVER

TEXT:
BLACK TWO COLOR
FULL COLOR SEND MATCHPRINT SEND RANDOMS
HALF TONES
SPECIAL INSTRUCTIONS

DELIVERY:
SHIP TO EVANSTON PUBLISHING
SHIP TO AUTHOR USING ONLY EVANSTON PUBLISHING LABELS
LABELS ENCLOSED LABELS TO BE SENT WITH CORRECTED BLUELINES
DO NOT SHIP UNTIL ADVISED
SHIP TO DISTRIBUTOR (SHIPPING AND LABELING INSTRUCTIONS ENCLOSED) AMOUNT
SEND ESTIMATE OF SHIPPING CHARGES LOCATION/ZIP

SPECIAL INSTRUCTIONS:
SEND SIX SAMPLE COPIES TO EVANSTON PUBLISHING FOIL STAMPING
VARNISH

rising every month, it is getting difficult to obtain even standard paper stock for short runs.

6. When you send in your camera-ready material, send it by Federal Express, UPS, or any other delivery service that will track its delivery.

7. When you receive your proofs from the printer, keep a copy of the changes you request. All changes asked for, whether author's alterations (AA) or printer's errors (PE) must be in writing to the printer. You should subsequently see some sort of proof that those errors have been corrected (a fax works very well for small corrections). If there are many corrections to the book, then order a new set of bluelines. It is worth this small extra cost to make sure that everything is the way you want it to be.

8. When working with a printer, your goal is to produce a quality book for a reasonable cost. Choosing the lowest possible bid for the printing of your book is often not the best way to obtain value for your money. Especially for the novice, it is important to build a strong long-lasting relationship with a printer who will guide you through the intricacies of printing a book and take responsibility for the quality of the book his or her company produces. Such an association may also help you to negotiate reduced freight, extended credit terms, or specialized customer services. A sympathetic printer may be able to set up a "gang" printing with another book that has the same specifications as yours, so that both books are printed at once, and both publishers receive the lower per unit cost that comes with a larger run.

9. Do not set unrealistic goals for the production or printing of your book. The finished product may have a few books with a speck of ink on the page, or the cover color may be off by half a shade from the matchprint. These are natural occurrences when translating design and typesetting to ink. However, if the binding glue is sloppy, or the pages are not each set with the same margins you indicated on the camera ready pages, or the pages are falling out of the book, then certainly you are entitled to a new press run at no cost, or a full refund for the books.

10. Once the book has been delivered, do not throw away any of the camera-ready material, called "artwork," your production scheduling paperwork, or the original quotations and all bills. Set up a morgue for storage of this important information plus some sample copies of the book itself. When the project is completed, make sure the printer sends you back all of your artwork. You may need it again to reprint the book

with another printer. You also own the film that was used to make the printing plates, but because it is bulky and most U.S. printers will store it free for a few years, it is probably better to let the printer keep it. You can always send for it if you need it (foreign printers often destroy the film at the end of a project, so if you are printing overseas, get the film returned with your artwork).

Types of Printing Presses

Presses are either sheetfed or web (roll) fed. They may be single color or multicolor, with each color requiring a separate printing unit consisting of inking, plate, and impression sections. A perfecting press, whether web or sheetfed, prints both sides of the paper in one pass through the press. *There are many types of presses within each category of sheetfed and web.*

Sheetfed Presses

As their names signify, these presses are fed one sheet of paper at a time. They work with sheets of paper from about 25 by 38 inches, to 55 by 78 inches. Most short run books (under 5,000 run) are printed on sheetfed presses. These presses are smaller than other kinds, and printing adjustments and corrections can be done more easily on them. There are two kinds of sheetfed presses: letterpress and offset presses.

Letterpresses have the type set onto plates so that typeface is raised up and inked. When the paper goes through the press, the type makes an impression on the paper. Handmade books are often run on letterpresses to give a more tactile appeal to the books. *Offset presses* do not print directly on the paper. A rubber cylinder pulls the image from the plate and then prints it on the paper using less ink and allowing for a crisper image than is possible from the letterpress.

Web Offset Presses

A web press uses a roll of paper that feeds paper continuously onto the press, making it a very fast press. Web presses have very precise specifications for paper size because of the way the paper must be cut from the roll. Therefore, depending on the size of your book, you would have to choose a printer with a web press with a specific "cut-off," so there would be no paper waste. Web presses are usually used for books with large print runs, because their speed more than makes up for their long set-up time.

Cameron Belt Presses

This press is actually a type of letterpress which has an attached adhesive binding system that prints the test, attaches the cover, and perfect (adhesive) binds the book in one operation. Its drawbacks include those of the letterpress, in that halftones and screens do not print well, so it is usually used for books of straight black text, such as academic treatises.

Cover Coatings

Covers and dustjackets of books require a coating to protect them and to enhance their appearance. The choice of a coating will be a cost factor in producing a book, but it should be the eventual use of the book that determines what coating to use.

Varnish

This is the least expensive of the coatings, and the one that is the least durable. It is applied when the color goes on the cover or dustjacket as if it were a colorless ink. It is available in matte or gloss finish.

Liquid Laminate Ultraviolet (UV)

This laminate is hardier than varnish and is also available in matte or gloss finish. It is applied in a separate operation from the printing, because the liquid coating needs to be cured with a high temperature. This heat can cause the cover or dustjacket to dry out so that it becomes brittle when folded.

Film Lamination

Film lamination is the most protective of all the coatings used for books. It is a very thin plastic sheet which is glued directly onto the cover or dustjacket. Depending on the process used, it can be applied cold or hot. Like the other coatings, film lamination can cause a cover to curl in damp conditions. However, there is now a non-curl film lamination on the market that costs little more than regular lamination and it corrects this problem.

Long Range Strategies

Many self-published authors will not be content with publishing and marketing a single title. It is a fact that it is always easier to publish and market your second book and subsequent titles. Self-publishers become familiar with the book trade, its mechanics, and realities. They have made contacts and found confidence in promoting and marketing their book. They have made mistakes and learned from them.

So how do you make the leap from single-title publisher to small publishing house? Certainly not all at once. No matter how successful your first book is, there is no way that you can bring out more than one new title and expect success. Until you can expand your business to include skilled employees or an experienced partner, it is a good practice to stick to bringing out one book at a time. This allows you to focus on production and still meet your marketing goals once the book is finished.

If you are going to bring out a second title, there are very strong advantages to keeping it closely related to your original title. First, and most obviously, you already have a working marketing plan, which should fit another book of the same genre. Another good reason for keeping with the same subject is that this leads to *specialization.* Specializing in a particular area allows you to service the same customer base with a new product, to build on media relations you have already established, cross-market your titles to conserve money, and perhaps even issue a catalog. Specialization has some positive connotations in the book business and can be the key to establishing a lasting identity in the book community.

If you find that you want to expand to become a publishing house, but do not have the time, money, or number of titles to support growth, consider joining with other single title authors to form a small press identity. Several independent publishers pooling their resources to produce a catalog, mass mailing, or marketing campaign can accomplish a great deal more than those same individuals could alone. In this situation, diversity can be as helpful as specialization, because there is more chance that at least one of your titles will be appropriate for any contact or outlet you target with marketing and promotion. Every campaign, mailing, venture, and exhibit will cost less, require less work, and undergo more scrutiny than is possible in a one- or two-person operation. Even if you are not going to be establishing a lasting organization, you can get mileage out of linking up with other author/publishers.

Rather than write and/or publish a second title, you may want to experiment with new forms for your original book. From audio tapes of the book being read aloud, to videos, foreign language translations, electronic books, seminars, special reports, workbooks, activity books, screenplays, and adaptations, your book can generate potentially profitable offspring. Adapting your book to non-book markets (for example, producing a video) can be lucrative and can even renew interest among book buyers. However, this is not a decision that should be made arbitrarily, and should not be undertaken unless there are definite signs that there is interest, a demand, or an established market for the proposed book-related product.

Audio Adaptations

Audio adaptations can be done very easily and inexpensively, simply by using a stereo tape deck (or other reliable recording unit) to record yourself reading the book aloud. Time your reading progress, so that you know roughly where to leave off at the end of each tape. Also check the running time on the tapes you are using in your deck; as individual decks will speed up or slow down the running time of a tape cassette. Once you have a satisfactory set of tapes recorded, use these as masters. You can then re-record with a twin tape deck with a "dubbing" feature or use a professional tape duplication service. Packaging can be very simple, perhaps a photostat of the book's cover shrunk to fit into the cassette case. You do not need to invest in a large quantity of tapes all at once. Due to the ease of duplication and the relatively low costs involved, you might choose to duplicate your master only to fill orders as they come in.

You can also opt to take the more professional approach in an attempt to sell larger quantities and to more professional outlets. This requires that you first rework your book to better fit the oral format. You may also have to pare down the material to fit into specific time constraints. For example, the book may have to fit on both sides of two 90 minute tapes, with room for an introduction, clean breaks at the end of each side, a promotional trailer for your next book, and ordering information. You may want to hire professional talent to do the voice work, and perhaps find a director experienced in voice-over work. You might want to add background music (make sure you have permission to use it), and some instructions for the listener. Listen to a few audio books from the big presses and you will get the idea. A reasonably-priced sound studio can record, mix, and produce a master tape of the work for you. This master is then used to make duplicate copies onto cassette tapes. You will need to design labels for the tapes, as well as a J-Card (the "album cover" for cassette tapes). The process of adapting a book to audio can cost as much as a traditional press run, and can take as long. And though audio books are popular, convenient, and potentially profitable, bear in mind that not all books are appropriate for, or make a good crossover into, the spoken word format.

Seminars and Workshops

Seminars and workshops provide a wealth of opportunity for profit and for making connections and contacts. If your book can support such an event, if you have considerable experience in a popular field, and/or if you can get well-known or experienced experts and panelists, you may want to develop an event around your book.

These events are not as difficult to plan and produce as you might think. However, the costs of advertising and hosting (rent for the facilities, food and materials) an event can be substantial. Bear in mind that while it is possible to develop a seminar that will show a profit, it is easy to miscalculate, and unexpected expenses and problems will keep you in the red. The best way to avoid a costly mistake is careful planning. Develop a workshop or seminar locally and then build up to a full-scale operation.

Sequels and Updated Editions

There are several types of books, such as mysteries, annual guides, and time-sensitive how-to books, that carry with them the expectation of updated editions, sequels, or further installments in a series. Mystery writers, for example, are generally expected to have at least two sequels following their flagship title. If your book falls into one of these categories, it is a good idea to continuously work on new manuscripts. In the case of annual guides and other time-sensitive resources, you should be updating your information from the moment the first edition goes into production. How-to books that rely upon industry advances or developing technologies (such as a book about the Internet) may be dependent upon significant advances to warrant updates. If this is the case, you may want to focus on preparing new materials and marketing plans for such a title while further development of the actual text is on hold. Actively market these forthcoming titles and keep book trade and media contacts aware of your plans. The more advance marketing you do, the more momentum the title will have when it reaches its publication date.

Electronic Books

Electronic books on CD-ROM disks are a very recent development. The implications and applications of this technology are very exciting. One such product on the market is an interactive version of Shakespeare's *Othello,* which allows you to not only watch animated clips of *Othello* productions with sound, but also to read aloud any part in the play, karaoke-style, with the computer delivering the lines for the other characters. Adapting a book to CD-ROM requires hard work, detailed planning, experienced programmers, high-end computer equipment, a lot of money, and a fine-tuned marketing plan. In short, this is not something you should try to do yourself. There are ways to get your book on CD-ROM, but they generally require that you either entice a large press to buy the rights, pay someone a lot of money to do it for you, or go for a bare-bones electronic adaptation, with none of the bells and whistles.

Electronic publishing on the Internet is a another way of selling your book. By putting your book into a common digital form, such as ASCII text, or as a file (or set of files, each a whole chapter) formatted in a word-processing program specialized for the

Internet, you can sell your book directly to the consumer without reprinting the book. This option should only be considered by authors who have already successfully published and promoted their titles, as it is almost impossible to adequately promote an electronic title. In addition, this option requires specific computer hardware, software, and a home page on the Internet World Wide Web, as well as some very specific experience with online operations and marketing.

Video Adaptations

Video adaptations of a book can take on just about any format. How-to books lend themselves to visual demonstrations, histories to a documentary format, children's stories to live-action or animation, tour guides to footage of the journey and sights. A video adaptation is a full-scale production, and requires detailed advance planning and specialized skills. There are hundreds of video production companies that can help you with every stage of the production. This is not to say that you cannot make a video adaptation of your book without hiring expensive professional help. But if you do try to make the video yourself, any lack of expertise on the part of you or the crew is going to show up clearly in the final product. There are other ways to secure a video adaptation of your book, including finding publishers who specialize in video books, or recruiting semiprofessionals from your local access cable station or local college or university.

Expansion

The key to expanding your publishing operations is to take it slowly and develop each new step thoroughly, rather than shifting all of your focus too quickly to the next project. If your first title is not taking off, committing yourself to the development of a second title will not help. Taking the time to develop an existing title into a strong seller can only help your chances for a successful second title. As an independent publisher, you are not constrained by "shelf life" considerations that plague the large presses. Also be aware that once you have a book in publication, you are an industry player. Take advantage of this by interacting with experienced book trade contacts, and putting their experience to work for you. You would be surprised how much information, support, and cooperation you can tap into.

The Ten Commandments of Marketing Your Self-Published Book

1. Thou shalt make five promotional efforts a day to get your book noticed.

Send a press kit, call a program director, enter your book for an award, fax a sell sheet, and set up a book signing. Five a day and your book will get noticed.

2. Thou shalt carry copies of your book around with you at all times.

Get used to presenting and pitching your book. Opportunity may knock at any time of the day or night. Be prepared.

3. Thou shalt not sell books to bookstores on consignment.

Some trade outlets (jobbers, wholesalers, distributors) work exclusively on consignment, but do not let bookstores or small retailers put your books on consignment. You'll probably never see a check, or the books again.

4. Thou shalt not sell your book to consumers for less than its cover price.

Unless you are dealing with a wholesaler, retailer, or offering a special promotion, do not back down from the price of your book. This may seem trivial, but once you devalue the book in your mind, it will affect your ability to sell the book confidently.

5. Thou shalt pay special attention to friends, family and associates when marketing.

This segment of the book market is golden. They want to buy the book and brag about it to their friends. Give them every opportunity to do this, and enjoy the momentum this creates.

6. Thou shalt not waste your money advertising.

Do not pay for advertising unless it serves a higher purpose, such as complementing a book review, or playing a part in a larger strategy to woo a tight, niche market. It takes average consumers seven sightings of the same ad before they respond. Unless you plan to stay in the paid ad game for the long haul, keep away.

7. Thou shalt monitor newspapers, magazines, trade journals, television, and talk radio.

Keep your eyes, ears, and mind open for news stories and issues to piggy back on. Get to know the local radio hosts and their interests. Keep looking for new places to plug your book.

8. Thou shalt not waste time trying to sell directly to librarians.

Branch libraries will buy a maximum of two of your books each. A bookstore will buy an average of ten. A wholesaler will buy 100. Bookstores and wholesalers reorder. Do the math.

9. Thou shalt be crafty, bold, imaginative and controversial.

Do anything and everything you can to get attention and publicity. The more extreme and outlandish, the more attention you'll attract. Once you have their attention, follow through with a precision pitch for your book.

10. Thou shalt keep special days, holidays and events holy and observe them with a special promotion and offerings of press kits to the media.

The media are forced to observe traditional and quirky holidays, events, and special days with offbeat stories. Give them something to write about.

GLOSSARY

Every profession has its own language and it is important to understand this jargon, especially if you are paying for specialized services. This glossary is not only a reference, but is an abbreviated textbook of the terms used in publishing.

AA (Author's Alteration) Used to indicate that a change to typeset copy is the author's change. Such an alteration is usually charged to the author.

Acknowledgment A thank you by the author to those people who helped with the book.

Alteration Any change to copy or cover once the prepress work has begun.

Appendix Information that is relevant to or supports the main text, usually technical material or figures. It is usually the first section of the back matter.

Artwork Generic term for illustrations and copy used to make film and plates.

Autograph Party A gathering at a bookstore where the author gets to meet people interested in his or her work and autographs the books they buy.

Back Flap Inner panel of dust jacket that traditionally contains a photo and short biography of author.

Back Matter All the informational pages following the main text.

Back Order An order for a book taken even though the book is not yet published or is out of stock.

Base Line The imaginary horizontal line that runs under the letters of words to keep them aligned.

Bastard Title Another name for the half title page.

Binding The way the pages of a book are held together — by glue, stitching, staples, or combs.

Binder's Board A stiff paper board used as a cover for a case bound book.

Bleed Color or type that is printed to the edge of a page.

Bluelines/Blues Contact prints made from the printer's film and used for final proofing. Depending on the process used, such proofs are also called silvers or browns.

Bulk The thickness of paper, usually expressed in ppi (pages per inch).

Bulk Mailing Large quantity of mail sent out third class according to specifications set up by the post office. More reasonable in price than first class, but must be a minimum amount of pieces and carefully sorted.

Bullets Dots or dingbats set above the baseline of text and next to items in a list to make them stand out.

Camera-Ready Any material, from the artwork to finished board (mechanical), that is ready to be filmed for printing.

Caption/Cutline The title and explanation under a photograph or illustration.

Card Deck A form of direct mail advertising using reply post cards to be sent back by the buyer. The card decks are usually sent out in loose-deck or booklet format.

Casebound Book Hard cover book.

CIP/PCN Cataloging in Publication/Preassigned Card Number Number assigned by the Library of Congress to aid in cataloging a book.

Coated Paper that is coated with clay to improve the clarity of ink on the paper.

CIS Coated one side paper stock used as a cover in perfect bound books.

C2S Paper stock coated on two sides.

Cold Type Type which is set by computer in contrast to setting type with hot metal casting.

Colophon A publisher's trademark, sometimes called an imprint. It can also refer to the description at the end of the back matter that describes how the book was printed — what typeface and paper was used.

Color Keys/Color Flats Color proofs in which each color is on a separate overlay and that, when placed in registration, show the way the cover or page will actually look.

Color Separation Any page, including the cover, that is printed in more than one color and arranged by the designer so that each individual color is on a separate overlay. For more complicated full-color photographs or illustrations, separations are done electronically.

Composite Proof/Comp This is a proof with everything, including artwork, in position.

Continuous Tone Photo Photograph without screens.

Cooperative Advertising Advertising in which the cost and profits are shared by the author/publisher and the publication.

Copy The text of a book.

Copyright Ownership of a creative work.

Copyright Page The left-hand page (verso) following the title page and containing information about the copyright and previous copyrights, "All rights reserved" statement and any other restrictions, the publisher and publisher's address, the print code, the ISBN, the Library of Congress number, and the country in which the book was published.

Cover The cover of a book is considered to be made up of four pages: the outside front is cover one; the inside front is called the second cover; the inside back is called the third cover; the outside back is called the fourth cover.

Crop Marks Fine lines drawn to indicate trim size so the printer knows where to cut a page horizontally and vertically.

Cropping Showing exactly the parts of the photograph to be used and those to be deleted.

Dedication Page The page on which the book's dedication is placed. It is included in the front matter.

Die Engraving stamp used to emboss the copy or artwork on the cover or dustjacket of a book or blade used for cutting irregular paper shapes.

Direct Mail Form of marketing which uses the mail to send out promotional material and order forms.

Display Ad Advertisement which is designed and usually contains graphic elements rather than just typeset copy.

Dot Gain This is the result of dots printing larger than they appear on the proof.

Dummy A pasteup of or computer generated layout, using sample text and artwork to indicate the way the finished work (cover, pages, etc.) will look.

Duotone A photo produced using two negatives and usually using two different inks.

This technique adds depth and subtle color to a photograph.

Dustcover Paper jacket covering a book, usually printed in color, and with flaps that are used for information about the book and author.

Dylux Type of paper used in making a blueline proof. Bluelines are sometimes called dyluxes.

Edition Each printing of a book.

Em A measurement which uses the width of the letter m as its basis. An em-dash is a dash the size of an "m." Its actual size is dependent on the font.

Enamel Paper This is paper with a gloss coating. It is often recommended for books with many photographs.

Endpapers Decorative heavy weight papers at the beginning and end of a casebound book. One end of each page is glued to the inside cover board.

Epigraph A short quotation from another book or a poem that sets the overall tone or theme of the book. It should include the name of the author and the work from which it is taken.

Errata Errors found in a book can be revised by inserting an errata sheet listing the corrections rather than reprinting the whole book.

Estimate The anticipated cost of printing based on a book's specifications.

F & G Folded and gathered signatures of the book

Foil Stamping Used to stamp an image on a cover with a metallic film. This can include the title and author's name.

Folio Page number

Footband These are strips of cloth at the bottom of the spine of a casebound book.

Foreword/Preface The foreword or preface, usually written by someone other than the author, about the book or author.

Four Color Process to print four colors, magenta, cyan, yellow, and black, which simulate the full color spectrum.

Front Matter All the introductory pages before the main text.

Galleys In the traditional method of printing, type is set in long galley sheets one column wide before being prepared to conform to the page layout.

Ghosting This is a shadow image behind the printing. It is a printer's error.

Glossary Glossaries supply the definitions of terms and jargon used within the text.

Graphic Any type of artwork used.

Graphic Design This can include the total look of the book, including cover and page layout, or just one illustration.

Gripper Edge This is a leading edge (a blank area, usually about ¼ inch) that must be left for feeding a sheet of paper through a sheet fed press, where the paper is held by grippers.

Gutter The margin next to inside edge of page.

Half Title The first right hand page (recto) of the book with copy on it, containing only the book's main title. It does not contain the subtitle, author's or publisher's names. This page is the first to be omitted if the book length has to be cut.

Halftones Photographs must be changed into halftones in order to be printed. Halftones use small dots to produce gradations of light and shade.

Hard Copy Pages printed from a computer.

Head Abbreviation for headline. The head is any a word or copy that introduces a chapter or section of a book. It is designed to stand out from the text following it.

Headbands These are the strips of cloth at the top of the spine of a case bound book.
House Paper This is paper a printer buys in quantity and keeps in stock at all times. It is usually cheaper than paper that must be ordered for a printing job.
Imposition This is the arrangement of the pages in a signature so when folded, they will be in the proper order.
Imprint The name, address, and logo of a publisher.
Index Listing of subjects within the book and page numbers on which they can be found.
Indicia Printed information on envelope used in place of a stamp.
ISBN Acronym for International Standard Book Number, which assigns identifying numbers to books.
Italics A slanted font of a typeface.
Justified Type that is even on both right and left margins.
Keyliner The person who pastes the elements of the page together into a camera-ready board.
Knock Out When color is dropped out of a background.
Layout Visual representation of the design of a book, including how a page looks. It should contain kind and size of type for body copy and heads, where artwork and halftones are placed, margins used around and between columns of type, and where and what colors are to be used.
Leading The space between lines of type. Type is specified by the use of a fraction with the size of the type above and the amount of leading below. This page is set in 11 point type with a leading of 14 points, or 11/14.
Lines per Inch The measurement of rows of dots within a screen.
Line Art This is an illustration in pen and ink with no shading or tonal values.
Mechanical/Board The pasteup of all the elements of a page or cover into camera-ready form.
Media Kit Information packaged for book promotion. It usually includes a media release, author's photograph (head shot) and biography, information about book, and reviews about book.
Moiré This is the pattern caused by incorrect alignment of screens.
MS The abbreviation for manuscript.
Net The price to be paid after all discounts.
Offset When there is a transfer of an image onto the reverse side of a page because the ink is still wet when the pages are stacked and/or folded. This is a printer's error.
Overlay A sheet, often of clear acetate, laid over a board (mechanical) and lined up with register marks. It is used to separate colors on a page or cover, or separate out other modifications.
Overrun When a larger than ordered amount is printed to off set printing and binding spoilage.
PE (Printer's Error) An error made by printer and marked for change. Such changes are made at no extra charge to the author during any stage of production.
Perfect Bound A form of binding where the pages of a book are glued into the spine.
Permissions To ask for use of copyrighted material, usually for a fee.
Photostat/Stat A photographic process used to make camera-ready copies, usually of artwork. The stat camera can reduce and enlarge the original and make positive or negatives.
Pica/Points Measurements used by printers and designers. A pica is made of 12 points. There are six picas or 72 points to the inch.
PPI Pages per inch is a measurement indicating how many pages of a type of paper

are needed to equal one inch. The lower the number, the bulkier the paper.

Press Check When the designer or editor goes to observe the printing of a book and check for color and registration.

Print Code A list of numbers on the copyright page which indicates how many times the book has been printed by dropping the lowest number with each new press run.

Publication Date The official date the book is offered for sale. This is not the same as the delivery date, which can be two or three months in advance of the publication date.

Ragged Right Right margins of text are not even (non-justified).

Ream Five hundred sheets of paper.

Recto Right-hand page.

Register Marks Lines on film or camera-ready copy to guide printers for proper registration.

Reverse To change the black values of artwork or text to white and the white values to black.

Remainders Overstock that is sold for much less than original price.

Roman Type that is not italic (slanted).

Running Head/Foot A headline/baseline or caption that is repeated on every page of a chapter. Many books are designed with a running head or foot of the book title on all verso pages and the chapter heading on the recto pages. Running heads and feet can be placed before the page number, centered, or next to the inside margin of the page.

Saddle Stitch/Wire Stitching A form of binding where the pages of a book are stapled with wire. There is no spine.

Scanning Symbols The bar code with the ISBN and price of the book, usually placed on lower right of back of book or dustcover.

Self-Cover A publication that has a cover of the same paper stock as the body pages.

Serif The crossbar at the top and bottom of letters. This book uses a body typeface with serifs. A typeface without serifs is called sans serif.

Short Discount A minimal discount given for small orders, especially to libraries and schools.

Signatures This is one printed sheet of paper coming off the press consisting of many pages which are folded, trimmed, and combined with other signatures to form the book. Signatures are usually 16 or 32 pages each, and the number of pages in a book are determined by a multiple of the signature.

Sizing When a photograph should be made larger or smaller to fit the layout of a page, this is called sizing.

Smyth Sewn The pages in a signature are sewn together and then sewn to the adjacent signatures.

Specs Type or layout specifications.

Spoilage All print estimates include an amount of paper that is wasted during the make ready and set up.

Stripper The person who puts together the film for printing.

Subsidiary Rights The use of a book beyond its original publication, such as reprinting, book club distribution, foreign translations, movie rights, or magazine serialization.

Tear Sheet A term in advertising for pages torn from a publication to show clients how their advertisements look.

Tipped/Tip-In A page, photograph, or illustration that is glued into a bound book.

Title Page The next recto page after the half title. It can include the title, subtitle, edition, author's or editor's name, address of the publisher, and the publisher's imprint or colophon.

Trade Books Books for the general public, as opposed to professional or religious books, marketed to bookstores and libraries.

Trap To print one color of ink very slightly over another color so that there are no gaps between the colors.

Trim Size This is the size of the trimmed (cut) pages as indicated by crop marks, and not including binding.

Typeface/Font The typeface is the name of a type and the font is each different size and style within a typeface.

Unjustified/Ragged Type Right-hand margin of the type is not evenly spaced, as opposed to justified type.

Verso A left hand page.

Web-Fed Press A press that prints from rolls of paper rather than individual sheets.

Weight Paper is sold by weight. Classification comes from the weight of a ream of the paper. Trade books are usually printed on 50 pound to 70 pound paper.

Wholesaler/Distributor/Jobber Suppliers of books who buy at a large discount from publishers and sell to book dealers and libraries. Distributors have their own sales force to sell books in their catalog.

BIBLIOGRAPHY

Brewer, Annie M., and Brewer, Donald T. *Talk Shows and Hosts on Radio,* Minneapolis: Whiteford Press, 1993.

Bruno, Michael H., ed. *Pocket Pal: A Graphic Arts Production Handbook,* 14th Ed., Memphis: International Paper Company, 1989.

Commercial Printing Guide, Seattle: Aldus Corporation, 1993.

Davis, Anita, ed. "7 Ways to Build a Page," *Publish,* October, 1995, pp.43-64

Goldsmith, Marianne, "Storytelling by Design," *Step-by-Step Graphics,* Vol. 11, No. 6, November/December, 1995, pp.56-65

Grants and Awards Available to American Writers, 18th Edition. New York: PEN American Center, 1994-95.

Hunt, Shane. "So You Call Yourself a Designer," *Corel Magazine,* April, 1995, p.55

Kavka, Dorothy. *Selling Your Book: The Writer's Guide to Publishing and Marketing,* Evanston: Evanston Publishing, Inc., 1993.

Kiefer, Marie. *Book Publishing Resource Guide,* Fairfield: Ad-Lib Publications, 1993.

Kremer, John. *1001 Ways to Market Your Books — For Authors and Publishers,* Fairfield: Open Horizons Publishing, 1993.

Library of Congress. *PCN Publishers Manual; Guidelines for the Preassigned Card Number Program,* Washington, D.C.: Cataloging in Publication Division, 1990.

Miller, Larry. "Mix Type," *Technique,* November, Vol. 2, No. 11, 1995, pp.70-71

Parker, Roger C. "Exploring Script and Decorative Typefaces," *Corel Magazine,* April, 1995, pp.32-34

Poynter, Dan. *The Self-Publishing Manual,* 8th Edition. Santa Barbara: Para Publishing, 1995.

Tinkle, Kathleen. "Classic Composition," *Aldus Magazine,* Vol. 4, No.7, September/October, 1993, pp.39-42

Tinkle, Kathleen. "Classic Composition, Part Two," *Aldus Magazine,* Vol. 5, No.l 1, November, 1993, pp.45-49

Walker, Priscilla. "A Lesson in Leading," *Aldus Magazine,* Volume 1, No. 3, March/April, 1990, pp.45-47

Williams, Robin. *The PC is not a Typewriter,* Berkeley: Peachpit Press, 1992.

Worchester, Robert L. *In Print: How to Plan, Purchase, and Produce Print,* Bloomingdale: Media Asociates International, Inc., 1989.

INDEX

This body of this book was typeset in Berkeley (11/14). The heads were set in Poppi-Laudatio Regular bold (18/Auto) and the subheads in Poppi-Laudatio Regular bold (12/15).

Clip art in this book is from Dynamic Graphics' Designer Club, Clipper, and Electronic Clipper.

Photographs by Matthew Rubinberg.